meaning to the processional elements in medieval cathedral architecture. Both poem and cathedral architecture, he maintains, are based upon overlooked processional iconography in the "world book."

He provides a full structural analysis of Spenser's *The Faerie Queene* as a Neo-Aristotelian-Platonic construct and as an imaginative reflection of that lost "antique" medieval world iconography embodied in texts and maps in, among other places, Gabriel Harvey's library. Spenser is seen as a Reformation poet one step removed from medieval cosmological and pilgrimage lore, aware of the new literature of exploration, and yet deeply influenced by the older iconography.

Milton projects new poetic structures and a transformed universe into *Paradise Lost*, Demaray shows, by combining revolutionary empirical methods of historical and cosmological depiction with traditional biblical representation. *Paradise Lost* is revealed as a new kind of universal epic dependent upon both empirical eyewitness accounts and inward spiritual vision.

About the Author

JOHN G. DEMARAY is professor of English and Renaissance Studies at Rutgers University, and was a recent visiting professor to the Universita degli Studi di Firenzi. Dr. Demaray's publications include *Milton's Theatrical Epic: The Invention and Design of "Paradise Lost"* (Harvard University Press, 1980), *The Invention of Dante's "Commedia"* (Yale University Press, 1974) and *Milton and the Masque Tradition* (Harvard and Oxford University Presses, 1968).

Duquesne Studies

LANGUAGE AND LITERATURE SERIES

[VOLUME ELEVEN]

GENERAL EDITOR:

Albert C. Labriola, *Department of English, Duquesne University*

ADVISORY EDITOR:

Foster Provost, *Department of English, Duquesne University*

EDITORIAL BOARD:

Judith H. Anderson
Donald Cheney
Patrick Cullen
French R. Fogle
A. Bartlett Giamatti[‡]
A. C. Hamilton
S. K. Heninger, Jr.
A. Kent Hieatt
Robert B. Hinman
William B. Hunter
Michael Lieb
Waldo F. McNeir
Thomas P. Roche, Jr.
John T. Shawcross
James D. Simmonds
John M. Steadman
Humphrey Tonkin
Robert F. Whitman

[‡] *It is with sadness that we note the death of Board member A. Bartlett Giamatti in July 1989.*

COSMOS AND EPIC REPRESENTATION

A human form, posed before lower steps of ascent and grasping a perfect circle above, as the measure of the earthly world. This ladder and T-and-O world icon, the first letter of the word "Terrates," appears in a discussion of the medieval earth's three regions in Isodorus Hispalensis's twelfth or thirteenth century *Etymologicon*, a work once housed in the monastery of Vallombrosa outside Florence. (*Bibliotèca Medicea Laurenziana, Conv. Sopr. 319*)

COSMOS
AND EPIC
REPRESENTATION

Dante, Spenser, Milton and the
Transformation of Renaissance Heroic Poetry

By John G. Demaray

Duquesne University Press
Pittsburgh, Pennsylvania

Published in the United States of America

by Duquesne University Press
600 Forbes Avenue
Pittsburgh, Pennsylvania 15282

Library of Congress Cataloging-in-Publication Data

Demaray, John G.
   Cosmos and epic representation : Dante, Spenser, Milton, and the
transformation of Renaissance heroic poetry / John G. Demaray.
       p.   cm.   — (Duquesne studies. Language and literature series;
   v. 11)
   Includes bibliographical references and index.
   ISBN 0–8207–0231–5 (cloth) : $48.00
   1. Epic poetry, English—History and criticism.   2. English
poetry—Early modern, 1500–1700—History and criticism.   3. Dante
Aleghieri, 1265–1321. Divina commedia.   4. Spenser, Edmund,
1552?–1599. Faerie queene.   5. Milton, John, 1608–1674. Paradise
lost.   6. Cosmology in literature.   7. Renaissance.   I. Title.
II. Series.
PR539.E64D4   1991   90–21022
809.1'32—dc20   CIP

For Hannah

Contents

Illustrations

Acknowledgments

The Proceedings of the American Philosophical Society has kindly granted permission to reprint portions of my study *Dante and the Book of the Cosmos* (Philadelphia, 1987). My gratitude is expressed to Painton Cowan for permission to reproduce photographs from his *Rose Windows* published by Thames and Hudson.

I am deeply indebted to the Huntington Library for a Resident Fellowship and to the National Endowment for the Humanities for a Research Grant in support of specialized work on this study in the United States and then in Great Britain, Europe and Israel. I am indebted as well to the Rutgers University Research Council and Rutgers University Graduate School for awards that facilitated overseas research and that made possible the inclusion of a wide range of illustrations. Special thanks are due the New York Public Library for use of the Frederic Lewis Allen Room, and the Princeton University Library for work space and access to rich collections. Appreciated also is assistance from individual staff members at the British Library, the Bibliothèque Nationale, the Bibliotèca Medicea Laurenziana and the Bibliotèca Vaticana.

Among colleagues whose insights or assistance contributed directly or indirectly to this book, I would like to single out for particular thanks William Anderson, John M. Steadman, Stanley Stuart and Elizabeth McLachlan. Most grateful acknowledgement is made to Julia Bolton Holloway and Joseph Tusiani for helpful criticism of a draft of the Dante section. Giuliano Pellegrini and Giuseppi Galigani generously offered learned aid at Firenzi; Geoffrey Ashe, at Glastonbury; and Fr. Sabino de Sandoli, at the Franciscan Biblical Library, Jerusalem. I am obligated to Albert C. Labriola for drawing upon his own revealing studies of Renaissance iconography in providing academic analysis and support, and to Susan B. Wadsworth for excellent editorial work. I am grateful as well to Lawrence Lader and associates in the Allen Room for their constant and spirited literary good counsel. Yet as always, I owe the deepest debts of all for literary advice, assistance, and encouragement to Hannah Disinger Demaray.

Introduction

In the late Middle Ages and Renaissance, the breakdown of the great ordering icons of medieval world cosmography and biblical representation—the labyrinths, ladders, crosses, circles, mounts, temples and pilgrimage "stations"—resulted in dramatic transformations in the structure and content of heroic verse. These transformations are here freshly examined in three major "epics": Dante Alighieri's *Commedia*, Edmund Spenser's *The Faerie Queene* and John Milton's *Paradise Lost*.

These strikingly different heroic poems embody iconographic forms that mirror those once thought to exist in two ultimate source books of truth: the Book of God's Works, the created world and wider universe; and the Book of God's Words, the Bible. Corresponding icons in the two source books were believed to point to the most important events in universal history. The icons accordingly served as a matrix for a range of late medieval and Renaissance poems and art works. Yet because today's modern Latin culture has waned and contracted in comparison with the international Latin-Byzantine culture of past centuries, it is a fundamental premise of this study that key iconographic markings in well-known Latin and Byzantine texts, illustrations, pilgrimage stations, and architectural structures have been overlooked by commentators; and that many source book iconographic "words" reflected in heroic verse have consequently been left unexamined.

Primary documents and illustrations from European and Near Eastern libraries are used for the first time to disclose this neglected biblical and worldly iconography, and then to show its fragmentation in the sixteenth century into diffuse emblems and empirical elements under pressure from the Reformation and from new scientific philosophies. World iconographic "centers" imaged in poetry are seen to shift from Jerusalem to English Glastonbury and even to India and the East.

Key structural and internal features of heroic poems, I argue, can best be critically registered by combining analysis of texts with a comparative study of the worldly and biblical core iconography

1

found both in verse and in early artistic, architectural, literary and geographical-cosmographical works. This core iconography will be seen in the overall design of certain late medieval European churches, in the paradigm of liturgical rituals, in iconographic pilgrimage stations replicated in Europe and England, in medieval cosmographical illustrations, in iconographic maps in the earliest English Bibles, in a voluminous body of tracts and biblical commentaries and allegorical works, and so too in the forms and content of late medieval and Renaissance epics.

The iconographic materials considered are clearly nominalist in their extraordinarily profuse, varied and changing individuation; yet at the same time, these materials have a capacity to synthesize, to coalesce and embody the changing and the many in subsuming icons pointing to ideas and values considered to be beyond change. While the nominalist quality of the materials precludes any holistic recall of past iconographic traditions, the materials' synthesizing quality, studies by iconographic critics have confirmed, give rise to identifiable, ordered arrangements of corresponding icons that, within the focus of this study, come into view in core worldly and biblical patterns.

Depictions of "external Nature" and biblical history nevertheless come down through the centuries in altering iconographic clothes. Poets and artists of earlier periods experienced the cosmos and Scriptures—the medieval Books of God's Works and Words—under the influence of changing fashions in ideology and iconography. "We really read 'what we see'," Erwin Panofsky has remarked, "according to the manner in which *objects* and *events*" are rendered "by *forms under varying historical conditions.*" Panofsky urged the critic to examine the *"intrinsic meaning"* of art and literary works against "the *intrinsic meaning* of as many other documents of civilization historically related to that work or group of works, as he can master"; and Panofsky accordingly evolved a critical method to uncover how *"objects"* and *"events"* are translated into artistic inventions encompassing "motifs," "concepts," "types," "stories" and "allegories," and then into fully developed iconographic creations having intrinsic symbolic values.

In recent years, comparative iconographic studies have offered illuminating insight into how, under given historical circumstances, symbolic values become manifest in medieval and Renaissance paintings, mosaics and architectural forms. Using many of the terms of art criticism while adding theoretical analysis, John M. Steadman has successfully applied a general iconographic approach to a reading of Renaissance poetic icons in the light of contemporaneous reference manuals. Other critics have unveiled new poetic meanings by drawing in comparative investigations upon a spectrum of constructed forms and iconographic paintings and illustrations: Giovanni Fallani, Jeffrey T. Schnapp and Anthony K. Cassell, for example, in relating early Italian art and architecture to Dante Aligheri's *Commedia*; S. K. Heninger, A. Kent Hieatt and Jane Aptekar in exposing correspondences in sixteenth century cosmography and art in Spenser's verse; and Roland Frye, Mindele Treip and Michael Lieb in demonstrating the influence of European and British visual arts and literature upon Milton's poetry.

These essays chart the comparative influence, function and meaning of worldly and biblical icons with attention to both recent specialized criticism and medieval-Renaissance views. The essays, while stressing early outlooks and ideologies, have benefited from the iconographic critical approach of Panofsky and others, and from those currents in European semiotic and literary criticism focused on the comparative analysis of early textual and artistic signs, figurae and structures. The essays seek to decipher and interpret—to use the terminology of Marcello Pagnini in the publications of the Milan International Semiotic Association conference— the "homologies to be found in a single work and characteristic structures of the same period," structures embracing core "literary" and "nonliterary" productions and events.

Remarks on extensive commentary that place the present volume's approach in perspective have on occasion been relegated, readers are forewarned, to some very long footnotes. This allows primary critical arguments to be more directly pursued in the main text. As the notes seek further to clarify, late medieval and Renaissance poetry is obviously not here privileged as a pure textuality, but rather as a textuality produced in the cross-disciplinary streams of altering medieval and Renaissance ideologies and myths of history, and of cosmographical, architectural, artistic and literary iconography. In the late Middle Ages and early Renaissance, the "noble numbers" of poetry were, after all, thought to correspond in essence to disciplines of the quadrivium; namely, to geometry, mathematics, astronomy and music; and poems were believed to correspond in form to the iconographic configuration and types of external nature. This study is therefore aimed at revealing the iconographic-ideological power of poetic form even as it records the power of iconography and ideology upon poetic form.

In past publications on the *Commedia*, I attempted to expand upon contemporary criticism that, without particularized reference to the iconography of the medieval World Book, concentrated upon the spiritual conversion of Dante through his acting out of typal events scored in the Book of God's Words, the Bible. *The Invention of Dante's Commedia* and related essays contained arguments recounting how the unfolding typology of Dante's *Commedia* corresponds in structure to iconographic typology in *both* the World Book and the Bible. A hierarchy of Old and New Testament events—events signified in the worldly iconography of the Egypt-Jerusalem-Rome pilgrimage stations, and in the words of the Bible—were found to have been reenacted by Dante, in an ascending spiritual order, in the progressive typological episodes of his pilgrimage poem. At the end of the *Paradiso*, Dante was seen recurrently to reenact the Transfiguration, the climactic biblical-pilgrimage event.

Recent publications have made possible an ever clearer delineation of the biblical-pilgrimage core of the *Commedia*, and they afford new perspectives on the structures and narratives of *The Faerie Queene* and *Paradise Lost*. William Anderson has defined how Dante's imitation beyond life of pilgrimage events conflates with the poet's inward spiritual growth in accord with the *Itinerarium mentis in Deum* of medieval meditative tradition. The ritualistic forms of Dante's reenactment of pilgrimage-biblical episodes, forms manifest in the yearly cycle of church liturgy and ancient Jewish feasts such as Tabernacles involving Temple processions, have been elucidated by, among others, Peter Armour, Jonathan Sumption and Julia Bolton Holloway. And the patterned iconographic typology of churches, in which such rituals were performed, has been demonstrated—by Jerome Mazzaro, Jeffrey Schnapp, John Lyerle, V. A. Kolve and others—to be mirrored in types evident in the verse of Dante and other late medieval and Renaissance writers.

In the present "processional reading" of central iconographic structures of Dante's *Commedia*, corresponding icons are examined in accord with their sequential representation in ascending or descending chains, circles or other formations; and with a view to their unfolding "operation" and "effect" upon characters and readers. Recent theories of iconographic typology, reviewed in notes and Appendix B, are applied to Dante's text with modifications in the light of primary sources and studies.

The iconographic structures of the *Commedia* and Gothic cathedrals are found to correspond—a view long held but never, I believe, developed using detailed medieval worldly representations—

because both are discovered to be based on previously neglected "source book" and Egypt-Jerusalem-Rome pilgrimage iconography. Dante's processional poem is seen in form, content and meaning to correspond to the processional elements of medieval cathedral architecture: the nave "Exodus" labyrinth floors, the "Jerusalem temple" altars, and in particular the "cosmic heavenly city" rota-rosa windows.

In central chapters on Spenser's *The Faerie Queene*, sequential "processional" iconographic analysis is largely supplanted by an examination of the meaning and structural relationship of dispersed but subsuming core icons in different poetic books. A full structural reading unveils the poem as a neo-Aristotelian-Platonic construct and as an imaginative reflection of that disintegrating "antique" medieval world iconography represented in *mappae-mundi* and texts found, among other places, in Gabriel Harvey's library. Faeryland Exodus emblems in Book I are reviewed in the context of Dante's Exodus typology and of Exodus pilgrimage "stations" in the Holy Land and at British Glastonbury. Sixteenth century "Glassenbury" with its terraced Tor surmounted by a tower, a British type of the New Jerusalem and a mythical haunt of the faery queen, is seen to be shadowed in Gloriana's core faery city Cleopolis with its tower of glass. The poet's emblematic House of Holiness, Mount of Contemplation, House of Alma, sacred temples, and globe of Merlin are also found to reflect patterned "world book" icons. A final chapter on Spenser discusses, in the entirely new perspective of his patron Leicester's masquing activities as a Red Cross Knight, the poet's lightly subversive view of medieval iconographic-cosmographical universal history.

Spenser is observed to display both a skepticism toward and a delight in the "old" medieval history and iconography. In *The Faerie Queene*, disparate and sometimes satiric fictional narratives embodying chivalric and other themes, and mirroring an external social and political world largely by analogy, are set within an ideological-cosmological structure developed from the "old" system of iconographic correspondences. Spenser is treated as a transitional poet one step removed from medieval cosmographic and pilgrimage lore, aware of the new empirical literature of exploration and yet deeply influenced by older traditions.

Finally, through an investigation of iconographic "counter-poised journey" structures in Milton's *Paradise Lost*, a new kind and pattern of empirical-typological iconographic representation is disclosed. Milton is seen sharply to reject that medieval iconography associated with "processional," collective religious pilgrimage

to the medieval world's supposed iconographic "center" at Jerusalem. Under the influence of revolutionary cosmographic and
historical conceptions that inspired works such as *Purchas his
Pilgrimage*, subtitled in 1619 *The Historie of Man*, and Luis de
Camões's *Os Lusiadas*, Milton projects into his poem, by employing
the viewpoint of characters who are cosmic travelers, a vast and
transformed universe. Traditional iconographic typology, bor-
rowed from earlier writers, is merged with original methods of
empirical depiction learned from the literature of discovery. Universal history is revealed using both "scientific" information and
traditional epochal events, and a special emphasis is now placed
upon interior spiritual experience and individual reason. Milton's
Paradise Lost is therefore seen as a new sort of universal epic
containing both traditional and revisionary elements, an epic with
iconography dependent upon empirical eyewitness accounts of
voyages as well as upon supposed inward spiritual vision of
immaterial essences and immortal realms.

Because in much recent formal criticism early iconographic and
contemporary world outlooks have often been confused or intermingled, and because modern cosmographical projections that
could not possibly have been known to early writers are still
employed to illustrate scholarly editions of their works, I call
attention here to the varying uses by epic writers of an embracing
medieval world iconography that entered into European art and so
was available to Western writers, arising from a wide Latin-
Byzantine international culture. This was the culture fired initially
by the crusades and then, in the thirteenth century, by the poets,
philosophers and artists from East and West gathered together in
Sicily by Frederic II. It was the culture enriched by the Mediterranean trade and the arts and sciences of the Italian city-states; by the
spiritual reforms of the Franciscans with their pilgrimage hospices
in the Holy Land, at the "New Jerusalem" of Santa Croce in
Florence, and on Italian Mt. La Verna; and by the theology,
learning and art of the clerics and scholars at the great Cathedral
School at Chartres, at the universities in Paris and in Oxford, and
at the religious houses of the international teaching orders scattered throughout Europe and England. As a result of this culture's
still pretending to the political organization of the Roman Empire,
much of the typology of late medieval and Renaissance heroic
verse points, not to modern empirical Mediterranean and earthly
cosmography, but rather to an inclusive medieval, iconographic

"world book" with Jerusalem at its geographic center, and with a primary pilgrimage path leading from iconographic station to iconographic station, and so circling from Europe "beyond the sea" to the Holy Land and Jerusalem, and then back across the sea to Rome.

Interdisciplinary analysis has been supported by my own on-site studies of the complete medieval iconographic chain of Egypt-Jerusalem-Rome pilgrimage stations and churches—a chain already centuries old in Dante's time—and by on-site inspections of typological imitations of elements of that chain at pilgrimage churches and sites in Italy, France and England, and at the British "New Jerusalem" of Glastonbury, the place associated in legend with mythical Avalon and with the tomb of King Arthur.

On these iconographic chains and circles of pilgrimage stations—and in iconographic cosmographical illustrations, architectural elements, art works, and many other objects and creations of the late Middle Ages and Renaissance—the icons representing most holy persons and places were often ordered in geometrical and hierarchical fashion in harmony with the presumed level of spirituality of their immaterial essences. It was this ordering of iconography by way of supposed essences—with chains and circles of unfolding icons placed to operate upon the reader-actor moving in procession or on a quest—that was imitated in the iconographic structures and typological narratives of heroic poems. By means of this "processional method of education," biblical events represented by the worldly iconography—the types—were fulfilled in the patterned meditative-physical activities, the antitypes, of the reader-actor.

During the Renaissance iconographic representations are shown to alter in consonance with altering iconographic visions of the "real." The extraordinary iconographic web of correspondences in Dante's *Commedia*, a culmination and *summa* of medieval cosmographical views, gives way in sixteenth and seventeenth century poems to a collage of diffusive emblems and new scientific elements which supplement or supplant the old iconography. Renaissance voyages of global discovery impress new contours upon world maps and lend new shadings to the history of the human race. The advent of the new empiricism and cosmography is seen to have a jarring effect upon heroic poetry, forcing a readjustment of metaphors, imagery and themes. But poets and "makers" from the late Middle Ages through the Renaissance continue also to depend upon the correspondences and structures of the old iconography.

That alterations in general iconographic outlook first preceded and then later influenced alterations in the form and content of heroic poetry seems to me clearly substantiated by the evidence. Dante in the thirteenth and fourteenth centuries, Spenser in the sixteenth century and Milton in the seventeenth, each in turn obviously elaborated upon and reflected in their works the distinctive biblical and worldly iconography, different in each period, that had been established well before they began their compositions.

In the *Commedia*, Dante mirrored that biblical world iconography developed in the fourth and fifth centuries from pilgrim tracts and from writings by clerics such as St. Jerome and Paulus Orosius. This iconography was given detailed form in the sixth through the twelfth centuries in works by Cosmas Indicopleustes, Pseudo-Beda, Sallust, Beatus of Valcavado and others and was disseminated in the thirteenth and fourteenth centuries by the Franciscans and the international orders of knights. This biblical world iconography was also incorporated into Brunetto Latini's encyclopedic *Tresor*, mentioned by name in the *Inferno*.

Elaborated "T-and-O" *mappaemundi* of the eighth and later centuries, typal icons now popularly named after their "spiritual" cosmographic design, serve as examples. Matter in these icons was rendered so as to conform to the assumed configurations of spirit. The "T-and-O" *mappaemundi* were flat projections with the land masses of Europe, Africa and Asia—the then-known world—contained usually in a circle, but on occasion in an ellipse or even a rectangle, with the Garden of Eden at the top-center of the circle at the farthest point east. Asia, harboring sites including Mt. Sinai, the Dead Sea and Jerusalem, was located in the upper half of the circle; Africa with the city of Babylon, modern Cairo, and the Nile River and Red Sea sites, in the lower right quadrant; and Europe containing Rome on the River Tiber, in the lower left quadrant. The medieval *Mare Internum*, the present Mediterranean Sea, divided the lower half of the circle in the form of an altar-like "T." The Pillars of Hercules, modern Gibralter, which gave access to the Great Ocean surrounding the entire circular land mass was situated in a low position at the base of the "T," while holy Jerusalem was placed, as might be expected, just above the "T" crossbar near or at the spiritual-physical "center" of the earth's round land mass. The holy city was in turn regularly drawn as a circle, bisected by two key streets in the form of a cross, nested within the wider circle of the world.

The 12 signs of the zodiac or the 12 wind signs often appeared around the outer perimeter of the circle beyond the encompassing

Great Ocean. On some icons—perhaps the most notable being the Ebstorf map (ca. 1235)—the head, hands and feet of Christ protrude beyond the circle; for the medieval earth was indeed frequently thought to be an icon for the body of God.

On the Hereford world map (ca. 1285) which G. R. Crone rightly believes may have been based on earlier projections of routes to the Holy Land, the labyrinth line of the Exodus leads from Babylon (modern Cairo) in the lower right African quadrant, across the Red Sea to the triangular drawing of Mt. Sinai in the upper semicircle of Asia, and on in a winding manner past the Dead Sea to a terminus near Jerusalem at the middle.

In adapting this sort of Latin-Byzantine medieval world perspective to the iconography of the *Commedia*, Dante, accepting a common medieval belief advocated by Brunetto Latini and others that the earth is a globe, depicted the circular land mass as bent like a concave shell over the northern hemisphere with Jerusalem at the center and summit, the "podes"; and the Great Ocean as extending over the convex southern hemisphere with Eden now an island at the bottom-center, the "antipodes." Other places mentioned by Dante such as Rome, Gibraltar and Exodus locales are in accord with their iconographic representation in early tracts, world icons and in the *Tresor* of Latini.

By the time Spenser was writing in the later sixteenth century, representations of the external world were being radically revised. Empirical irregularity and diversity were replacing the older, underlying iconographic order. Ptolemaic projections, rediscovered and then printed in 1482, added what were then considered new cosmographical forms and emblems to the medieval drawings of Europe, Africa and Asia. Gerhard Mercator's world projections and planispheres, published from 1538 through the end of the century, inspired sixteenth century cosmographers in their delineation of the strange and relatively exotic New World and its peoples to the West, as well as of the old continents and peoples of the East.

As will be seen, Edmund Spenser had access to books depicting both the old cosmography and the new. Spenser mentions the new in teasing fashion in *The Faerie Queene*; but he most prominently introduces into his poem, in a highly imaginative way, nonspacial "antique" ideological core icons in combination with reflections of the medieval "T-and-O" world replete with emblematic beasts, knights, giants, amazons, dwarfs and images related to St. George.

In the seventeenth century in composing *A Brief History of Moscovia,* John Milton appended a list of citations naming as his sources the empirical voyage accounts by British seamen collected in Samuel Purchas's *Purchas his Pilgrimage* (1613), a work written as a revision of the medieval world book. Milton not only followed the empirical citation method advocated in Purchas's unusual cosmographical history; he derived from it and other works, as will be shown, a historical method and a view of historical cosmography unique to his period that is reflected in important ways in the structures and themes of *Paradise Lost*.

In a comparative iconographic study of this kind, it is important to realize that a once influential ideology on the relation of the mind to things, an ideology that the new empiricism was changing, underlies much early biblical and worldly iconographic representation. This late medieval and Renaissance general epistemological theory emerges from, and can be seen to be implemented in, writings such as Dante's *Convivio* and *Commedia*, Kenelyn Digby's two published *Observations*, Edmund Spenser's minor poetry and *The Faerie Queene*, Julius Caesar Scaliger's *Poetices Libri Septem*, and John Milton's *Art of Logic* and *Paradise Lost*. Yet this older and shaping ideology—whatever might be the contemporary critique of its philosophical value—has been obscured and neglected amid the current lively linguistic disputations being conducted in today's highly theoretical and divisive philosophic climate, a climate in which an increasing number of evolving modernist critical movements foster variant epistemological-linguistic theories that are often sweepingly divorced from the theories of the past. In developing Ferdinand de Saussure's postulations on the arbitrariness, or immotivation, of linguistic signs, advocates of structuralism, poststructuralism and deconstruction have made a radical critique of language that has certainly enlarged the possibilities of poetic discourse; but it has also tended to disengage poems from their aesthetic, iconographic and even their ideological settings. Just as iconographic criticism needs to consider the powers specific to poetry, linguistic criticism needs to consider the powers of iconography and ideology upon poetry.

Influenced by neo-Platonic and neo-Aristotelian philosophical doctrines reinterpreted in the perspective of Christian rational and mystical theology, the three major writers reviewed here generally suggest through their works that the intuitive and logical rational powers and, to a lesser degree, imaginative powers of artists and poets as "makers" can conform to and—rather than simply "react to" or "refer to" existing things, or "copy" outward appearances—can also to some extent directly apprehend and immediately experience the supposed spiritually radiant immaterial essences or substantial forms and the related material and other accidental forms of external being. These works further suggest that artistic and literary creations, through their invention, disposition and ornamentation—though governed by conventions of making that are implicit to each artistic discipline—can correspond in underlying meanings and operational structures to the order and nature of the cosmos. Outward natural appearances, usually associated with philosophic accidental forms thought to have no existence apart from central essences or substantial forms, could be adjusted and recast by different artists and writers to best show forth the inward spiritual splendor of the central essences. The underlying meanings and structures of works such as poems, paintings, and even cathedrals are thus in general produced to correspond with the presumed immaterial constituants of external creation.

Iconographic representational concerns as well as rhetorical ones shaped the verse. Rhetoric was often employed in the service of ideology and of iconographic content and form.

This study seeks to acknowledge the functional or shaping influence of a neglected, early and dominating ideology and iconography upon literary form; and at the same time, it seeks to acknowledge in a clear and exacting way the recent iconographic art, literary and architectural criticism concerned with the specific subjects of these chapters. Primary texts and "antique" source materials are placed within a comparative iconographic framework with the aim of critically uncovering core structures and meanings in three major epic poems. It is hoped that these analyses will afford fresh and original insights into how writers adapted important but previously unnoticed biblical and worldly iconographic typology, sometimes in conventional and sometimes in innovative ways, to the demands of their heroic verse; and into how, with shifts in ideology and iconographic representation, Renaissance heroic poetry was transformed.

ONE

Cosmic Typology in Dante's *Commedia*

The Poem, the Cathedrals and the Source Books of God

> "La mente tua conservi quel ch'udito
>   hai contra te," mi comandò quel saggio;
> "e ora attendi qui," a drizzò 'l dito:
> "quando sarai dinanzi al doce raggio
>   di quella, il cui bell' occhio tutto vede,
>   da lei saprai di tua vita il vïaggio."
>
> *Virgil's words to Dante*
> *in the city of Dis*
> *(Inferno 10. 127–33)**

> "Let your memory recall what you have heard
>   against you," the Sage declared to me; "and
>   now mark here"; and he raised his finger:
> "when you shall stand before the sweet ray of
>   that Lady, whose bright eyes see all, from her
>   you shall know the journey of your life."

Two fervent desires underlie Dante's poetically rendered pilgrimage to Beatrice at the end of the *Vita Nuova* and in the *Commedia*: a passionate longing to overcome error and sin in this

---

* References are to book and lines.

life by finding, as a pilgrim, the true pathways to the holiest temples in the holiest cities associated with this lady; and, at the same time, an overwhelming yearning to transcend this mortal realm of suffering and death, to rise through pilgrimage to a vision of Beatrice in heaven. Such desires of intellect and will, giving strength to the rational conviction that pilgrimage on earth is a prefiguration of spiritual ascent in the world beyond, serve as the basis for the structure of Dante's *Commedia* and, when considered apart from Beatrice, of elements in contemporaneous medieval religious architecture. In its encyclopedic scope and its relation of the finite earth to eternal heaven, the poem is an analogue for pilgrimage temples and churches that in the late Middle Ages were widely considered architectural representations of the external physical and immaterial universe.[1]

The medieval conception of the universe as a figural model for religious buildings arose from many early sources, among them St. Augustine's discussion of the order of the cosmos in *De ordine* 2 and the remarks of Macrobius in *Commentarius ex Cicerone in somnium Scipionis* 1.14, in which he describes the universe as a "cosmic temple." Medieval builders of religious edifices were also clearly inspired by passages in Revelation 21.2–31, describing the descending heavenly city, the New Jerusalem, as resplendent in "pure gold, like to transparent glass." Influential too were passages in Proverbs 8.27 and Ezekiel 40.3; these were interpreted as alluding to divine architectural creation. Numerological proportions in medieval religious edifices were developed—though the exact degree of influence has been questioned and debated—using cosmic proportions cited in Plato's *Timaeus* and supposedly advanced also by Pythagoras, and by referring to biblical passages on the size of Solomon's temple.

The *Commedia*, it should be recalled, depicts a pilgrimage in this life and beyond in the Easter season of 1300, a period when, according to Giovanni Villani in his *Croniche Fiorentine*, 200,000 pilgrims thronged to temples and basilicas in Rome during the Church's first Jubilee Pilgrimage. Villani states that it was his own participation in this important event—together with his reading of Virgil, Sallust, Paulus Orosius and other "masters of history" who recorded important events of times past—that inspired him to write his chronicle.[2] The first page of a contemporaneous manuscript commentary on the *Commedia*, produced in Pisa in 1335, contains a drawing of pilgrims bowed before Boniface VIII, the pope who granted exceptional Jubilee indulgences in 1300 to pilgrims visiting the holiest basilicas of the eternal city.[3]

Like the processional architecture of these and other Byzantine-Romanesque basilicas of the fourth through the eleventh century, and of numerous Italian and northern European reconstructions of the round "temple" of the Holy Sepulchre largely of the eleventh century and later, Dante's processional poem contains representations of pilgrimage "stations" and holy "centers" in the medieval iconographic Book of the earth or world. The pilgrim passes through these representations, reenacting and fulfilling in his own spiritual life past biblical events that had occurred far away at the signified holy sites. And like Tuscan and French Gothic processional cathedrals of the twelfth century and later with their comprehensive pilgrimage elements, Dante's poem is constructed to depict a pilgrim's fulfilling movement, not only through stations in this world, but also within the larger Book of the Cosmos that comprises the spheres and the Empyrean. In cathedrals, it was the arrangement of iconographic "types" or *figurae* that made such processional movement possible. Designs in nave floors and associated icons often signified the Palmer's pathway to Jerusalem; altars through their iconography represented the holy "temple altars" in that city; the great wheel windows above, flooded with heavenly light illuminating the ordered icons of the elect, pointed to the Church Triumphant in heaven.

Medieval biblical "typology" or "figurism" was thought to provide, as is well known, a means through which artists and others could apprehend and depict the "true" structure of external reality and universal history. The "true" words of Scripture, church fathers such as Origen, Augustine and Gregory of Nyssa affirmed, could in their literal sense point to and so objectively signify true epochal events—events considered as "types" or *figurae* and represented by artists in appropriate verbal or visual forms—involving "historical" persons, places and things. Applying what came to be known as the "allegory of the theologians" to biblical texts, the church fathers bound together Old and New Testament history by indicating how, in the chain of universal Hebraic-Christian history, each epochal event—the type or *figura*—foreshadowed and then was fulfilled in the next—the antitype. Thus the epochal event of the Exodus, the type, was seen to prefigure the epochal event of the Redemption, the antitype. The Redemption then became the type or *figura* that was next observed to foreshadow the Transfiguration, the antitype, and so on to the end of the world and the eternal bliss of souls in heaven. Abstract or "mystical" meanings could then arise from what was considered the fact of Scripture's literal historical sense.

Just as "historical" figural or typological events were thought to be pointed to by the language of the Book of God's Words, the Bible, so too were these same "historical" events believed to be signified by iconographic markings—visual "types" in the form of relics, stones, rivers, mountains and landmarks, and heavenly bodies—in the corresponding Book of God's Works, the created world and cosmos. The patterned "historical" iconography pointed to by the "words" and markings of these absolutely "true" divine source books was then replicated by artists and builders in the iconographic *figurae* of paintings, mosaics, sculpture, stained glass windows, cosmographical illustrations, church architecture and literature. The churches and other works were designed in part to motivate persons to try to comprehend and reenact the depicted episodes through spiritual meditation and ritualistic action, and thus to fulfill in the events or *figurae* of their own lives the spiritual pattern and meaning of true divine history.

Architectural-literary figural criticism of the *Commedia* has in general concentrated upon comparisons of individual architectural elements in Dante's poem and in medieval churches, exposing, for example, how the iconographic types in earthly floral wheel windows, such as the one in the basilica of San Zeno, Verona, are fulfilled in Dante's transcendent rose of heaven.[4] Yet the sheer volume of iconographic subject matter, together with the difficulty of establishing an encompassing critical perspective, has to a large degree limited comparisons of overall typology to an analysis of Gothic elements of number, structure, multiplicity and unifying *figurae*.[5] The influence upon Dante of that very popular medieval architectural form, the Byzantine "temple" round church, has been neglected, as has the influence of processional-pilgrimage architectural iconography in general.[6]

Recently the medieval Book of God's Words, the Bible, and the medieval Book of the World, with Jerusalem at the supposed center of the northern hemisphere's landmass, have been related to the iconographic figural structure of the *Commedia*. Dante's journey beyond life in the Jubilee Pilgrimage year of 1300 has been interpreted as a fulfillment of corresponding events foreshadowed both in biblical history and in a Great Circle long pilgrimage over 42 stations of the Exodus leading from worldly Egypt to holy Jerusalem, next over a ring of stations of the Redemption in Jerusalem, and then on to the enactment of a ritual of Transfiguration before the gate of Old St. Peter's Basilica on the stations of eternal Rome.[7] The biblical-pilgrimage typology of world and poem, however, can be further illumined through comparison with the parallel typology of medieval churches and temples of Byzantine and Romanesque as well as of Gothic design. Close investigation is, in fact, still required of Dante's integrating "cosmic" light and wheel icons—among them, the circles of the stars alluded to by the poet as an "angelico templo" (*Paradiso* 28.53) and the circular court of heaven called "nostra basilica" by Beatrice (*Par.* 25.30)—as they coalesce with wider church and temple iconography and with the figural structure of *Purgatorio* and *Paradiso.*[8] These circular icons, drawn in part from earthly round church, basilica and cathedral architecture, are types that have their ultimate fulfillment in an all-inclusive "volume": the Book of the entire "Cosmos" viewed by Dante during the Beatific Vision (*Par.* 33.86).

The Book of the created universe is dramatically unveiled to the poet in the Empyrean when he looks upon what, to his finite human faculties, appears as "the universal form of this knot" (*Par.* 33.91: "La forma universal di questo nodo"): the simple flame, or "semplice lume," that unites in a single volume, bound together by love and ingathered in Godhead, all the leaves of the universe:

> Nel suo profondo vidi che s'interna,
>   legato con amore in un volume,
>   ciò che per l'universo si squaderna;
> sustanze e accidenti, e lor costume,
>   quasi conflati insieme
>
> (Par. 33.85–89)

> Within its depths I saw ingathered, bound by
>   love in one volume, the scattered leaves
>   of all the universe;
> Substance and accidents and their relations,
>   as though together fused

"S'interna" can possibly be associated with "terno" or "trinity" which holds together, as commentary has suggested, the pages of the cosmic book with the number three of spirit.[9] The words "si squaderna," meaning scattered or unbound, imply "quaderni"— four each—and so connote the number four of matter, the physical substance of the universe. "Si squaderna" also connotes the four sheets of parchment, the "quaderno" or quire of medieval manuscripts, which were folded and cut to make eight leaves of a book.

Because of the increasing power of Dante's vision, the simple flame that is the "forma universal" then transfigures into one paradoxical simple semblance ("simplice sembiante") that appears as three rotating circles ("giri") of light that finally reflect within themselves our human image ("nostra effige") (*Par.* 33.109–31).

Dante's poetic narrative will be seen ultimately to derive from the transcendent, subsuming Book of the Cosmos ingathered in Godhead. Concurrently, Dante's narrative will also be seen to derive from figural centers of journey, associated with biblical history, in this physical world. By ingeniously inverting and yet preserving figural bonds that join earthly and heavenly types, the poet makes those types in *Paradiso* refer most directly to the transcendent light and wheel icons signifying God, and he makes those in the *Inferno* and *Purgatorio* refer to this transcendent center but also to figured centers on earth.[10]

The icons of Godhead sustain, fulfill and synthesize the antithetical or complementary earthly centers: the central interior "tomba" of Satan within the physical globe (*Inferno* 34.128); the tomb and cross of Christ, the second Adam, in a Jerusalem temple at the center of the northern hemisphere (*Inf.* 34.1–3, 112–17); the nest or "nido" of the human race and the traditional tomb of the first Adam in Eden at the center of the southern hemisphere (*Purgatorio* 28.78; 32.37); and the tomb and temple of St. Peter, the Father of the Church, in an earthly eternal city that is a type for the heavenly city in which the saint appears enthroned on high (*Par.* 27.22–27; 32.124–30).[11]

Satan, in falling to his "tomba" within the earth, caused the land of the southern hemisphere to flee, Virgil explains in *Inf.* 34; this land then gathered in the northern hemisphere with the temple and tomb of Christ at the geographic center (*Inf.* 34.124–29). Dante, in turning from the northern to the southern hemisphere on the hairy sides of Satan, is informed by Virgil that, though in hell, he is under Jerusalem where Christ was "consunto," obviously "consumed" through Redemption on the cross (34.114).

The iconographic-figural relationship between the Jerusalem and Rome temples is illustrated by St. Peter's words among the stars. St. Peter, in fact emphasizing the true sanctity of his temple and tomb in Rome by denouncing their desecration under Pope Boniface VIII, echoes the phraseology and words of Jeremiah (7.4), who three times used the term "temple" in crying out against the despoiling of the holy Jerusalem Temple of the Lord. Peter decries Boniface, who, the saint insists, "usurps upon earth my place, my place, my place" (*Par.* 27.22: "usurpa in terra il luoco mio,/il luoco mio, il luoco mio"). Peter then states that Boniface "has made my burial ground a sewer for blood and stench, whereby the apostate one who fell from here above, is soothed down there below" (*Par.* 27.25–27: "fatto ha del cimitero mio cloaca/ del sangue e della puzza, onde il perverso,/ che cadde di quassù, laggiù si placa").

At the "temple" site of Christ's tomb and cross at the Christian geographic "center" of Jerusalem, anonymous pilgrims of the twelfth and later centuries recorded, a conduit in the rock of Golgotha allowed Christ's blood to flow upon the supposed skull of Adam in the cave beneath (see note 6, chapter 2). And in the *Commedia*, at the old prefiguring pagan world geographic center of Crete, where a chaste pagan king is said to have once ruled over the world, the idol of an Old Man signifying humanity is entombed within Mt. Ida. With eyes turned toward Rome and shoulders toward Egyptian Damietta, the idol weeps red rivulets that flow down to the lake of Cocytus that entombs Satan (*Inf.* 14.94–120). Now in Rome at the temple and tomb of St. Peter, the Apostolic successor of Christ, a sewer rather than a conduit exists through which blood and stench passes and so soothes Satan in the pit of hell.

Dante, in creating and locating his earthly tomb and temple figurism to accommodate the assumed spiritual iconographic order of this physical world, thus becomes the consummate exponent in poetry of an actual medieval architectural mode studied at length by Andre Grabar: the figural Martyrium temple-tomb marking a spiritual-geographic center, related through earthly types and antitypes to the tomb of Christ in Jerusalem.[12]

THE WORLD BOOK AND CORRESPONDING TYPES: NATURE AND ART

An analysis of Dante's culminating temple and circle icons requires preparation. At first, the diversity and multiplicity of medieval pilgrimage typology may seem bewildering. To gain perspective, some preliminary suggestions are needed on a complex subject: how corresponding typological structures can be discerned in the iconographic Book of the World, the Bible, medieval churches and Dante's *Commedia*. A unifying point of view is indeed possible. While medieval pilgrimage typology is nominalist in its encyclopedic multiplication of individual types, it is mystical in its attempts to absorb and harmonize this multiplicity in patterned structures of synthesizing antitypes. These antitypes are eventually represented as merging in the oneness of Infinite

Being. The corresponding structures of antitypes in the world, the Bible, churches and Dante's poem come into focus when types are examined, not in "static" and sometimes confusing one-to-one comparisons, but in terms of their sequential, progressively unfolding operation and effect upon the acting reader, worshipper or pilgrim.

In his famous lecture on the desire of the human intellect and will to move toward true objects of love in *Purgatorio* 18, Virgil cites the substantial forms of objects and carefully explains in philosophic terminology the medieval "operational principle" of progressive perception and apprehension:

> Ogne forma sustanzïal, che setta
>   è da materia ed è con lei unita
>   specifica virtute ha in sé colletta,
> la qual sanza operar non è sentita,
>   né si dimostra mai che per effetto,
>   come per verdi fronde in pianta vita.
> Però là onde vegna lo 'ntelletto
>   de le prime notizie, omo non sape

(Purg. 18.49–56)

> Every substantial form, which is distinct from
>   matter and is in union with it, has a specific
>   virtue contained within itself
> which is not perceived save in operation, nor is
>   manifested except by its effects, just as life
>   in a plant by the green leaves.
> Therefore man knows not whence the understanding
>   of the first cognitions may come

Similarly, a person could gain knowledge of medieval types through the operation and effect of these types, even though the sources of certain "first cognitions" were incomprehensible. In the world, the Bible, churches and Dante's poem, unifying types were arranged—or were conceived as being arranged—progressively to enlighten the reader-actor who was engaged in external processional and interior meditative activity. Thirteenth and fourteenth century religious humanism placed stress upon each person's acting out the journey of this life, the journey of decision on earth that foreshadowed the person's fulfilled eternal destiny. When viewed from the perspective of the moving reader-actor, the multiple elements of pilgrimage typology become ever more coherent and can be seen to guide the reader-actor in a spiritual ascent from "station" to "station," and from associated meditative step to step, toward hoped-for union with God.

This processional outlook is essential to a critical appreciation of the range of pilgrimage typology. By placing recent architectual criticism of medieval churches in the perspective of medieval processional pilgrimage literature; by making processional on-site inspections of stations and churches on the Egypt-Jerusalem-Rome route and in Europe; and then by using pilgrimage typology to gain insight into the unfolding typology of the *Commedia*, all-embracing figural patterns in the world, the Bible, churches and the poem come to light.[13] The reader-actor is almost invariably directed, by the corresponding forms of pilgrimage typology, from a reenacted Exodus conversion of the soul from sin to grace, to a Redemption of the soul through a figured reception of Christ, to a Transfiguration of the soul through figured visions of the elect and of God.[14]

Past studies have revealed how the poetic sequence of Dante's actions beyond life is joined through figural "back references" to events recorded in the Bible, to corresponding pilgrimage events scored in the iconographic Book of the World, and to personal episodes in Dante's own *Vita Nuova*. The *Vita Nuova*, a book of personal remembered history, discloses a pattern of prefiguring personal events by associating these, through typology, to biblical episodes. From this pattern, the fulfilling otherworldly pilgrimage of Dante arises.[15] The *Vita Nuova* recounts the love of Dante for Beatrice as a type of Christ, his spiritual separation and "turn" from his lady after her death, and his partial spiritual regeneration through consciousness of pilgrims, especially of Palmers and Romers.

In the manner of medieval religious buildings with earthly types below and heavenly antitypes above, Dante constructed the *Commedia* from two figurally related but reversed viewpoints. The heavenly inceptive cause of the poem, Dante's experience of a vision inspired by Beatrice in the Empyrean, is recorded in the final chapter of the *Vita Nuova*; the poet tells of a "miraculous vision in which I saw things that made me resolve to say nothing further of this most blessed one, until a time when I could discourse more worthily about her" ("mirabil visione, nella quale vidi cose, che me fecero proporre di non dir più di questa benedetta, infino a tanto che io potessi più degnamente trattare di lei").[16] The earthly cause of the *Commedia* is Dante's awareness of the pilgrimage of Romers through Beatrice's city on their way to Old St. Peter's basilica in the eternal city to view the Veil of Veronica: the "blessed portrait left to us by Jesus Christ as a copy of his most beautiful face" ("imagine benedetta, la quale Gesù Cristo lasciò a noi per e esempio della sua bellissima figura"; *Vita Nuova* 41). This earthly pilgrimage to Rome suddenly stirs Dante to conceive of a sonnet, "Oltre la spera" ("Beyond the Sphere"), describing the pilgrimage of his "sospiro" or sigh to Beatrice in heaven. The sigh charts the otherworldly pathway that Dante will someday take in the *Paradiso*; it ascends through the spheres to the Empyrean where it gazes upon Beatrice who, in turn, is looking upon God.

In chapter 41, Dante then reflects upon the different kinds of travelers, including those known as "peregrini" going to the shrine of St. James in Galicia; he here writes of those whose journeys, when joined, comprise the full Great Circle pilgrimage. According to the poet, "They are called Palmers who go beyond the sea eastward, whence they often bring back palm-branches ("Chiamansi *Palmieri* in quanto vanno, oltremare lá onde molte volte recano la palma"). Dante adds that the other pilgrims are "Romers in that they go to Rome" (*Romei* in quanto vanno a Roma").

Despite the fulfilling journey of the poet's sigh and the poet's brief, final allusion to a mysterious vision, the spiritual "turn" of Dante away from Beatrice in the *Vita Nuova* is decisive. The poet, having fallen into sin and wandered from the direct spiritual path to his lady, is revealed at the beginning of an extended twofold "long pilgrimage" in this life and beyond. Every important spiritual "turning point" in the otherworldly journey of Dante in the *Commedia* is in some measure a development of events in the *Vita Nuova*; for example, his encounter with Virgil on the low desert, his "turn" on the hair of Satan toward Eden and his lady, his meeting with dead souls who are about to climb Mt. Purgatory, his vision of Beatrice in the Earthly Paradise, his growing comprehension from the height of the fixed stars of earthly pilgrimage routes below, his gazing upward in the Empyrean toward Beatrice in the celestial rose. Again and again the memory of the reader—and, frequently but belatedly, of Dante—is swept to the past as events beyond life recur in new and yet strangely familiar patterns. Then in a flood of revelatory association, memory, imagination and reason take a sudden leap, and the meaning of the new event is illumined in the full perspective of Dante's past love and changing relationship to his lady. At the same time, every "turning point" in the poet's journey beyond is inevitably related, by means of typology that points forward as well as back, to Dante's vision of Beatrice in the heavenly rose as she guides the poet's eyes upward toward God. In the Earthly Paradise, Dante's memory of past sin is washed away in the river Lethe. In the Empyrean, certain of Dante's lesser faculties weaken or fail even as the poet's rational intuitive powers increase. But throughout, the poet's imitative figural actions and experiences give an interrelated structure to the work as it successively unfolds before the reader.

How Dante's pilgrimage beyond imitates events in the world book and the Bible has been precisely charted.[17] Just as a fore-shadowing Palmer on earth in the pilgrimage year 1300 moves "uphill" from worldly Egypt over the Sinai deserts, past a "gate of confession" and up the stone terraces and steps of Mt. Sinai, and on to the geographic center of the northern hemisphere at Jeru-salem; so Dante, in an otherworldly reenactment of the Exodus journey, moves uphill over a desert strand, past a gate of confes-sion and up the stone terraces and steps of Mt. Purgatory, and on to a summit Eden situated at the geographic center of the southern hemisphere. Then in a fulfillment of the presaging terrestrial movement of a Palmer to the temple, tomb and cross of Redemp-tion on the Jerusalem pilgrimage way of the cross, Dante in Eden moves to figural representations of the Jerusalem temple, tomb and cross in encountering Beatrice, a type of Christ. Finally, just as a prefiguring Palmer—now taking the name Romer—on a pilgrim-age of return sails through the waters and reflected light of the Mare Internum to the shore near Rome, and then traverses the stations of the eternal city to the gate and tomb of St. Peter and to the relic of the Veil of Veronica; so too Dante, acting out the journey in part through inverted typal correspondences, soars through the light of "the great sea of being" (*Par.* 1.113; "lo gran mar de l'essere") to a "riva" or shore of right love (*Par.* 26.63), and then experiences transfiguring visions of a heavenly eternal city that are compared to the experiences of travelers to Rome.

Past studies have also shown how, within the recurrent narra-tive of the *Commedia*, each of the three central biblical events reenacted in the world beyond is foreshadowed within the pat-terned action of a preceding otherworldly event.[18] When Dante is driven backward after his attempted ascent of the delectable mountain in *Inferno* 1, it is within the matrix of this failed Exodus pilgrimage action, which prefigures true figured Exodus pilgrim-age on Mt. Purgatory, that Dante learns of Beatrice's intercession with Virgil in the vestibule of hell. Beatrice's descent to the vesti-bule presages Dante's figured Redemption before Beatrice in Eden. Then within the redemptive pattern of action in the Earthly Para-dise, Dante sees a miraculous tree that renews itself in a prefiguration of the Transfiguration. Having fallen asleep before the tree, the poet compares his spiritual illumination upon awakening to that of the three Apostles on Mt. Tabor (*Purg.* 32.38–60, 73–84). Dante begins his own Transfiguration in the stars in the presence of the manifested hosts of Christ Triumphant, hosts prefigured to some degree in Eden through the procession that represents books of the Bible and the earthly Church Militant. Among the stars, Dante sees and speaks to the Apostles of the Transfiguration; his spiritual revelations in this realm foreshadow his final Transfiguration before the Cosmic Book ingathered in God.

During Dante's visionary encounters with his lady that are also pivotal junctures in the figural design of the *Commedia*—the final Exodus pilgrimage conversion of the poet before Beatrice in Eden, his later Redemption before his lady also in the Garden, and his interior Transfiguration initially inspired by gazing upon Beatrice in the celestial rose—the poet calls conspicuous attention to his three primary "source books": the Bible, the Cosmic Book that includes the world book, and the *Vita Nuova*. By moving his own and his reader's consciousness backward and forward by alluding to foreshadowed and realized events signified in these three "source books," he provides through the "operation" of his figurism an index to just where in the twofold pilgrimage he has been, where he is in the remembered "present" of his peregrinations, and where he has yet to go.

Dante's awareness of famed "world book" typology associated with Redemption in Jerusalem and Transfiguration in Rome can be readily understood, it seems to me, by modern readers. Yet because the fifteenth century geographic revolution dramatically displaced Mt. Sinai and other Exodus sites from their preeminent locations near the medieval world's "center," readers and commentators, accustomed to modern maps of Italy and the Mediterranean basin that appear in recent editions of the *Commedia*, may find it somewhat difficult to appreciate the earlier and very different typological outlook of Dante and his contemporaries toward the Exodus pilgrimage route and the legendary thundering mountain of God.

In Dante's period, biblical and worldly typology were inseparable. As early as the sixth century, the Sinai monk Cosmas Indicopleustes, in his influential *Topographia Christiana*, had illustrated geographical-biblical "truth" by placing Jerusalem at the world's geographic center and the Sinai sites close to that center. By the eighth century, psalters and biblical commentaries were regularly illustrated with world T-and-O maps of the Sallust and Beatus type showing the Sinai area next to the central Holy City. From the tenth through the thirteenth century, world T-and-O maps— culminating in the detailed projections by Isidore of Seville, Henry of Mainz, Richard of Haldingham, and the creator of the Ebstorf world chart—regularly included triangular drawings of Mt. Sinai on the sometimes marked Exodus path leading through the Red Sea or to Jerusalem at the center.

The fifteenth century empirical geographical revolution transformed Mt. Sinai from a famed spiritual-geographic "type" near the center of the world into a merely physical topographical "feature" now far removed toward the equator somewhere at the southern tip of the Sinai peninsula. Following the Crusades, many western pilgrims continued to visit the thundering mountain of God. It was therefore left largely to the sixteenth century Protestant Reformation attack upon the veneration of relics and pilgrimage sites to end the traditional importance of Mt. Sinai as a type and station on the actual pilgrimage pathway to Jerusalem. The Reformation also helped to create the nearly total modern breach, based upon evolving doctrinal and cultural differences, between the Greek monastic establishment at Mt. Sinai and the Latin West.

THE TEMPLES, LABYRINTHS AND WHEELS OF EARTH

Although the *Commedia* demonstrates Dante's comprehensive knowledge of Great Circle pilgrimage typology—doubtless gained from pilgrimage literature and Patristic commentary, from world T-and-O icons containing illustrations of Mt. Sinai and selected Holy Land stations, and from the pilgrimage and crusading oral traditions fostered by the Franciscans, the Knights Templar and other groups—the poet inevitably was influenced by the pilgrimage art and architecture of medieval churches. What immediately and powerfully confronted Dante as an Italian artist of the late Middle Ages was the international Byzantine-Romanesque-Gothic iconography of long pilgrimage, an iconography richly manifest as part of a living pilgrimage tradition through art works in the temples and churches of Florence, Bologna, Pisa, Rome, Venice, Ravenna, Assisi, and other Italian and northern European cities. Though modes of architectural figurism and iconography differed, the major kinds of religious buildings—the round churches or "temples" largely based in form on Constantine's Holy Sepulchre, the rectangular Romanesque basilicas adapted from the design of imperial Roman law courts, and the cruciform stone-and-glass Gothic cathedrals constructed to receive and project heavenly light—all contained figured pilgrimage stations and altars and relics signifying, with varying degrees of comprehensiveness, earthly and heavenly personages, objects and realms. In Gothic cathedrals, elaborate stone structural systems and structured wheel windows to a large degree replaced Byzantine mosaics and paintings as types for the earthly and the eternal. However, even the famed Byzantine temple of the Holy Sepulchre, as described in pilgrim texts after the sixth century that elaborated upon the fourth century account of Eusebius Pamphila, embodied cosmic iconography in the structural elements of its perfect-circle Resurrection building or Anastasis, its Anastasis hemisphere covering or dome, and its central tomb surrounded by what Eusebius claimed were 12 pilasters representing the 12 Apostles.[19]

In criticism relating such medieval architectural features to Dante's pilgrimage poem, one fascinating subject has yet to be seriously explored: how both the *Commedia* and early temples and churches, in their overall iconography and processional figural structures, are based upon and reflect the core iconography of the "true" source books of God and of pilgrimage stations. It was in the fourth century, it should be remembered, that the first Christian emperor, Constantine, constructed for the use of pilgrims the round Anastasis—or possibly a semicircular Anastasis that was reported to be round in the seventh century and later—after his mother Helena "discovered" key stations and relics while on a Holy Land pilgrimage. The circular design of the Anastasis was then reflected in the circular ground plan with octagonal outer walls of the Dome-of-the-Rock Sanctuary (Kubbet-es-Sakhra) in Jerusalem, erected in the temple area of the city in the seventh century, and associated by pilgrims with the Old Temple of Solomon. In Rome during the fourth century, Constantine is credited with building the basilicas of Old St. Peter's, Old St. Paul's, St. John Lateran and other churches. These structures were built both to house the tombs of apostles, saints and imperial relatives—many of whom had traveled to the eternal city from the Holy Land—but also, according to tradition, to contain Exodus and Passion relics that had supposedly been carried to Rome by Helena.[20] In France during the mid-twelfth century, Abbot Suger— who stated in his *De Administione* that he regularly conversed with travelers from Jerusalem—constructed the "first" Gothic cathedral, St. Denis, as a royal pilgrimage and crusading center, thus, in the words of architectural critic and historian Otto von

Simson, "linking the religious heart of France with Jerusalem, the navel of the world."[21]

Worshippers in the round churches, basilicas and cathedrals moved over the earthly nave floor, or through ambulatories, to the high altar which usually signified temple altars at Jerusalem. At many medieval churches—St. Maris in Acquiro and St. Maria in Trastevere in Rome; St. Vitale and St. Giovanni Evangelista, Ravenna; St. Martino, Lucca; San Giovanni al Sepolcro, Brindisi; St. Savino, Piacenza; and at Amiens; Rheims; Chartres; Sens; St. Michele Maggiore, Pavia; Bayeux; Potiers and a host of others—inlaid stone labyrinth nave floors or labyrinths carved in stone contained intervolved, directional pathways that pointed worshippers to central rose or other medallions. Such medallions usually represented, particularly in church pilgrimage iconography of the thirteenth and fourteenth centuries, the fulfilled and "true" spiritual-geographic "station" of Jerusalem.[22]

A number of the core medallions were scored, within containing floral or geometric iconographic forms, with small minotaur and pagan icons signifying the "old" spiritual-geographic centers of Crete or Troy, foreshadowing types of the "new" Hebraic-Christian center of the Holy City. The minotaur at the core of labyrinths also served as an icon indicating a spiritual-geographic center of evil in the underworld, a foreshadowing type of hell and the figural antithesis of the Holy City. The mazes themselves quite clearly represented the sinful earthly realm. In their configurations as a type of this world, the mazes appear also to have suggested a prefiguring antithetical or corresponding pagan form for the fulfilled and transcending "temple" architecture of Jerusalem, and through wider typological association, for the Christian church architecture of Europe.[23]

Some medieval worshippers could have shown contempt for evil and this world by stepping upon mazes marked with the minotaur. Still, in many pilgrimage churches, the lowly floor labyrinths with their directional pathways would doubtless have conveyed to medieval worshippers not only a sense of a single journey, but also a sense of a hierarchy of earthly journeys to evil and to holy spiritual-geographic centers, with the earthly Exodus pilgrimage to Jerusalem being the fulfillment of prefiguring pagan travels. By moving over "true" labyrinth paths leading to central floral, circular or otherwise geometrically shaped medallions, pilgrim-worshippers on nave floors, after confessing their sins, could have reenacted *in figura* the wandering journey of conversion through the maze of this world to the Holy City. Given the dimensions, the apparent typological function, and the iconographic positioning of the largest of the circular or otherwise geometrical floor labyrinths in pilgrimage churches such as those at Rheims and Chartres—labyrinths extending completely across the main aisles not far from entrance portals—it seems very likely that medieval pilgrims actually fell to their knees on the mazes and so acted out figural journeys to Jerusalem before rising and proceeding down the aisles to main altars. Commentators have long suggested this but have been unable to prove it conclusively.

Inscriptions preserved on extant reproductions of two central "station" medallions identify church architects. Jean d'Obais, first Master Builder of Rheims, and Robert Luzarches, first Master Builder of Amiens, have their names and those of their immediate successors "humbly" scored at the center of the labyrinths in their respective cathedrals. This apparently signified that they had built fulfilled types of Hebraic-Christian "temples" transcending foreshadowing pagan structures of the past, and that they had *in figura* reached the "new" earthly world center of Jerusalem and had yet remained in a lowly spiritual position. Recent studies of the inlaid and carved church labyrinths, particularly the inclusive work of Hermann Kern who discusses 51 such church structures in Italy, northern Europe and Britain, reveal how numerous and popular were these figural pathways to foreshadowing "old" pagan centers and to the earthly Holy City, a type for the heavenly city of God.

Writing of the great cathedral of Chartres in which Dante's last guide in the *Commedia*, the mystic St. Bernard of Clairvaux, had accepted leadership at the urging of Abbot Suger of the planned third crusade to Jerusalem, architectural critic Painton Cowen presents a striking but unelaborated comment on the cathedral's giant 13.36-meter west wheel window; the cathedral's huge, circular 12.885-meter inlaid stone labyrinth in the nave floor; and the pilgrimage of Dante in the *Commedia*.

> Below the rose is the labyrinth, set into the nave at such distance from the west door that if the rose were to be "hinged down" it would almost fit over it. Labyrinths generally symbolize the path of the soul through life, and medieval pilgrims reenacted this, following the path of the labyrinth in the cathedral on their knees, symbolizing the journey to Jerusalem. The rose window superimposed on this labyrinth suggests the mandala, the viewfinder of meaning, projected on to life, as a means not only of finding one's way but also of differentiating between the forces of good and evil. In the *Divine Comedy* we can see identical symbolism in Dante's journey through the spheres of Hell, Purgatory and Paradise on a journey

that, he himself says, could be interpreted four different ways, one of which was that of the Christian through life. On arrival at the last circle of Paradise, Beatrice offers Dante a rose; so too at Chartres the labyrinth weaves its way (there is only one path) through concentric circles and at the centre there is a six-petalled rosette into which the path leads: it unmistakably echoes the rosette at the centre of the rose window that overlooks it.[24]

In Italy in Dante's period, circular twelfth century labyrinths of the Chartres design also existed in churches in Lucca, Pavia, Piacenza and in St. Maria in Aquiro, Rome; and a drawing of a Chartres-type labyrinth illustrates a manuscript copy of the *Commedia* (ca. 1419) now in the Vatican library.[25]

A limited figural analogue, however, will later be substituted for Cowen's sweeping symbolic identification. Cathedral wheel windows and related nave-floor labyrinths will be seen as figural elements generally similar, but not identical, to heavenly and earthly types in the *Commedia*; and movement over an earthly nave floor near entrance portals will be viewed as a type for only specified stages of a long twofold earthly and heavenly pilgrimage.

Worshippers at the main, figured "Jerusalem temple" altars in medieval churches received Christ in the form of the Eucharist and so acted out their Redemption by the Son. In Gothic cathedrals and basilicas of cruciform design, the main altar with a crypt tomb underneath was located, of course, at the cross point of the nave and the transept or *bema* and, in Gothic structures, often orientated toward Jerusalem. Here at the Gothic "Jerusalem temple" altars, the ritual of the reception of the Eucharist was performed between iconographic representations of the Books of the Old and New Testament. Old Testament biblical personages traditionally appeared in the cosmic wheel window of lesser radiance located in the north transept; New Testament personages were represented in the cosmic wheel window made bright by direct sunlight in the south transept.[26]

In round churches, the main altars rested at the centers of the circular naves usually over a crypt tomb. This plan was derived from pagan tomb and temple structures but also from the design of the "temple" of the Holy Sepulchre with Christ's altar tomb at the center of the round Anastasis.[27] The fifth century church of Santo Stefano Rotondo in Rome takes this circular form, and in a general way, so do the medieval figural imitations—either round, hexagonal or octagonal—of the Church of the Holy Sepulchre at Pisa, Bologna, Milan, Borgo S. Sepolcro, Brindisi and other Italian cities. In sixth century mosaics behind the main altar in the apse of

St. Pudenziana, Rome, the round Anastasis is directly represented along with other Jerusalem pilgrimage stations, including Golgotha surmounted by a huge cross of a kind mentioned by the fourth century pilgrim St. Silvia; but the mosaics signify, too, the heavenly Jerusalem by showing an enthroned Christ in the foreground in conclave with his disciples.[28]

At altars where worshippers acted out their Redemption, Passion relics abounded. For example, Last Supper relics and a great variety of others, a number of them said to have been brought to Rome by St. Helena, rested in the *Sancta Sanctorum* altar in the Chapel of St. Lawrence, St. John Lateran. The chapel was located in a separate hall of St. John Lateran that survived the burning of the basilica in 1308. Fragments of the true cross, again believed to have been carried to the eternal city by St. Helena, resided in altars of the fourth century basilica of S. Croce di Gerusalemme, formerly the Sessorian Palace, and were associated with the Jerusalem station, within the Holy Sepulchre, of Helena's finding of the cross.[29]

Worshippers moving toward and gazing upon the lofty paintings, mosaics or glowing wheel windows that often showed Christ at the center of the Cosmos—icons fully visible only from the central main altars of the "temples"—were then in a spiritual and physical position to attain *in figura* a transfiguring vision of personages in the heavenly city and of God. This figured vision could be reinforced by the holy ritualistic movements of clerics below in typological imitation of the radiant images above that were often joined in dynamic designs representing divine procession or circular dance. In the eternal city of Rome, cosmic icons in Old St. Peter's basilica, including a sixth century wheel window, encircled the high altar of the supposed Vicar of Christ. This altar, located over the tomb of St. Peter, was near spiral columns, said to be from the Temple of Solomon, at this new western spiritual center of the Latin Church.[30]

Worshippers in Old St. Peter's engaged in a most spiritually transfiguring action that was considered to be a prefiguring earthly type for Beatific Vision. At designated times usually at the end of long pilgrimage, they briefly viewed one of the holiest relics in Christianity: the Veil of Veronica imprinted with the visage of Christ. Writing of the Jubilee Pilgrimage of 1300, Giovanni Villani observes that, during the period of the pilgrimage activities, "for the consolation of the Christian pilgrims, every Friday and every solemn feast day, was shown in St. Peter's the Veronica, the true image of Christ, on the napkin."[31]

In keeping with the practice of disclosing *in figura* at the center of pilgrimage temples some visual representation of transcendent religious experience, the apses behind the main altars at SS. Cosma and Damiana, Rome; of St. Apollinare in Classe and St. Vitale, Ravenna; and of many smaller Byzantine-Romanesque churches shimmered with mosaics depicting the Transfiguration of Christ. These apse mosaics in Rome and Ravenna have been found to be of the same style, technique and period as the sixth century Transfiguration mosaics. Lateral Old Testament scenes depicting Moses before the burning bush and receiving the Law are found in the apse of the Church of the Transfiguration, St. Catherine's Monastery, at the base of the ring of pilgrimage stations on Mt. Sinai.[32] In the seventh century through Dante's period, there was a steady and pronounced communication over established land and sea routes between the international pilgrimage monastery and ring of stations, controlled by Greek monks, and the Latin West. The Church of the Transfiguration at Mt. Sinai had its own chapel dedicated to SS. Cosma and Damiano, another chapel reserved in Dante's time for the use of Latin pilgrims, and yet another chapel dedicated to Constantine and his mother Helena. She, by tradition, had journeyed to Mt. Sinai as well as to Jerusalem and Rome.[33]

Christ's Transfiguration on Mt. Tabor, as dramatically portrayed in Byzantine apse mosaics of pilgrimage churches at Mt. Sinai, Rome, Ravenna and elsewhere and in a west window at Chartres, was *in figura* the recognized fulfillment of Old Testament events involving Moses on Mt. Sinai and New Testament events involving Christ on Mt. Sion. Many worshippers in cathedrals and basilicas reenacted these events during the Jubilee Pilgrimage Year of 1300 and at other times. In moving over earthly nave floors, they reenacted the Exodus; in receiving the Eucharist at main altars, the Redemption; and in gazing upward upon mosaics or wheel icons of Christ and his elect, the Transfiguration. These were also the events that Latin pilgrims on Great Circle journeys progressively acted out: first, they sought spiritual conversion on the stations of the Exodus; next, Redemption on the stations of Jerusalem; and finally, Transfiguration through viewing the relic of the Veil of Veronica at St. Peter's on the stations of Rome.

Through references in the *Commedia* to that holy person who in life acted out the journey of the Israelites and the Passion and visionary illumination of the Son—"serafico" St. Francis—Dante presents an exemplum of sacred imitative conduct. He also demonstrates a knowledge of that pilgrimage mountain in Italy that served as a local type for those distant, hallowed mountains of the Exodus, Redemption and Transfiguration in the Near East (*Par.* 11.37). According to contemporaneous documents, St. Francis in fact made a pilgrimage from Damietta, Egypt, to the Holy Land in 1219–1220. Early in 1221, the saint journeyed to Rome. Then on Mount La Verna in Italy in September 1224, in an extraordinary reenactment of biblical events originally occurring on Mt. Sion and figurally associated Holy Land mountains, St. Francis is said to have fasted, prayed and meditated for 40 days and 40 nights before finally experiencing a vision of the Crucifixion and being marked with the Stigmata. In November 1224, the saint and his disciples traveled 19 miles to the southeast from Mount La Verna to the medieval town of Borgo San Sepolcro, so named because it harbored yet another Italian figural reproduction of the temple of the Holy Sepulchre. St. Francis stayed there for several days in a hermitage above the town.[34]

With its caves, stone steps, grottoes and ascending paths, Mount La Verna is situated on the eastern border of Umbria overlooking the Ravenna plain. The mountain rises preeminently to the approximate height of Mt. Vesuvius in the region of the Italian Camaldolese hermits. Like the Vallombrosan hermits outside Florence, the Italian Camaldolese were influenced by the hermitical practices of the Sinai and Egyptian desert fathers.[35] In the tenth and eleventh centuries, Greek anchorites from Mt. Sinai and the surrounding desert had come to Italy and Sicily and stimulated the Italian Camaldolese movement, a movement dating by tradition from the fourth century when St. Athanasius visited Rome and addressed his *Life of St. Anthony* to Western anchorites. In 1294 the Mt. Sinai and La Verna eremitical traditions were further joined. As J. P. Migne records, the Franciscan Friar Angelo de Cingulo, employing Latin renderings by "Ambrosio" of the Camaldolese, produced in that year presumably for the use of monks and pilgrims the *Scala Paradisi*, a Latin translation of Sinai Bishop John Climacus's seventh century work the *Heavenly Ladder* (Κλίμαξφείαςαγόδου).[36] Climacus's book of 30 meditative steps to God represented the traditional 30 years of Christ's life before baptism. To a large degree the work was inspired, as exempla in the text confirm, by the spiritual experiences of anchorites on Mt. Sinai's ladder to God. Over 3,000 stone steps, two stone gates and numerous pilgrimage stations, all established by at least the sixth century, enabled medieval pilgrims and monks to move upward from St. Catherine's Monastery at the base to the mountain's summit. To encourage comparable pilgrimages up the pathways and steps of Mount La Verna to sites made holy by St. Francis, the Italian Franciscans in the mid-thirteenth century established various stations on the mountain, built the main church La Chiesina, and constructed in 1263 the Stigmata Chapel over the craggy, ribbed rock on which the saint was said to have been scored with the wounds of Christ. To foster long Holy Land pilgrimages over the route followed by St. Francis, in the early and mid-thirteenth century they founded a chain of at least nine pilgrim hospices in the Holy Land, which were staffed with Italian clerics, that were operating in Dante's period.[37]

Particularly significant is the fact that during this period the seventh successive general of the Franciscan order, St. Bonaventura, came under the influence of the pilgrimage stations to holiness in composing his study of inward steps to meditation: *Itinerarium mentis in Deum* (ca. 1259). Bonaventura, while residing at La Verna, in the mid-thirteenth century, is credited in La Verna tradition with having regularly prayed and meditated in a small oratory constructed against the rock of the Stigmata, an oratory reached by stone steps leading down one side of the rock. The oratory was formally dedicated to Bonaventura in 1509.[38]

In the *Paradiso* Dante precisely identifies that "harsh rock between Tiber and Arno" (11.106: "crudo sasso intra Tevero e Arno") on which "serafico" St. Francis received the Stigmata, "l'ultimo sigillo," after returning from the Near East to gather spiritual "fruit from Italian herbage" (11.105: "frutto de l'italica erba"). The poet thus alludes—possibly as one who had actually climbed to and seen the rough rock in the Stigmata Chapel—to an Italian pilgrimage site and mountain that had become associated, in part through St. Francis, with Mt. Sion and, through figural and historical relations, with Mt. Sinai and Mt. Tabor. In the circle of the sun of *Paradiso*, moreover, Dante as a pilgrim beyond life sees the blazing form of Illuminato (*Par.* 12.130), that follower of St. Francis who accompanied the saint from Egypt to the Holy Land. Presenting St. Francis, after Beatrice, as a type of Christ, Dante learns from Thomas Aquinas that the saint of the Stigmata was born on that slope from which there rose into the world "a sun, even as ours at times rises from the Ganges" (*Par.* 11.50–51: "un sole,/ come fa questo talvolta di Gange")—that is, due east from Jerusalem on medieval T-and-O world iconographic maps. The place of St. Francis's birth, Aquinas continues, should not be called Assisi, but "Oriente" (*Par.* 11.54).

In the thirteenth and fourteenth centuries before the Protestant Reformation, such veneration of earthly relics and of blessed earthly stations, mountains, temples and cities was an accepted part of religious practice in the West. Most substantial forms, as Virgil states in *Purgatorio* 18, were believed to be in union with matter. More important, the spirit had been made flesh. Icons of the Incarnate Christ of this physical world often dominated the typanums and altars of the new Gothic cathedrals, just as references to the Incarnate Christ frequently dominated the typological commentary of the period.[39] True imitation in poetry, architecture or pilgrimage consisted, of course, not in representational invention or action that primarily replicated the accidental forms of matter, but in a conformity of the immaterial intellect with the immaterial substantial forms underlying the veil of matter, and in a revelation of those immaterial forms through personal action or through the "making" of some object or structure. But in this mortal world most substantial forms were necessarily disclosed through the instrumentality of matter.

While abstract meditation with the aid of grace was a paramount means to "true spiritual illumination," medieval meditations usually included the recollection of holy places and events employing remembered visual images. And the religious practices of the period made obligatory the acting out of events through liturgical ritual culminating in the reception of the sacraments.[40] Local or long pilgrimage involving veneration, worship and reception of the sacraments was both a source for and an extension of that ritual. Even the eremitical Camaldolese did more than engage abstractly in the spiritually demanding "steps" of meditation outlined in works such as St. Bonaventura's *Itinerarium mentis in Deum* or St. Bernard's *De Gradibus Humilitatis* (ca. 1121), tracts related through monastic and pilgrimage tradition to John Climacus's *Scala Paradisi* and consequently to the stone pilgrimage steps of Mt. Sinai. Some form of figured action, physical as well as spiritual, was required. A religious ritual was physically performed, or the pilgrim's staff was in effect physically grasped, and a foreshadowing, concrete, historical biblical event was reenacted and fulfilled in the concrete, historical life of an individual.

HISTORICAL PILGRIMAGE "FULFILLED": EXODUS, REDEMPTION, TRANSFIGURATION

Important directional references to Dante's own "historical" twofold pilgrimage to Beatific Vision in the *Commedia* are intro-

duced during the poet's acted-out Redemption in Eden and beginning spiritual Transfiguration at the outermost edge of the physical
universe. At the summit of Mt. Purgatory, Dante imitates scriptural events before a procession signifying the Bible and the
Church Militant; and at the summit of the physical universe, he
further imitates scriptural episodes before earthly pilgrimage paths
and the city of Rome, which are visible in the Book of the World
below.

The Book of God's Words—represented by holy Elders and a
strange beast, the griffin, signifying Christ—is included among the
personages accompanying Beatrice into the Earthly Paradise when
she reencounters Dante midway in his pilgrimage beyond life.
Beatrice appears in a chariot drawn by the griffin, and the Elders
turn to her and sing, among other things, "Come to me from
Lebanon, my spouse" (*Purg.* 30.11: *"Veni, sponsa, de Libano"*), a
biblical passage traditionally referring to the marriage of Christ to
his Church. "Blessed is he that comes" (*Purg.* 30.19: *"Benedictus qui
venis!"*), the procession members later cry, words quoted in all four
gospels as being called out by the multitude when Christ entered
the temple area of Jerusalem. And before Beatrice speaks, nearby
angels in the Earthly Paradise establish the redemptive nature of
Dante's actions in the garden by singing the first part of the
thirtieth psalm, *"In te, Domine, speravi"* (*Purg.* 30.83), which includes the words:

> In manus tuas commendo spiritum meum;
> redemisti me, Domine, Deus veritatis
>
> Into your hands I commend my spirit, you
> will redeem me, O Lord, O faithful God

Then Beatrice, for the first and only time in the *Commedia*, calls
the poet by his name, "Dante," and refers to his "vita nuova"
(*Purg.* 30.55, 115). She next strives to bring the poet's mind and
memory to a realization of the direct but lost spiritual pathway to
God that had once been open, a pathway that in the new life was
such that "every good talent would have made wondrous increase
in him" (*Purg.* 30.116–17: *"ogni abito destro/ fatto averebbe in lui
mirabil prova."* It was, of course, Dante's sigh that was described
in the sonnet "Oltre la spera" in the *Vita Nuova* as ascending to
Beatrice in fulfillment of the prefiguring pilgrimage of the Romers.
And Beatrice here calls this lost spiritual pathway to mind by
referring to the surrounding angels in Eden as the powers controlling the "operations of the mighty spheres that direct each seed

to some end, according as the stars are its companions" (*Purg.*
30.109–11: "ovra de le rote magne,/ che drizzan ciascun seme ad
alcun fine,/ secondo che le stelle son compagne"). Remarking that
"he did turn his steps by a way not true" (*Purg.* 30.130: "volse i
passi suoi per via non vera"), Beatrice then recapitulates, not the
direct journey of the sigh, but the poet's long otherworldly journey
to Eden. She ends with the demand that Dante, in what is clearly a
final act in the conversion of his soul, show "penitence" (*Purg.*
30.145: "pentimento"). After Dante confesses his sins and is drawn
through the spiritually cleansing waters of Eden's River of Leth, he
gazes into Beatrice's eyes and, in a redeeming vision, sees in them
the reflected image of the griffin. The poet is then said to taste of
that "food which satisfying of itself, causes hunger of itself" (*Purg.*
31.128–29: "cibo/ che, saziando di sé, di sé asseta").

Only after presenting visions of the history of Church and
empire does Beatrice, repeating the description of the Palmers
given in chapter 41 of the *Vita Nuova*, associate the poet's completed pilgrimage to Eden beyond life with the completed pilgrimage of Palmers to Jerusalem on earth. She insists that Dante
remember all that he has seen and heard "for the reason that the
pilgrim's staff is brought back wreathed with palm" (*Purg.* 33.77–78:
"che 'l te ne porti dentro a te per quello/ che si reca il bordon di
palma cinto").

In receiving Beatrice as a type of Christ among character-types
signifying the Bible and the Church Militant in Eden beyond life,
Dante has fulfilled the foreshadowing actions of a Palmer on earth
who, in possession of the truths of the Bible, experiences a conversion of the soul on Exodus pilgrimage pathways and then, moving
on to pilgrimage stations in Jerusalem, reenacts the Redemption by
receiving Christ as the Eucharist at a temple in the Holy City.[41] The
poet's actions in Eden are prefigured too, by means of more
immediate "home-city" typology pointing to long pilgrimage: in
the acted-out Exodus conversion of a pilgrim on the earthly nave
floor of a medieval pilgrimage church; in the acted out Redemption
of that pilgrim before a clerical procession, within view of wheel
windows or mosaics and paintings of Old and New Testament
personages; and finally, in that pilgrim's reception of the Eucharist
at a central "Jerusalem temple" altar. In the context of Dante's
poem, the prefigured and fulfilled events take place during the
Easter season of the Jubilee Pilgrimage year 1300.[42]

In Eden Beatrice also enlarges upon the opening statements of
Virgil and Dante in the *Inferno* about the direction of journeys to
the heavenly city and to earthly Rome (1.128; 2.13–33). She now

announces with increased figural lucidity Dante's final heavenly and earthly goal: citizenship with her forever in an eternal kingdom, a realm identified with Christ and with Rome. "You shall be with me forever," Beatrice declares, "a citizen of that Rome whereof Christ is a Roman" (*Purg.* 32.101–02: "sarai meca sanza fine cive/ di quella Roma onde Cristo è romano").

Dante, however, is consistently behind in his grasp of his position as a pilgrim, and in the Earthly Paradise Beatrice declares that his mind has turned to stone (*Purg.* 33.74).[43] Yet when the poet in *Paradiso* ascends to the realm of the stars, when from this spiritual and physical perspective he looks down upon true and false pilgrimage routes upon earth, he is directly confronted with certain literal "truths" about the first stage of his twofold earthly and otherworldly long pilgrimage. These are the "truths" that Beatrice sought without success to convey in Eden by mentioning the "vita nuova" and by pressing the poet to recall alternate short and long pilgrimage pathways both on earth and beyond life that were first revealed in the earlier work. Amid the stars Dante is now in a position to understand in retrospect, and even more completely to fulfill, what Beatrice had suggested and what events in the garden confirmed. Speaking to Dante in a fashion that embraces the "historical" literal sense of an allegory of the theologians, Beatrice unmistakably declares before the Apostle St. James that

> "La Chiesa militante alcun figliuolo
> 　　non ha con più speranza com' è scritto
> 　　nel Sol che raggia tutto nostro stuolo;
> 　però li è conceduto che d'Egitto
> 　　venga in Jerusalemme per vedere,
> 　　anzi che 'l militar li sia prescritto."
>
> 　　　　　　　　　　　　　　　　　(*Par.* 25.52–57)

> "Church Militant has not a child richer in hope,
> 　　as is written in the sun which irradiates all
> 　　our host,
> 　therefore was it granted him to come from Egypt
> 　　to Jerusalem to see, before the term of his
> 　　warfare is completed."

Through the literal sense of her words, Beatrice is clearly saying that during his lifetime Dante has come, not from the earthly world to the world beyond life, but from "Egypt" to "Jerusalem." She calls the poet a child, not of the heavenly Church Triumphant, but of the earthly Church Militant. By means of these typological back-references to prefiguring "historical" earthly events, Beatrice authoritatively reminds the poet that, in acting out a twofold "historical" journey, he has made *in figura* the foreshadowing earthly pilgrimage of the Palmers that was first mentioned in chapter 41 of the *Vita Nuova*. It is this foreshadowing earthly pilgrimage, in imitation of the biblical Exodus of Moses and the Israelites, that has been the historical type and the "true" existential base for Dante's fulfilled "historical" journey beyond life from hell, the antitype for earthly Egypt, to the "milizia" or soldiery of the Church Militant in Eden, the antitype for earthly Jerusalem (*Purg.* 32.22). Beatrice's remarks carry with them the additional typological suggestion that the poet's otherworldly pilgrimage to Eden, in the manner of other recurrent biblical imitative actions in the poem, is in turn foreshadowed and now in some respects is further fulfilled in the poet's ascent to the stars. Here in this stellar realm of the Book of the Cosmos, Dante, as a true child of the Church Militant, learns that his hope is "written" in the sun.[44] This blazing orb shines upon what Beatrice declares to be the "hosts of Christ's triumph" (*Par.* 23.19–20: "schiere/ del trïunfo di Cristo"), that is, the hosts of the Son rather than of the entire Trinity.

These hosts of Christ's Triumph are an unusual and often misinterpreted figural amalgam, representing fully neither the earthly Church Militant seen in the physical world below in the Earthly Paradise nor the heavenly Church Triumphant later to appear above in the immaterial Empyrean. The hosts are there to exalt the Son of medieval Incarnation theology, a Divine-Human Being of flesh and spirit and the Second Person of the Trinity. In this outermost extremity of the physical universe bordering immaterial realms, they appear in the form of stars, those luminously spiritual and yet "mediating" physical objects that direct humanity from the material cosmos to the eternal. The bright central sun, a type for the Human-Divine Christ, is actually said by Beatrice to have a power and might that opens "the pathways between heaven and earth" (*Par.* 23.38: "le strade tra 'l cielo e la terra"). And among the stars, the earthly mother of Christ, the Virgin Mary, appropriately reenacts her bodily Assumption into heaven. This illustrates the way from the earthly to the divine and confirms the union of matter and spirit (*Par.* 23.88–120). "There is the Rose," Beatrice says of the Virgin, "wherein the Divine Word made itself flesh" (*Par.* 23.73–74: "Quivi è la rosa in che 'l verbo divino/ carne si fece").

The stellar hosts and the blazing sun thus figure forth the

fulfilled realm of the Incarnate Christ at the material-spiritual border of the cosmos. This realm is the transcendent antitype of some events and personages of the Church Militant in an Eden figuring the Redemption in Jerusalem, and a prefiguring type and partial embodiment of events and personages of the Church Triumphant in the Empyrean figuring the Transfiguration in Rome. Some typological references, viewed retrospectively, point back first to the "milizia" in the Earthly Paradise and then to the Holy City on Mt. Sion; other selective references point forward to the heavenly city of the rose that is the fulfillment of the Italian city of Church and Empire. Yet the stars in their all-important midway region serve in themselves as spiritual-physical guiding lights, lights to which Dante strikingly alludes by ending each canticle with the word "stelle." It is the dazzling light of the sun, however, that most powerfully guides Dante—and, by implication, all humanity— from the physical universe into immaterial regions of eternal vision.

In the Earthly Paradise, the four nymphs of the cardinal virtues had drawn Dante into their dance, singing, "here we are nymphs and in heaven we are stars" (*Purg.* 31.106: "Noi siam qui ninfe e nel ciel siamo stelle"). But the three dancing nymphs of the theological virtues, prefigurations of the three circling Apostles of the Transfiguration in the stellar heavens, had in Eden only moved toward the poet without reaching him (*Purg.* 31.131–32). Now, by answering questions posed by the Transfiguration Apostles Peter, James and John, Dante defines and embraces each of the theological virtues and so takes a final step toward spiritual union with the Son. The poet also enters into a period of transfiguring visionary experience when he raises his eyes to the blinding but spiritually illuminating light of the Apostle John (*Par.* 25.119). For Dante, in this middle realm of the stars, transcendently confirms his earlier position as a child of the earthly Church Militant, becomes a member of the hosts of the Second Person of the Trinity, and begins his admission to the heavenly Church Triumphant of the triune Godhead.

Dante finally ascends from the stellar sphere to the shore of right love that is the immaterial Primum Mobile, the region where the angels who move the spheres have their "tempio." Here, the poet learns from his lady that twofold directional influences indeed emanate from these realms at the physical-spiritual border of the universe. In the words of Beatrice:

"Questi ordini di sù tutti s'ammirano,
  e di giù vincon sì, che verso Dio
  tutti tirati sono e tutti tirano."

(Par. 28.127–29)

"These orders all gaze upward, and downward
  have such conquering might that toward God
  all are drawn and all draw."

The poet in fact has already demonstrated an implied knowledge of the true figural pathway to the Church Triumphant and the Creator. In defining faith before St. Peter in the sphere of the stars, Dante elaborates upon his earlier assertion in *Inferno* 2 on the journey of St. Paul. The poet had noted that St. Paul traveled over the general route of Aeneas to the "holy place, where the Successor of the greatest Peter sits" (23–24: "loco santo,/ u' siede il successor del maggior Piero"). Among the stars the poet again alludes to St. Paul, the "dear brother" of St. Peter, and to Rome:

" . . . Come 'l verace stilo
  ne scrisse, padre, del tuo caro frate
  che mise teco Roma nel buon filo,
fede è sustanza di cose sperate
  e argomento de le non parventi;
  e questa pare a me sua quiditate."

(Par. 24.61–66)

" . . . As the veracious pen of your dear brother
  wrote of it, who with you, father, put Rome
  on the good path,
Faith is the substance of things hoped for
  and the evidence of things not seen;
  and this I take to be its quiddity."

When Dante reaches that eternal Church Triumphant of the rose, which is compared to earthly Rome (*Par.* 31.31–36), Beatrice extends allusions both to Florence and to the final stage of twofold Rome-heaven pilgrimage that was initially recorded in the *Vita Nuova*, chapters 40–42. She unequivocally declares what, in the literal sense of Dante's journey beyond to the eternal city of heaven, can only now in context be considered "true": that the poet has traveled to the "divine from the human, to the eternal from time. . . . and from Florence to a people just and sane" (*Par.* 31.37–39: "divino da l'umano,/ a l'etterno dal tempo . . .,/ e di Fiorenza in popol giusto e sano"). Beatrice's assertion in its literal sense could not have been made before the hosts of the Christ Triumphant in the material stellar heavens; her pronouncement is reserved for Dante's actual arrival at the celestial rose in the immaterial Empyrean.

From combined allusions in the *Vita Nuova* and the *Commedia*, it can be seen that Dante journeyed from Beatrice's city of Florence, in a realm of time and change, to a hell figuring Egypt, to an Eden figuring Jerusalem, and then to a just and timeless heavenly city figuring Rome. After writing of his journey to the heavenly city, Dante hopes to return, as he confesses to St. Peter and Beatrice amid the stars (*Par.* 25.4–12), to the font of his baptism in the "fair sheepfold" or "bello ovile" of Florence, there to be crowned poet laureate.[45]

FROM EGYPT TO JERUSALEM: SPIRITUAL CONVERSION ON EARTH AND BEYOND

A cultural gulf separates the modern historical consciousness, dependent upon empirical "fact," from the medieval typological and iconographic consciousness that, as can be seen in the *Commedia*, molds personal life to a divine figural framework. A central interpretive problem arises from this separation.

The *Commedia* is frequently and, in my view, correctly interpreted in general as an allegory of the theologians that, in its literal sense, is considered as if historically true. However, Beatrice's pronouncement about Dante's journey from Egypt to Jerusalem in the poet's lifetime (*Par.* 25.52–57)—a statement unsupported by empirical biographical "fact" and seemingly symbolic in meaning—is often regarded in its literal sense as a fiction or "beautiful lie," an allegory of the poets pointing to abstract ideological-spiritual "mystical" senses. Usually an annotation is presented only of the assumed abstract anagogical sense of this supposed "beautiful lie," namely, that the poet in his lifetime traveled from the physical world, signified by the supposed fictional term Egypt, to the heavenly Church Triumphant often said to be represented by the hosts manifest in the material stellar sphere, signified by the supposed fictional term Jerusalem.

Yet this declaration by Dante's lady (*Par.* 25.52–57) is the clearest and most direct accommodation in all of the *Commedia* of the Exodus theological allegory, disclosed in the passage on Psalm 114 (113 in the Vulgate) of Letter X to Can Grande della Scala, a letter now commonly regarded as written by Dante or reflecting his views. The statement is also one of the clearest and most direct extensions in the poem of the twofold earthly and heavenly typology introduced in the final chapters, 40–42, in Dante's *Vita Nuova*. Are readers, then, in effect being asked to suspend disbelief, to accommodate an "adjustment" in the figural pattern of Dante's life, and to accept that the poet in his "historical" lifetime made *in figura* the earthly Exodus pilgrimage of a Palmer?

That is exactly the point. Displaying a medieval typological consciousness foreign to modern attitudes, Dante orders the details of his past life and of his poetic cosmos to conform with biblical figural patterns, just as he so orders the depiction of his earthly life in the *Vita Nuova* by using holy numerological relations and biblical allusions, and just as medieval persons so ordered the structure of the geographic world and of medieval cathedrals by discovering or constructing chains of iconographic stations in holy figural arrangements. Dante employs the kind of medieval figural back-signifiers analysed by Erich Auerbach in discussing souls beyond life in *Dante: Poet of the Secular World,* and by A. C. Charity in discussing the poet in *Events and their Afterlife.* In the literal sense of the *Commedia,* then, Dante discloses that he has made *in figura,* possibly through liturgical-pilgrimage rituals in Rome churches or other Italian churches, or perhaps even at stations in the Franciscan La Verna region of Umbria, an earthly figured Egypt-to-Jerusalem Exodus journey that is fulfilled in his pilgrimage beyond life. He thus follows well-established medieval figural traditions in insuring that matter manifests the truths of spirit; and in inventing a work that both embraces and transcends the personal, he graphically illustrates those essential typological biblical patterns to which, he believes, his own life and, by inference, that of the reader and all persons should conform.

Dante so joins the great host of actual and legendary medieval "pilgrims" whose journeys to Jerusalem or the Holy Land— journeys made in fact, *in figura,* or recounted in medieval fictional works and oral tradition—gave expression to a spiritual pattern in life that was aspired to by great numbers of medieval people. Among these pilgrims in fact and in medieval legend were St. Francis, St. Jerome, St. Silvia, Paulus Orosius, St. George, King Arthur, Charlemagne, St. Helena and Constantine; and through the centuries the actual Palmers from Italy and other parts of Europe. Included too were those persons who can be associated with Dante, both as figured pilgrims to a "station" of Jerusalem and as "makers" of great medieval figural constructs that pointed the way to the Holy City: Master Builders Jean d'Obais of Rheims and Robert de Luzarches of Amiens. Of course, the ultimate typological model for all actual, figural and legendary peregrinations of conversion was the original Exodus journey of Moses and the Israelites as recorded in the Bible and as scored by God in the holy sites of the Sinai.

Like the dead souls in the *Commedia* whose existences in the other world can be seen as extensions, in an altered state, of previous mortal life, Dante's foreshadowed earthly life—gradually remembered and revealed as an acted-out past sequence of ever more holy biblical-pilgrimage events that serve as types—is continued and intensified through the poet's repeated acting out of the same sequence of events in the remembered "present"; these events are now uplifted to a transcendent, otherworldly plane and serve as antitypes. Dante obviously differs from the dead souls in that he is alive. But in an audacious poetic maneuver, the poet in his role as pilgrim imposes upon this foreshadowed world and upon the imagined details of the realms beyond—realms that he nonetheless obviously believes are actually there—the deep-rooted medieval experience of "true" existence as a continuing imitation in body and soul, in appropriate locales, of the same crucial biblical episodes found in universal Hebraic-Christian history.

Through recurrent participation in the cyclical calender of church services centered on Easter, through recurrent actual or figured pilgrimage to holy sites, and through meditation on the cycle of holy occurrences in divine revelation, the same scriptural events were imitated again and again. Such actions, when constantly performed in ever more virtuous fashion under the illumination of grace, were thought to transport a few extraordinary mortals to the spiritual level of the angels in eternity. Each repeated fulfillment of biblical history in the life of an individual, moreover, was in itself necessarily a true, historical event. And from the literal sense of Dante's past foreshadowing pilgrimage in life, as well as from the literal sense of the poet's "present" journey beyond life affording fulfillment on a higher spiritual plane—both the past types and the "present" antitypes being considered in their sequential unfolding as historically "true"—the same senses of the Exodus, outlined in Letter X, arise. The allegorical sense, serving as the figural in theological allegory, points to the historical Redemption through Christ; the moral sense abstractly signifies the conversion of the soul from sin to grace; and the anagogical sense abstractly signifies the movement of the soul from the corruption of this world to the eternal glory of heaven.

lurif invia pphibebant · Denicq̃ uia hoc de ei facre murtinif poffibilitate pfua
fii· qd cu antea natura terrif maria difpararet· ac tuto cingi circuitu firma
per oceanu montiu pdictoru effoffif radicib; divullfoq̃ confufio camporu:
deuerif lacunif q̃ terrarii· improuifum pelagifin ufu impigre mortalitauf ad
nufit· pmutauif orbif facie naturaq̃ diferimina· Hoc igitur freto tuorfu eu
ropa diftendatur· ufq̃ in tanaif fluminif curgit· a quo mehoant ufia· nili m
dem aluea limitat · & ut quide iulluf eande africaq̃ difrumpenf· telluruf com
pleeu interfecauf multitudine fluvioru· europa tamen interminari ppon
tidif faucib; dicere quia plurimiq̃ que apponidif pangufta defcendenf· ad meo
tide quoq̃ perfertur·

1. An unusual twelfth century *mappamundi* originally from the
Dominican monastery of San Marco, Firenze, where Dante probably
studied. Jerusalem appears as a dot at the center, and the Mare
Internum is seen as a T-shaped form curving upward in an arc to the
right. The *mappamundi* illustrates Marianus Capella's *La visione del
mondo. Courtesy of Bibliotèca Medicea Laurenziana (S. Marco 190).*

2. Twelfth century illustration of the Book of God's Works from Sallust's *Bellum Iugurthenum*. A low circular iconographic earth in T-and-O form corresponds with a high, more spiritual circular iconographic heaven with seven planets and a zodiac. This correspondence was imitated by Dante in his representation of a T-and-O earth and a seven-planet heaven, just as it was imitated in the earthly nave floor designs and the heavenly rota-rosa windows of churches. *Courtesy of the British Library.*

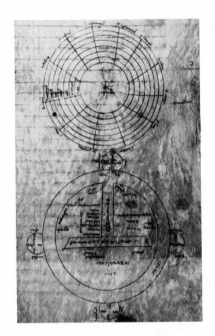

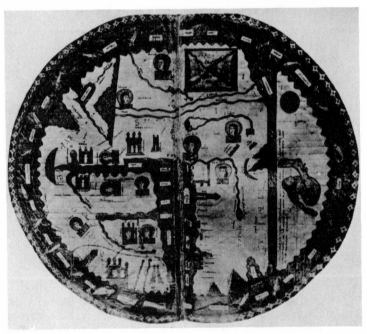

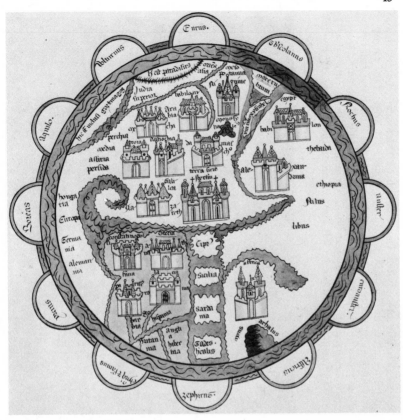

4. Mappamundi (ca. 1380) encompassed by the 12 signs of the zodiac showing "Babylon" in Egypt, the Red Sea, Mt. Sinai (upper right to left), Jerusalem (center), Rome (lower left-center), and Paris (lower left). *From* Grandes Chroniques de St. Denis, *courtesy of the British Library.*

3. (Opposite page, bottom) On this Osma Beatus T-and-O world iconographic map (ca. 1203), the heads of the 12 Apostles each appear in the land where that Apostle preached, surrounding the central region of the Holy Land and Jerusalem. The River Jordan flows into the Dead Sea (upper right). The map illustrated Beatus of Valcavado's commentary on the Apocalypse. *Courtesy of Biblioteca Medicea Laurenziana (Cod. Plut. 64.18).*

46

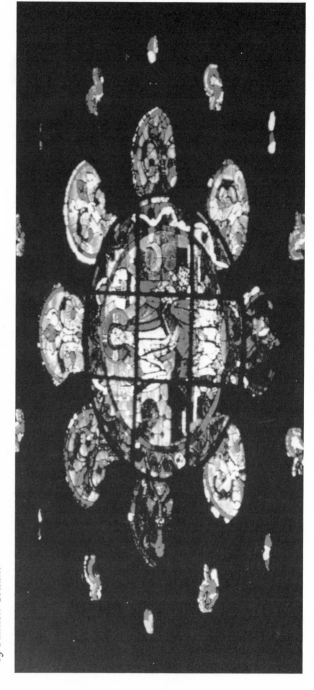

5. The two ultimate medieval source books of "historical" truth, upon which Dante based the "historical" figuralism and structure of the *Commedia*, are depicted in this mid-thirteenth century rosette window at Chartres. Christ as the Logos sits enthroned at the center of the circular cosmos, with the circular world in his left hand and the Bible lying half open on his left knee, giving a blessing and presenting the Books of His Words and Works. At the middle of the world in Christ's hand, a spired building marks the place traditionally used to signify Jerusalem. Enveloping Christ within the round window design are white and yellow stars, red planets, the sun on the left and the moon on the right. *Photograph by Painton Cowan.*

47

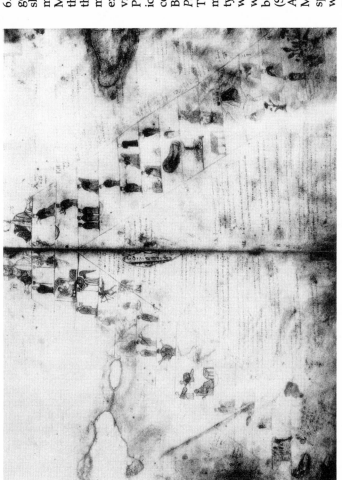

6. Detailed eleventh century geographic icon of Mt. Sinai, shown in its traditional mappamundi location between the Mare Mortuum (left of center) and the Red Sea (dark projections on the right). Personages on the mountain's steps to God serve as exempla of specific virtues and vices—Charity, Avarice, Gluttony, Pride, Lust and Penitence. The icon appears as the table of contents for a manuscript of Sinai Bishop John Climacus's *Scala Paradisi* (late thirteenth century). The pilgrimage pathway up the mountain of Exodus, a figural type for Dante's Mt. Purgatory, was described in numerous western pilgrimage tracts beginning with that of St. Silvia (St. Etheria) in the fourth century. At the monastery of St. Catherine, Mt. Sinai, medieval pilgrims who spoke different languages, but who were joined together by the common experience of ascending the holy mountain's stairs, could view many early icons depicting the ladder to God. *From the Monastery at Patmos (Cod. 122, fol. A–B).*

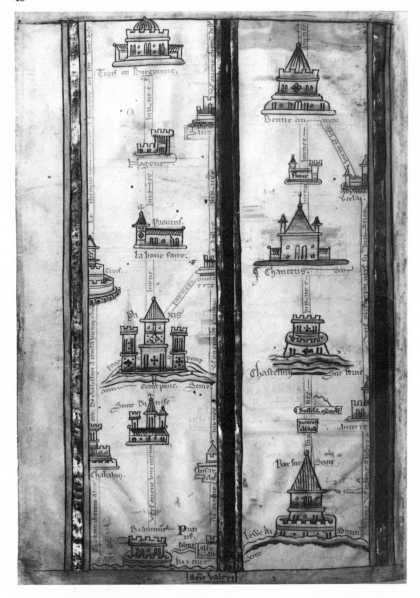

7. The long pilgrimage pathway is shown as a straight line, passing through the city of Paris, in Matthew of Paris's *Itinerary* (thirteenth century). The author, a St. Alban's Abbey monk, records and illustrates the pilgrimage from England, through Canterbury and Dover, across France to Italy, and then includes a map of the Holy Land. Paris's direct line contrasts with the wavering line used in early texts to delineate the path of the Exodus. *Courtesy of the British Museum.*

8. The stone Gate of Confession and some of the approximately 3,400 stone steps, on the medieval pilgrimage pathway up Mt Sinai to the summit chapel of Moses. *Photograph by O. F. A. Meinardus.*

9. Stone steps ascending from the grotto of St. Francis on the medieval Franciscan pilgrimage pathway on Mt. La Verna. This mountain rises over the Ravenna plain that was an Italian antitype for the Holy Land pilgrimage mountains of vision and Redemption. In *Paradiso* 9, Dante refers to the "l'ultimo sigillo" that marked St. Francis on the "crudo sasso" of Mt. La Verna. *Photograph by the author.*

10. Detail from the Ebstorf mappamundi (ca. 1235) illustrating the place of the Israelites' Red Sea crossing, Mt. Sinai and the medieval summit chapel of Moses on the mountain. *Courtesy of the New York Public Library.*

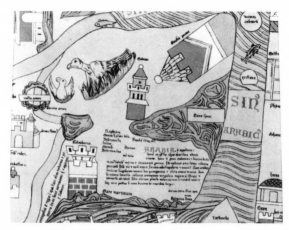

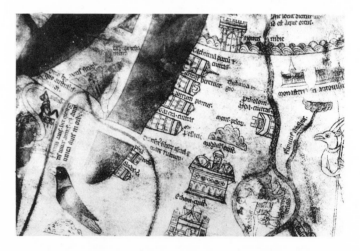

11. Detail from the Hereford mappamundi (ca. 1285) by Richard of Haldingham showing the line of Exodus (lower left). In accord with tradition, the line moves across the Red Sea to a triangular drawing of Mt. Sinai and ends southeast of the "center" of the world at Jerusalem (not shown here). The Nile River is rendered as a vertical line on the right. In a twelfth century *Descriptio* still used as a pilgrim guide book in the seventeenth century, the pilgrim Fetellus identified 42 stations of the Exodus along a pathway corresponding to the Hereford map. Anonymous pilgrim VI (twelfth century) made the same identification. *Photograph by P. Dean. Courtesy of the Dean and Chapter of Hereford Cathedral.*

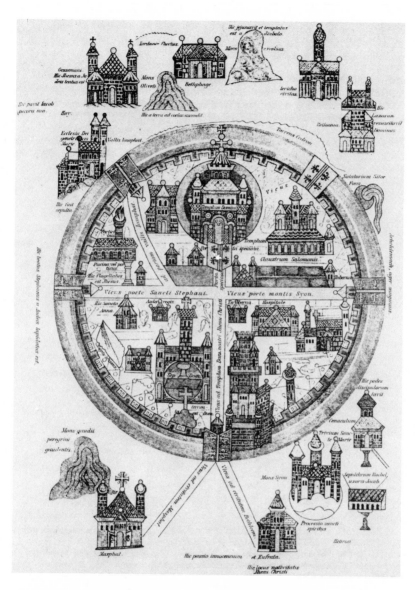

12. In consonance with the accounts of pilgrims, the famed medieval cross of Redemption on Golgotha and the round urn-shaped stone marking the center of the world within the Holy Sepulchre are reproduced on this map (ca. 1180) from *Itinera Hierosolymitana Crucesignatorum*. The major streets of Jerusalem form a cross within the perfect circle of the city. *From ZDPV, Bd. XV, fol. 1 (Leipsig, 1892).*

13. Apse of St. Pudenziana, Rome. Late fourth or early fifth century Byzantine mosaics depict Christ and the Apostles before the actual medieval pilgrimage stations of the Redemption in Jerusalem. The earthly Jerusalem serves as a foreshadowing type for a fulfilled immortal realm. At the left is the round Anastasis of the Holy Sepulchre. At the center is the huge jeweled cross, erected on Golgotha in the fourth century by Emperor Theodosius I, that was regularly reproduced on medieval icons of the Holy City.

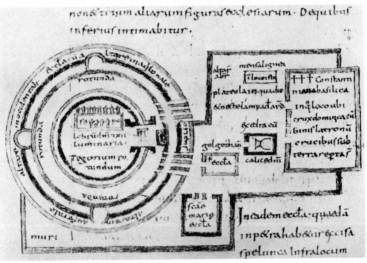

14. The earliest detailed ground plan drawing for the Holy Sepulchre. *From the Holy Land pilgrimage narrative of Arculf (ca. 670), Vienna, ms. 458, fol. 4v.*

15. The urn-shaped stone marking the medieval "center of the world" as it stands today in the choir of the Holy Sepulchre in Jerusalem. Dante reflects medieval iconographic views in *Purgatorio 2*, writing of Jerusalem's position at the center of the earth's circular land mass in the northern hemisphere. *Photograph by the author.*

16. At the medieval "New Jerusalem" of San Stefano, Bologna, an urn-shaped stone stands before an Italian figural reconstruction of the temple of the Holy Sepulchre, replicating the stone at the world's center in Jerusalem. From the tenth through the twelfth century, a chain of pilgrimage stations—fulfilled types of those in the Holy City—were established at San Stefano so that persons could reenact a Jerusalem pilgrimage while remaining at home. *Photograph by the author.*

54

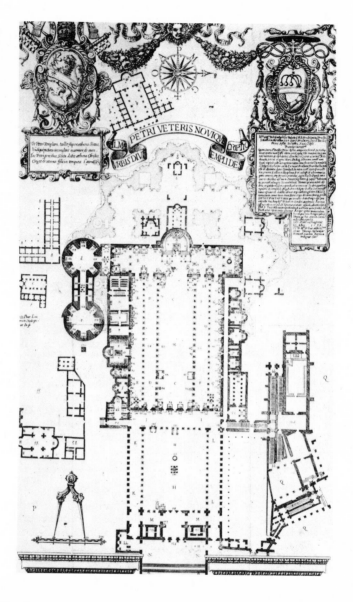

17. The Constantinian basilica of Old St. Peter's from a sixteenth
century ground plan of Alpharanus. In Dante's time, the basilica
included the two circular martyria on the south, columns near the main
altar supposedly from Solomon's Temple, and a sixth century wheel
window in the eastern facade. *From* De basilicae Vaticanae, *pl. I.
Courtesy of the Bibliotèca Vaticana.*

18. The mosaic of the Transfiguration in the apse of St. Vitale, Ravenna.

TWO

The Temple, Wheels and Rose of Dante's Heaven

Transfiguration and the Cosmic Book

The radiant eyes of Beatrice lead Dante on the journey of his life to the Cosmic Book unified in God. In Eden, the eyes dazzlingly shimmer "like the sun in a mirror" ("Come in lo specchio il sol")[1] with the twofold form of a holy beast, the griffin, signifying Christ. Among the fixed stars these eyes, beaming vast distances, give a startling and transcendent clarity to Dante's own vision:

> così de li occhi miei ogne quisquilia
>   fugò Beatrice col raggio d'i suoi,
>   che rifulgea da più di mille milia.

(Par. 26.76–78)

> so Beatrice dissipated every mote
>   from my eyes with the ray of her own
>   that shone for more than a thousand miles.

In a passage of extraordinary poetic power, Beatrice's eyes flash in the Primum Mobile "as a taper's flame in glass" (*Par.* 28.4: "come in lo specchio fiamma di doppiero") with the reversed image of the entire physical universe. And they last gaze down upon Dante, before turning to the eternal fountain of light, from the distant celestial rose. So clear is Dante's vision of Beatrice in this immaterial realm that the poet writes, "her image descended to me not mingled with any medium" (*Par.* 31.77–78: "süa effige/ non discendëa a me per mezzo mista").

The radiance in Beatrice's eyes, like the lesser glow in other substances, is of a special kind. Early in the *Paradiso* when Dante

asks his lady about the light passing through the partially translucent and yet spotted substance of the moon, Beatrice replies that
the moon does not reflect light as do medieval looking glasses
composed of "glass which hides lead behind itself" (*Par.* 2.89–90:
"vetro/ lo qual di retro a sé piombo nasconde"). She offers a
metaphysical explanation. "Divers virtues make divers alloy" (*Par.*
2.139: "Virtù diversa fa diversa lega"), Beatrice explains:

> Per la natura lieta onde deriva,
>   la virtù mista per lo corpo luce
>   come letizia per pupilla viva.
> Da essa vien ciò che da luce a luce
>   par differente, non da denso e raro
>
> (Par. 2.142–46)

> Because of the glad nature from which
>   it flows, the mingled virtue shines
>   through the body as gladness does through a living pupil.
> Thence comes what seems different between light and light
>   not from density and rarity

It is the virtue of the object, not its physical constitution, that
determines the level of its spiritual illumination.

Later in the Primum Mobile, Beatrice tells Dante how the threefold light of God instantaneously created the angels just as light
passes instantaneously through glass and virtuous stones. On this
occasion she adds no comment about the "vetro" or glass being
coated on one side with lead to form a reflective surface on the
other. She instead uses the world "vetro" in its primary sense to
denote a virtuous transparent substance which light illumines and
through which it is conveyed.

> E come in vetro, in ambra o in cristallo
>   raggio risplende sì, che dal venire
>   a l'esser tutto non è intervallo;
> così 'l triforme effetto del suo sire
>   ne l'esser suo raggiò insieme tutto,
>   senza distinzione in essordire.
>
> (Par. 29.25–30)

> and as in glass, in amber, or in crystal, a ray
>   so glows that there is no interval from its
>   coming to its prevading all;
> so the threefold effect rayed out all
>   at once from its Lord into its being,
>   without distinction of beginning.

Though the radiance of Beatrice's eyes, like that of glass, must be understood in a metaphysical sense, John Leyerle and James L. Miller have persuasively advanced an interrelated philosophic-naturalistic explanation of the peculiar power of this lady's eyes to be internally illumined and to reflect, transmit, focus and "ray" divine light.[2] Their explanation is based upon the thirteenth century optical knowledge of Roger Bacon, Albertus Magnus, Thomas Aquinas and others. Dante's lady, Leyerle and Miller maintain, gazes with the optical powers discovered by Robert Grosseteste (ca. 1168–1253) and largely embodied by medieval glaziers in the layered "specula,"optical glasses or lenses, that conveyed sharp beams of heavenly light through lofty rota-rosa windows down to worshippers in twelfth and thirteenth century cathedrals. The round transept windows at Lincoln cathedral, Leyerle notes, were actually referred to as the "two eyes of the church" ("Ecclesiae due sont oculi") in an anonymously written thirteenth century poem on the life of St. Hugh, Bishop of Lincoln.[3]

Knowledgeable references to optics appear in a number of late medieval literary works, the most notable being Jean de Muen's continuation of the *Roman de la Rose* (ca. 1280). In Prosa IV of the continued poem, the author introduces the figure Nature who, in presenting a discourse on optics, explains the many optical effects that result from light striking or passing through glass which is transparent, polished, coated on one side, or formed into different kinds of lenses. The discourse has rightly been interpreted as suggesting that the poem itself, referred to as a "miroure" by Jean de Muen, is both a reflecting glass and lens radiating and deflecting light upon love and lovers.[4]

Dante's use of the words "speglio," "specchio" and "speculum," given poetic contexts and medieval meanings, also appears usually to connote both a reflective "looking glass" and a transparent "optical glass" or lens. When Beatrice's eyes in the Primum Mobile are compared to a "specchio" (*Par.* 28.4), for example, Dante seems to be signifying that they simultaneously retain, mirror and "beam" light in accordance with their metaphysical virtue but also in a way consonant with the optical knowledge of the period. Yet the radiance of Beatrice's eyes would doubtless have been widely suggestive to early readers, calling to mind an unearthly medieval metal mirror that is forever untarnished, or a crystal prism through which light rays, or a stained glass window panel transformed by internal or external darkness from a lens into a bright, reflective surface. And always Beatrice's eyes would be observed to glimmer with the light of God's love and grace.

Dante's more general "rota" and light icons, as they embrace and synthesize both the physical universe that is mirrored in Beatrice's eyes and the figured "wheels" of the celestial city and of Godhead, surely have medieval architectural sources. Throughout Italy, Europe and the Near East, the perfect circles of the earthly wheel windows, as numerous commentators have confirmed, manifested the entire cosmos. The concentric rings with a divine image at their center often contained *figurae* variously showing the earthly paradise, moon, planets, sun, stars, zodiac and immaterial heavens. The "rosa" form of the windows, by tradition, signified both the Virgin Mary and heavenly love; translucent colored icons of the Virgin, frequently appeared in the center or summit panels of the windows, glowing in the heavenly light that also illumined other panels traditionally depicting Old and New Testament personages. The "rota," with its tracery of spokes and petals, was conceived of as a complex geometrical-theological model of divine cosmic order, and also signified the dynamic nature of an active, creative Godhead and universe. Uplifted high in the cathedral facade and transepts, the "rota" windows served as types of the cosmos that both fulfilled and subsumed the circular icons of just the physical earth represented in T-and-O altar icons and in the round "mazes" inlaid in stone in the nave floor.

Just as Dante gave form to the iconography of the Book of the World in the *Commedia* by using the popular literature of "spiritual geography" and pilgrimage, he gave form to the transcendent Book of the Cosmos in his poem by employing the popular art of cathedral architecture.

Like Abbot Suger, the twelfth century builder of the "first" Gothic cathedral St. Denis, Dante was inspired by a number of celestial cosmographers, including St. Paul and pseudo-Dionysius. In the immaterial Primum Mobile, Dante poetically constructs a "wondrous and angelic temple" (*Par.* 28.53: "miro e angelico templo") according to the divine order manifest in musical harmony and in the metrics of number, "as a song with its measure" (*Par.* 28.9: "come nota con suo metro"). But taking his inspiration from the "perfect" architectural forms of the classical and Byzantine Orient, the poet creates a transcendent temple having "only love and light for boundary" (*Par.* 28.54: "solo amore e luce ha per confine"), the kind of temple of which Suger could only dream.

Dante's version of the cosmic temple comes just after the poet, in the lower sphere of the fixed stars, has viewed pilgrimage routes in the physical world and has been told by his lady of the Egypt-to-Jerusalem foreshadowing segment of his long pilgrimage. Now having ascended to the Primum Mobile, his mind "imparadised" by his lady (*Par.* 28.3), Dante experiences a wider vision of the physical book of the universe that has its being in God. It is at this juncture that the poet sees what is called the "volume" (*Par.* 28.14) of the material cosmos reflected, reversed and glowing like a flame from his lady's eyes.

In a passage of extraordinary economy and striking poetic power, Dante describes how he turns his gaze from the eyes of Beatrice to a "temple" that gives form to the physical universe:

> come in lo specchio fiamma di doppiero
>   vede colui che se n'alluma retro,
>   prima che l'abbia in vista o in pensiero,
> e sè rivolge, per veder se 'l vetro
>   li dice il vero, e vede ch'el s'accorda
>   con esso come nota con suo metro;
> così la mia memoria si ricorda
>   ch'io feci riguardando ne' belli occhi,
>   onde a pigliarmi fece Amor la corda.
> E com' io mi rivolsi, e furon tocchi
>   li miei da ciò che pare in quel volume,
>   quandunque nel suo giro ben s'adocchi,
> un punto vidi che raggiava lume
>   acuto sì, che 'l viso, ch'elli effoca,
>   chiuder conviensi per lo forte acume;

(Par. 28.4–18)

> as one who sees in a mirror a taper's flame
>   lighted behind him before he has it
>   in sight or in thought
> and turns around to see whether the glass
>   tells the truth, and sees that it accords
>   with it as song with its measure,
> so my memory recalls that I did,
>   gazing into the beautiful eyes in which
>   Love made the noose to capture me;
> and when I turned, and my own were met
>   by what appears in that volume whenever
>   one gazes intently on its circling,
> a point I saw that rayed forth light so keen
>   that the vision on which it blazes needs
>   must close because of its strong power;

Dante now observes one-by-one, in an unfolding vision, nine angelic circles of fire that comprise the temple; these circles whirl around this penetrating point of brightness. The inmost and brightest circle wheels so rapidly that it surpasses in speed the motion of the outermost and fastest moving sphere of the physical universe; the other angelic circles turn at ever slower speeds in proportion to their increasing distance from the central light. Dante sees that in the physical universe the reverse is true; the innermost corporeal spheres move at ever slower speeds in accord with their nearness to the earth.

The poet understands at once that the immaterial angelic temple is the model or "essemplo," and the physical universe is its copy or "essemplare" (*Par.* 28.55–56); but he expresses puzzlement over why the movements of these circular immaterial and material divine constructs differ. Beatrice declares that in the physical universe, the outermost spheres have greater speed because they possess greater virtue in accord with their greater size; while in the angelic temple, the innermost spheres closest to the central light have the most virtue and spiritual brightness and so move with the greatest rapidity. But even in this inversion of speeds and virtues, Beatrice perceives a marvelous correspondence in design.

> "tu vederai mirabil consequenza
>   di maggio a più e di minore a meno,
>   in ciascun cielo, a sua intelligenza"
>
> (*Par.* 28.76–78)

> "You will see a marvelous agreement of greater
>   to more and of smaller to less, in each
>   heaven with respect to its Intelligence."

And identifying the intense point of light with Godhead, she announces that "On that point the heavens and all nature are dependent" (*Par.* 28.41–42: "Da quel punto/ depende il cielo e tutta la natura").

Dante's vision of the angelic temple directs the reader's awareness backward but also forward to a figurally related sequence of light icons. Disclosed within or through the movements of Beatrice's circular eyes, these icons are manifest as ever more distinguishable and more dazzlingly illumined concentric circles and points of brightness. The foreshadowed and fulfilled light icons lead Dante spiritually upward from the reflected image of the griffin—blazing in his lady's round eyes as the sun in a looking glass, and seen in the round "nido" or "nest" (*Purg.* 28.78) of Eden figuring Jerusalem—to the penultimate vision of Godhead, first observed as a single flame and then as three rotating circles of light. After leaving the Earthly Paradise at the beginning of *Paradiso*, Dante had followed Beatrice's gaze aloft, "like a pilgrim whose will is to return" (*Par.* 1.51: "pur come pelegrin che tornar vuole"), to the luminescence of the round sun. In the sphere of this orb, his power of sight was increased through the "splendor" of his lady's eyes (*Par.* 10.62); and he had witnessed twin sparkling circles of dancers that included St. Francis and St. Benedict, circles that wheeled about himself and his lady "like stars neighboring the fixed poles" (*Par.* 10.78: "come stelle vicine a' fermi poli"). And in this realm he had again seen, now at closer range, the blazing sun. "Give thanks, give thanks," Beatrice had asserted, "to the sun of the Angels, who of his grace that to this sun of sense exalted you" (*Par.* 10.52–54: "Ringrazia/ ringrazia, il Sol de li angeli, ch'a questo/ sensibil t'ha levato per sua grazia"). Among the stars, the poet had been briefly blinded when the Apostle St. John approached nearer still like "the sun eclipsed a little" (*Par.* 25.119: "eclissar lo sole un poco"). The icons of the physical sun that signify divine light, each icon prefiguring the next, are largely fulfilled in the Primum Mobile in the concentrated point of spiritual light mirrored in Beatrice's eyes. This light foreshadows the final, refulgent, circular icon of Beatific Vision.

The progressively developed figurism of the *Commedia* also explicitly reveals the circular iconographic models—found in both the physical Book of the Cosmos and the earthly Book of the World—for the round, immaterial temple of the angels. The typology of the poem implies that the nested spheres of the universe of sense or "mondo sensibile" (*Par.* 28.49) are a grand, cosmic physical temple formed after the angelic original. This temple is rendered throughout *Paradiso*, consonant with the medieval texts of Sallust and others, as being comprised from low to high of the spheres of the Moon, Mercury, Venus, the Sun, Mars, Jupiter, Saturn, the Fixed Stars and the Primum Mobile. Yet the temples of the angels and of the material spheres are in turn prefigured in the circular "nest" of Eden, at the center of the southern hemisphere, that contains types of the Old and New "circular" Temples in what was considered the circular city of Jerusalem. Thus, Dante did not create the angelic temple according to the Latin cruciform plan; he followed the circular classical-Byzantine design used both in the medieval Old Temple and in the Anastasis of the New Temple of the Holy Sepulchre and in their figural replication in Italy and Europe.

At the center of the angelic temple, Dante placed the point of light, surrounded by moving circles of sparks signifying Godhead. Through typology this point of light refers forward to the central light and nested circles of the Beatific Vision just as it refers back to the tomb of Christ at the center of the nested-circle design of the Holy Sepulchre's Anastasis. The angelic temple's point of light can even be seen to refer back farther still to the monstrous, antithetical type of all that is unholy: to Satan entombed at the earth's center at the core of the infernal city Dis, the figural opposite of the heavenly city of the rose.

It has been shown that Dante meets Beatrice, a type of Christ, when she appears in a chariot in the figured setting of the Old Temple on sacred Mt. Sion. In Eden as the poet faces east toward the point of the rising sun, he observes the divine pageant accompanying Beatrice glide into view at the moment dazzling light flashes and heavenly voices sing "Osanna" (*Purg.* 29.51). This is the chant cried out by the multitude—as recorded in the Gospels of Matthew, Mark and John—when Christ descended the Mt. of Olives, climbed the western hill of Mt. Sion and entered into the Old Temple enclosure of Jerusalem. It is also the chant sung by the nine angelic orders in the fulfilled round angelic temple of the Primum Mobile, as they move in perfect circles about the central light of Godhead (*Par.* 28.94). In terrestrial Eden, Dante proceeds in procession with Beatrice from the figured site of the Old Temple to a place where a spar of the chariot of the Church is bound to the tree from which the spar came: Eden's tree of life that was said to have supplied the wood for Christ's Cross. Associated with the Cross, this place signifies the New Temple of the Holy Sepulchre that enclosed both the traditional Golgatha, with the alleged burial site of Adam's skull beneath, and the traditional tomb of Christ.[5] Just before the spar and tree are bound together and so presumably crossed, voices in Eden murmur the name "Adamo" (*Purg.* 32.37), thus emphasizing the Redemptive nature of the Cross of Jerusalem in overcoming the sin of this First Parent. In fact, the New Temple of the Holy Sepulchre also sheltered the supposed cleft rock through which, according to pilgrims, Christ's blood flowed down from the Cross upon the skull of Adam below.[6] Both the Old and New round Temples of Jerusalem were restored in the Middle Ages to contain nested rings of stations about which pilgrims and others circled, in imperfect but solemn imitation of divine movements like those of the angels, to the holiest points at the center: the rock of the altar of Solomon at the Old Temple and the tomb of Christ at the New Temple. Both of these holy stations were venerated as sources of spiritual light.

When Dante initially writes of seeing the angelic temple mirrored in Beatrice's eyes, he appears to refer to the Knights Templar. Until the destruction of their order in 1310, these knights took oaths to protect the Holy Sepulchre and other holy shrines and, in medieval myth, they were said to have been the builders of Latin cruciform glass temples such as Chartres.[7] Earlier on Mt. Purgatory's terrace of the avaricious, Dante had heard Hugh Capet denounce French King Philip the Fair, the leader of the successful movement to crush the Templars and to take possession of their holdings, as the "nuovo Pilato" or "new Pilate" who "bears his greedy sails into the temple" (*Purg.* 20.93: "portar nel Tempio le cupide vele"). Then in the Primum Mobile of *Paradiso*, in looking from the ideal immaterial angelic temple back to Beatrice, Dante confirms that he has accurately seen its reversed and reflected image in her "beautiful eyes in which love had made the noose to capture me" (28.11–12: "belli occhi,/ onde a pigliarmi fece Amor la corda").

The "corda" here appears to be the rope of honor worn by the Templars rather than the Franciscan "capestro," or cord of humility, that serves as a girdle for the Franciscan Guido da Montefeltro in the *Inferno* (27.92).[8] Dante is captured by the divine love that bound the knights to their vows as guardians of the Jerusalem temple. The power of Beatrice's eyes over the poet is accordingly comparable to the power of the "corda" that, for the Templars, symbolized their military duty to overcome or to capture the infidel, or to die rather than accept defeat.

Circular processions and actual dances in earthly "temple" cathedrals came to be associated with transcendent celestial movements of a kind Dante describes in the angelic temple. Under the influence of the "angelic" theology of pseudo-Dionysius, Abbot Suger writes in *De Consecratione* (ca. 1146), for example, of a seemingly celestial "chorus" proceeding round and round the upper choir of the St. Denis "temple," the area between the nave and the main altar, during the Great Consecration on 11 June 1144. Suger enthusiastically declaims upon

> tot tantorum choream pontificum vestibus albis decoram, mitris pontificalibus et circinatis aurifrisiis pretiosis admodum comatam, pastorales virgas manibus tenere, circumcirca dolium ambire, nomen Domini exorcizando invocare; tan gloriosos et admirabiles viros aeterni sponsi nuptias tam pie celebrare, ut potius chorus coelestis quam terrenus, opus divinum quam humanum, tam regi quam assistenti nobilitati videretur apparere.[9]

how so great a chorus of such great pontiffs, decorous in white vestments, splendidly arrayed in pontifical miters and precious orphreys embellished by circular ornaments, held the crosiers in their hands, walked round and round the vessel and invoked the name of God by way or exorcism; how so glorious and admirable men celebrated the wedding of the Eternal Bridegroom so piously that the King and the attending nobility believed themselves to behold a chorus celestial rather than terrestial, a ceremony divine rather than human.

The song of this chorus, Suger adds, was considered "angelic rather than human" ("potius angelicus quam humanus").[10]

Processions such as these, illumined by moving circles of light from the flaming candles that, as Suger notes, were carried by celebrants,[11] became associated with what in the cosmic temples of Rheims, Chartres and other cathedrals were said to be cosmic dances. In *Rationale divinorum officiorum* (1164), Joannes Belethus writes of the relation of liturgy to the pilgrimage "stationes" of Jerusalem and mentions the dances performed in churches during ceremonies each December. He is critical of these customary dance performances, observing that although celebants in "great churches, that is as of Rheims, observe this custom of playing, it nevertheless seems to be more praiseworthy not to play" ("magnae Ecclesiae, ut est Remensis, hanc-ludendi consuetudinem observant, videtur tamen laudabilius esse non ludere").[12]

The tradition of the divine dance has been linked to the Gnostic Gospel of pseudo-John, a work known to St. Augustine.[13] Pseudo-John writes of how, at the command of Christ, he and the other disciples joined hands and moved, singing and dancing, around the Savior who stood at the center. The 12 disciples and their dance were then compared in Judaeo-Hellenic tradition to the 12 moving signs of the zodiac. In Dante's period the tradition of celestial song and dance had become a motif in architectural iconography as well as in popular and religious ritual. In the dynamic wheel-rose window designs signifying circular motion, the 12 apostles were often depicted on the inner petals of the rose; the corresponding signs of the zodiac on the outer petals; and Christ at the hub or center. Ceremonies on the labyrinth floors or altars below were then conducted in figural imitation of the divine order and movement represented by the cosmic wheels above.

Although Suger was extremely conscious of the figural significance of holy liturgical movement, he described the St. Denis consecration procession as taking place in a choir that was constructed as a rectangle. Circular processions of seemingly celestial participants, performed to song amid the movement of flaming tapers, would have been better realized in terms of geometric form by the Knights Templar in their circular, nested ambulatories in the round and octagonal temples of Florence, Bologna, Pisa, Milan and other cities.

In the Primum Mobile, the angels dance in nine, individuated, sparkling and rotating rings. Their "ternaro" or triad formations (*Par.* 28.105) lack the unity of the Trinity, each triad mathematically representing three vectors brought together but not combined, and musically representing three tones of a chord composed of the root tone with its third and fifth, with or without the octave. At Chartres, Chancellor Thierry had gained fame by presenting theological conceptions in such geometric formulations, reducing all geometrical and musical relations to derivations based upon the unity of a geometrically conceived Trinity.

In the first triad of the angelic dance, the "cerchi primi" or "first circles" (*Par.* 28.98), closest to the central light, are the swiftest and most fiery. According to Beatrice, this triad is composed of Seraphs and Cherubs who "succeed in measure as they are sublime in vision" (*Par.* 28.102: "posson quanto a veder son soblimi"). In the circle of the sun, Dante had identified St. Francis as "all seraphic in his ardour" (*Par.* 11.37: "tutto serafico in ardore") and St. Benedict as bathed in the splendour of cherubic light (*Par.* 11.39: "cherubica luce"). This earlier dance, performed by these two most angelic churchmen and their holiest followers and associates, is fulfilled in the whirling dance of love now performed by the Seraphim and Cherabim of the inner circles. In the outer circle of the first triad, Beatrice identifies the Thrones who dance with divine aspect. The angelic orders in this first threefold formation had been associated by Dante in the *Convivio* (2.7–11) with the Holy Ghost. Beatrice significantly remarks that true blessedness is founded on "the act of vision, not on that which loves, which follows after" (*Par.* 28.110–111: "l'atto che vede,/ non in quel ch'ama, che poscia seconda").

Beatrice then points out in the "altro ternaro" or "second triad" the angels who primarily sing: the Dominations, Virtues and Powers. This heavenly choir unceasingly utters "Hosannah" with "three melodies which sound in the three orders of gladness, whereof it is three-plied" (*Par.* 28.119–120: "tre melode, che suonano in tree/ ordini di letizia onde s'interna"). Dante in the *Convivio* had identified these orders with Wisdom and the Son.

In the final triad, Beatrice indicates, the Principalities and Archangels "girano" or whirl; and in the outermost ring, she observes "all of Angelic rejoicings" (*Par.* 28.126: "tutto d'Angelici ludi"). Though the text does not clearly signify abstract meaning, Dante had noted in the *Convivio* that this last ring represents the Father and Power.

As a prelude to Dante's final visions, the "trïunfo" or triumph of the angelic temple slowly fades as stars disappear at dawn (*Par.* 30.7–10); and the beauty of Beatrice appears to transcend all measure, surpassing even the description of her in the *Vita Nuova* from that first day Dante had seen his lady "in this life" (*Par.* 30.29: "in questa vita"). From the commanding statements of Beatrice, Dante discovers that he is now in the Empyrean in a realm of "pure light, light intellectual full-charged with love" (*Par.* 30.39–40: "pura luce:/ luce intellettüal piena d'amore").

Viewing and then drinking from a luminous river that showers sparks on flowery banks—elements identified by Beatrice as "the shadowy prefaces of their reality" (*Par.* 30.78: "di lor vero umbriferi prefazi")—the poet at last sees that reality in a vision of the celestial city that combines astonishing amplitude, delicacy and spiritual energy. The river, the sparks and the flowers seem to transform, in a marvelous fulfillment of a multiplicity of foreshadowing types of the Church Triumphant, into a glorious and subsuming garden wheel-rose: a great circle of light that sweeps over the Empyrean with a circumference (*Par.* 30.104) so vast that it outreaches the orbit of the sun and contains the "more than a thousand ranks" (*Par.* 30.113: "più di mille soglie") of those blessed in the celestial city of God. Dazzling light from the upward curvature of the lower edge of the wheel-rose above reflects the downward curvature of the upper edge of the Primum Mobile below, casting beyond the distant extremities of the celestial city a mirrored image of the outermost sphere, "as a hillside reflects itself in water at its foot" (*Par.* 30.109–10: "come clivo in acqua di suo imo/ si specchia"), that radiates outward through the Empyrean. This great wheel is created from a fusion of iconographic elements in cosmic wheel windows on earth. Yet with poetic daring, Dante dramatically transforms these elements even as he relies upon them.

Earthly wheels have long been recognized as signifying a dynamic, active cosmos; icons representing changeable Fortune were sometimes placed on the exterior of wheels such as those at Saint-Étienne, Beauvais; San Zeno, Verona; and the modified wheel of Fortune at St. Denis.[14] But unlike the rotating wheel dances and icons of the *Commedia* that appear in Eden, the circle of the sun, the Primum Mobile and elsewhere, the great wheel rose of the Empyrean remains changeless and serene. The only movement is that of the "milizia santa" or "holy militia" (*Par.* 31.2) of descending and reascending angels who, "like to a swarm of bees" (*Par.* 31.7: "come schiera d'ape"), appear divinely to invert and yet correspond to the natural order by carrying sweetness, not as in nature from the flower to the hive, but from heaven down to the ranked heavenly hosts in the petals of the flower (*Par.* 31.7–12). The celestial wheel-rose, moreover, is a divine and virtuous white, not multicolored like those most intricate earthly wheels that employed stained or painted glass to disclose in greatest iconographic detail the multitude of the blessed.

When Dante's gaze traverses within the rose the "two courts of heaven" (*Par.* 30.96: "ambo le corti del ciel") thronged with the personages of the Old and New Testaments together with other triumphant hosts, he sees an amalgamation of images that uniquely includes the fulfilled form of the Book of God's Words that had appeared in the foreshadowing procession in Eden. In earthly temples throughout Europe, the two courts of heaven, as has been noted, were widely separated with Old Testament personages in the north transept wheel and New Testament personages in the south transept wheel. Dante unifies the courts in a single circle. Also, the iconographic images of Christ, the Virgin, or a divine figure—images traditionally placed at the center of the earthly wheels—are now gone from the hub of the white rose of the Empyrean. The mysterious, empty hub glows yellow. Only through Beatific Vision will Dante gaze into this whirling center of all creation.

The unfolding action of the poem, derived in part from a knowledge of wheel-rose configurations, is extraordinary. The astounded Dante is drawn by Beatrice into an exalted position: directly into the yellow hub of the rose. The wonder of the poet before the celestial city is then captured in a comparison that points back to the foreshadowing earthly experience of travelers arriving before the eternal city of Rome, a comparison that points back as well to the initial starting place of Dante's long pilgrimage as recorded in the *Vita Nuova*.

> Se i barbari, venendo da tal plaga
>   che ciascun giorno d'Elice si cuopra,
>   rotante col suo figlio ond' ella è vaga,
> veggendo Roma e l'ardüa sua opra,
>   stupefaciensi, quando Laterano
>   a le cose mortali andò di sopra;

ïo, che al divino da l'umano,
   a l'etterno dal tempo era venuto,
   e di Fiorenza in popol giusto e sano,
di che stupor dovea esser compiuto!

(Par. 31.31–40)

If the Barbarians coming from such a region as
   every day is spanned by Helice, wheeling
   with her son towards whom sh.e yearn,
on seeing Rome and her mighty works—when
   the Lateran transcended mortal things—
   were stupefied;
what then of me, who to the divine from the
   human, to the eternal from time had passed,
   and from Florence to a people just and sane,
with what amazement must I have been filled!

Contemporaneous accounts reveal that during the Jubilee Pilgrimage of 1300, travelers, upon reaching Monte Mario overlooking the earthly eternal city, kissed the ground and cried, "Roma, Roma."[15] But such exultation, though suggested by Dante's simile, is represented as a grossly inadequate measure of the transcendent stupefaction of the poet before the celestial rose. Dante has journeyed from Florence beyond life on a pilgrimage of conversion, Redemption and Transfiguration through three realms to an eternal city of the sane and just; and he has thus fulfilled in the *Commedia* a prefiguring earthly pilgrimage of Palmers and Romers, first mentioned in the *Vita Nuova*, from "d'Egitto/ venga in Jerusalemme" (*Par*. 25.55–56) and then to Rome. Now before the heavenly city, despite his spiritual regeneration and his acceptance of divine gifts of grace, he is still like a barbarian yearning for his beloved and caught in the whirl of time. His simile deftly defines his spiritual inadequacy as a pilgrim.

The comparison also extends a remorseless criticism of the papacy of Dante's time, a criticism voiced earlier in the poem by St. Peter within physical view of Rome among the fixed stars. Although the poet's journey takes place in the Jubilee Year of 1300, the Rome to which Dante refers is the Rome of the past, the imperial city of genuine spiritual and temporal authority in which the Lateran, the palace of the papacy, transcended mortal things and was in harmony with heaven. It is this imperial and spiritual Rome, Dante announces through his poem, that will be reborn. Yet here and in other passages, Dante shapes the foreshadowing earthly journey of his life in concordance with epochal types that, while presented as sequential and "historical," are ultimately unaffected by the modern empirical details of time and place that fall outside the established figural matrix. Like Petrarch who, ignoring "objective" earthly time, wrote letters to the noble dead as if they were his living companions, so Dante through the typology of his poem merges the living and dead, as well as past and present places and events, into ideal figural patterns. The poet thus criticizes the papacy of his period while alluding to a prefiguring pilgrimage to the "true" Rome in the Jubilee Year of 1300.

In an analogy focused upon himself without reference to what he sees, Dante establishes a further relation between earthly and heavenly pilgrimage experiences, as he looks upward from his position beside Beatrice to the ordered personages of the rose:

> E quasi peregrin che si ricrea
>   nel tempio del suo voto riguardando,
>   e spera già ridir com' ello stea,
> su per la viva luce passeggiando,
>   menava ïo li occhi per li gradi,
>   mo sù, mo giù e mo recirculando.
>
>   (*Par.* 31.43–48)

> As the pilgrim who draws fresh life in
>   the temple of his vow as he gazes, and already
>   hopes to tell again how it be placed,
> so traversing the living light, I cast my eyes
> along the ranks, now up, now down, and now
> round circling.

The shared popular experiences that helped to give form to the medieval Book of the World, and that provided a primary source for Dante's typology, are indeed revealed in this concise simile. The foreshadowed earthly pilgrim stands beside his guide in the temple of his vow, moves his eyes upward along beams of light to ranked images and particularly those on lancet and wheel windows, and—as the enormous international body of pilgrim texts gives evidence—strives to remember all that he has seen, to recall the exact placement and the relative locations of the holiest pilgrimage icons, to relate or to write down the pattern of the icons so that persons at home may spiritually share in the pilgrimage. But then, as now, a most knowledgeable guide is needed to show and to explain the most important of the thousands of icons ranged in a pilgrimage temple. When Dante looks again for Beatrice, he discovers that she is no longer at his side. The mystic St. Bernard, the last guide, is now beside the poet.

Lifting his eyes to the great wheel-rose, Dante sees Beatrice within it making a crown for herself and reflecting the eternal ray. In chapter 38 of the *Vita Nuova*, it will be recalled, this lady was said to have been uplifted into heaven under the banner of the Virgin Mary. Now Beatrice actually appears to the poet in the "third circle from the highest rank" (*Par.* 31.67–68: "terzo giro/ dal sommo grado") below the Virgin Mary who is enthroned at the summit of the outermost ring. Dante writes of how his lady smiles upon him and then, assuming the posture in which she was last described in the earlier work, "turned her to the eternal fountain" (*Par.* 31.93: "poi si tornò a l'etterna fontana").

In chapter 40 of the *Vita Nuova*, the movement of pilgrims through Florence on their way to Rome to view "that blessed image which Jesus Christ left to us for a figura" ("la quale Gesù Cristo lasciò a noi per esempio della sua bellissima figura") was seen to foreshadow the pilgrimage of Dante's sigh to Beatrice who was looking upon Godhead in heaven. The "blessed image" or Veil of Veronica was indeed a *figura* of Beatific Vision; pardoners, as is revealed in *Piers Plowman*, and pilgrims returning from Rome sewed miniature *figura* of the veil on their garments and so carried the image throughout Christendom.[16] Francesco Petrarch, who described his own Jubilee Pilgrimage to Rome in book 2, epistle 9 of his *Familiar Letters*, composed sonnet 16 about an aging man's journey in his last days to this holiest of relics at Old St. Peter's Basilica.[17]

When Dante looks from Beatrice into the countenance of his nearby guide St. Bernard, the poet at this juncture is compared to a pilgrim from Croatia or some other distant land, a pilgrim still yearning for true vision, but one who grows doubtful upon viewing the briefly shown relic of the divine image.

> Qual è colui che forse di Croazia
>   viene a veder la Veronica nostra,
>   che per l'antica fame non sen sazia,
> ma dice nel pensier, fin che si mostra:
>   "Segnor mio Iesù Cristo, Dio verace,
>   or fu sì fatta la sembianza vostra?";
> tal era io mirando la vivace
>   carità di colui che 'n questo mondo,
>   contemplando, gustò di quella pace.

> (*Par.* 31.103–11)

> As is he who comes perhaps from Croatia
> to look on our Veronica, and whose old
> desire is not sated,
> but says in thought so long as it is shown:
> "My Lord Jesus Christ, true God, and was
> this, then, the fashion of your semblance?"
> such was I, gazing upon the living love of him
> who, in this world, in contemplation tasted
> of that peace.

The foreshadowing actions of an earthly pilgrim in an eternal city—actions distilled, intensified and merged in the fulfilled activities of Dante before and within the celestial city—have been specifically examined in other studies. Yet whatever earthly pilgrimage experiences Dante combined and "adjusted" to create "true," fulfilled events in the world beyond, the typology of the poem suggests the foreshadowing place and action of the final vision. Dante has *in figura* moved over the pathway taken by Aeneas and St. Paul to that earthly eternal city where the enthroned papal successor of St. Peter sits (*Inf.* 2.23–24); and in the world beyond in fulfillment of that foreshadowed journey, Dante has arrived before the city and the "alto seggio" or high seat (*Inf.* 1.128) of the divine Emperor of the eternal heavenly realm. In this twofold pilgrimage, the poet has come to his stated destination at the "gate of St. Peter" (*Inf.* 1.134: "porta di san Pietro") before the heavenly hosts in what Beatrice has called "nostra basilica" or our basilica (*Par.* 25.30). In his otherworldly actions he has embodied the prefiguring experiences of Romers on earth who view the relic of the Veil of Veronica at St. Peter's Basilica in the eternal city.

Although Dante's final vision of the celestial rose is so spiritually resplendent that it is only slightly suggested by earthly types, figural contexts having their origins in the *Vita Nuova*—but greatly expanded in the *Commedia*—point to a continued unfolding of prefigured action in an obvious earthly setting: the vast interior of the Byzantine-Romanesque basilica of Old St. Peter's. This basilica contained a sixth century wheel window installed under Pope Gregory III high in the eastern facade. Here, an earthly Romer, at the direction of a guide, could gaze upward from the basilica's holy "center" along a beam of light toward the heavenly iconographic forms and cosmic circles of a translucent wheel window illumined by the morning sunrise.

Beginning his experience of transfiguring vision, Dante raises his eyes, never to lower them to his guide again, toward the rose.

Its vast and shimmering brightness constantly appears to increase in luminosity "as at morn the oriental regions of the horizon overcome that where the sun declines" (*Par.* 31.118–19: "come da mattina/ la parte orïental de l'orizzonte/ soverchia quella dove 'l sol declina"). His eyes move "as from a valley . . . to a mountain" (*Par.* 31.121: "quasi di valle . . . a monte") past a middle region, where more than a thousand angels distinctly and individually glimmer, to the remotest far-flung reaches of the great wheel's summit. As Dante gazes, St. Bernard through his words points out the Virgin at the highest eminence, and then directs attention from "petal to petal" (*Par.* 32.15: "foglia in foglia"), naming a few among the biblical figures and the elect. Of the nonbiblical personages visible, St. Bernard identifies only Beatrice in the upper wheel and, in a descending row in the lower wheel, St. Augustine, St. Benedict and St. Francis.

The great wheel disclosed by St. Bernard is peerless in being vertically bisected, in a manner foreign to traditional wheel windows on earth, by what the saint calls a "muro" or wall containing a "sacre scalee" or sacred stairs (*Par.* 32.20–21).[18] The Virgin, in the central and highest place, appears in the outer ring along with, from Dante's viewpoint, St. Peter and then St. John the Evangelist on her right, Adam and then Moses on her left (*Par.* 32.121–32). The steps leading down from her to the hub of the wheel are occupied by the chain of her ancestors: first Eve and then the Hebrew women—Rachel, Sarah, Rebecca, Judith and Ruth (*Par.* 32.4–10). Dante's own lady, as an earlier reference reveals (*Inf.* 2.102), is enthroned in the third ring, outside the direct line of the Virgin's ancestors, to the right of Rachel and directly under St. Peter.

Again with striking poetic originality, Dante conflates wheel window elements and renders, in a new iconographic design strongly emphasizing female figures, the traditional wheel iconographic motif of the ancestry of the Virgin. In the great floral wheel of France in Chartres north (ca. 1233), for example, 12 diamond-shaped panels circle the central figure of the Virgin at the wheel's hub, illustrating her descent from Hebrew kings in the line of David.[19] The north wheel of Laon (early thirteenth century) contains at its core a stained glass representation of a woman holding a scepter of royalty, with her body divided by a ladder with nine rungs extending from her head to her feet.[20] The rungs of the ladder may signify royal ancestors, the nine spheres, the nine orders of angels, or other meanings. But whatever these open iconographic symbols suggest of divinely ordained hierarchical order, they compare in a general way to the design of Dante's "sacre scalee."

The straight line of the wall bisecting Dante's heavenly wheel rose is similar also to the straight, wide vertical and horizontal tracery lines that crisscrossed the circular Tuscan wheel windows in cathedrals such as those at Siena (ca. thirteenth century) and the Duomo of Florence—the last under construction without the wheel window in place when Dante was prior in 1300. These tracery lines, though never actually bisecting the circles, give the balanced pattern of oblong window panels a static quality that contrasts sharply with the effect of motion conveyed by the spokes of French Gothic wheels of a kind also evident at Assisi.[21]

Like the lesser but triumphant wheel of the angelic temple that synthesizes and fulfills the circles of the physical universe and the holiest of earthly temples, the circle of the celestial city has a form that reflects elements from a range of cosmic wheels on earth. This great wheel combines the petals of northern Gothic and Assisi basilica windows, the wide lines of Tuscan windows, the empty hub of early Gothic, the circles of Old and New Testament figures traditionally separated in north and south windows, and the seemingly static form of certain Italian windows. Yet through the serene and luminous immensity of the cosmic rose of Mary and of love, a rose that paradoxically fulfills even as it transcends all earthly models, Dante presents a brilliantly realized image of the eternal, Augustinian City of God ruled under the regency of Mary by the Imperial Emperor of heaven. And subsumbed within the city is the ultimate iconographic form, depicted through named or suggested biblical personages, of the Book of God's Words.

From the moment that his new life began until the moment of his final vision of his lady within the city, Dante has been individually guided on the journey of his life by Beatrice. Now a fulfilled pilgrim, Dante last looks upon his lady in the Church Triumphant as she sits, enthroned beneath St. Peter, reflecting the eternal light. The Father of the Church of Rome in turn sits at the right hand of Mary at the summit of the city of heaven.

Yet the Imperial Emperor of the celestial city is not fully manifest. The divine beam of the Emperor, though radiating down upon the city, has its source in mystical depths afar. And no iconographic image of the Emperor glows at the celestial city's yellow hub, now mysteriously occupied by Dante and St. Bernard, as it did in mortal wheels on earth. In the great circle of the celestial city, the "ancient and the modern folk" (*Par.* 31.26: "gente antica e in novella") must gaze upward toward the light of Godhead emanating from what appears as the threefold brilliance of a single star. Eulogizing the light in a *terza rima*, Dante writes:

> Oh trina luce che 'n unica stella
> scintillando a lor vista, sì li appaga!
> guarda qua giuso a la nostra procella!

> *(Par.* 31.28–30)

> O threefold light, which in a single star, glinting
> upon their sight doth so content them, look
> down upon our storm!

At a sign from St. Bernard, the poet of his own spiritual volition lifts his eyes to the Virgin Mary, and then follows the direction of the Virgin's gaze toward the divine illumination. With optical powers now purged and increased in virtue, Dante looks upward with ever greater depth and lucidity into the "beam of the deep light which in itself is true" (*Par.* 33.53–54: "raggio/ de l'alta luce che da sé è vera") that streams down upon him at the center of the rose. It is at this culminating moment of pilgrimage that the poet gazes upon what appears as the "semplice lume" (simple flame)— the unifying spiritual core and the ingathering, sustaining, and creatively moving infinite power underlying the book of the entire universe. This is the flame that is the fulfillment and transcendent form of the reflected light of Beatrice's eyes, of the radiance of the sensible sun, of the angelic temple's point of spiritual light, of the threefold and yet single beam raying down upon the blessed in the rose.

When in Dante's vision the flame transfigures into three rotating, fiery rings, these iconographic nested wheels fulfill and synthesize an extraordinary progression of multiple poetic images of primal light, mirrored light, movement, separate and merged color, and geometric and human form. Unlike all other wheel icons in the poem, the three luminous, whirling, mirroring wheels are equal in the magnitude of their light and the speed of their rotation. "Tre colori" or three colors (*Par.* 33.117), unnamed, shimmer in and from the three wheels, the colors reflecting from wheel to wheel "like rainbow from rainbow" (*Par.* 33.118: "come iri da iri"). The light and colors of the second wheel seem mirrored in the first, and those of the third wheel in both the first and second. Because the wheels are both sources and reflectors of light, even Dante is not entirely detached from the mirrored images he observes. For it is in the second circle that the poet finally sees, in its own color, "nostra effige" or our image (*Par.* 33.131).

Through the rational power of his creative intuition, Dante thus projects into his work a circular core icon that is comparable to visual images of Godhead at the center of wheel-rose windows. Yet through poetry the icon has dimensions of suggestiveness, beyond the purely visual, brilliantly signifying the unity of all creation in the oneness of triune Godhead: the Son proceeding from the Father, the Holy Ghost from the Father and the Son, and Christ incarnate mirrored in Dante's and in all humankind's image. In its motion, undefined colors, self-perpetuating and reflecting radiance, all-subsuming quality, and human and divine iconographic design, the icon comprehensively fulfills and transcends the motionless lower wheel of the rose and embodies the Book of God's Words in the dynamic, turning, perfect circles of the Book of Creation and of Godhead.

Dante's last mystical guide in the Empyrean, St. Bernard, had avoided using extended analogies and metaphors in his actual historical works when writing of his own beatific visions. Bernard, after first denying the possibility of such visions in his 1125 letter to the Carthusians, first began to refer to visions in composing, probably between 1129 and 1135, *De Gradibus Humilitatis*, a work of meditative steps in the anchorite-monastic tradition of John Climacus's *Scala Paradisi* and St. Bonaventura's *Itinerarium mentis in Deum*. Bernard, in steps seven and 21 of *De Gradibus Humilitatis*, writes from the assumption that human beings can experience vision; and in step eight, he argues at length that St. Paul had been "caught up" into the highest heaven and there gazed upon Godhead.[22] Then in 1137 in his twenty-third sermon on Canticles, Bernard made the first of many public announcements of his own mystical experiences.[23] Responding to questions about his visions, Bernard in sermon 85 on Canticles observes that they are beyond his own power as an adult to explain and are best revealed, through the gift of grace, in the experience of infants:

> O quisquis curiosus es scire quid sit hoc, Verbo frui; para illi non aurem sed mentem. Non docet hoc lingua, sed docet gratia. Absconditur a sapientibus et prudentibus, et revelatur parvulis.[24]

> O thou who art curious to know what it is to enjoy the Word, do not prepare your ear for this but your mind. The tongue does not teach this, but grace does. It is hid from the wise and prudent, and revealed unto babes.

Attaining in the context of the *Commedia* that grace and humility of which St. Bernard wrote, Dante gives poetic expression to his Beatific Vision through allusions to the earliest possible remembered experience of delight and to the popular "mother arts" of clothing and architecture. He defers to the medieval scholastic conception of the fine and practical arts as knowledge for the end of making, and humbly compares himself as a poet of "primo amore" or primal love to the "careful tailor who to the cloth he has cuts the garment" (*Par.* 32.140–41: "buon sartore/ che com' elli ha del panno fa la gonna"). And under the architectual influence of those earthly wheels of glass and stone that signified the immaterial realm of perfection, the physical circles of the spheres, the circle of the physical earth, and even the circle of the Garden of Eden, Dante realizes his poetic vision in an icon of rotating circles mirroring a human form. Still, in the presence of Godhead, Dante's finite human powers of speech and memory increasingly fail (*Par.* 33.106–08). And in the presence of the divine turning wheels, these two powers so diminish that Dante, like St. Bernard, can only compare the experience to that of an infant:

> Omai sarà più corta mia favella,
>   pur a quel ch'io ricordo, che d'un fante
>   che bagni ancor la lingua a la mammella.
>
> (Par. 33.106–08)

> Now shall my speech fall farther short even of
> what I can remember, than an infant's who
> still bathes his tongue at the breast.

The last analogy in the *Commedia* may seem disconcertingly logical to modern readers, for Dante raises an issue from medieval geometrical theology. Dante longs to know "how the image conformed to the circle and how it has its place therein" (*Par.* 33.137–38: "come si convenne/ l'imago al cerchio e come vi s' indova"). In seeking a solution, the poet compares himself to a geometer who tries to square the circle and "finds not, in pondering, the principle of which he is in need" (*Par.* 33.134–35: "non ritrova,/ pensando, quel principio ond' egli indige"). Divine-human Godhead, like the problem of squaring the circle, Dante notes, is logically unfathomable. Yet in focusing part of his question on how a divine-human image conforms to a circle, the poet raises, in a transcendental context, a problem exactly parallel to that actually confronted by medieval architectual masters and their apprentices in relating and placing one or more human images, formed in stained glass, within the intricate geometrical-theological tracery of the cosmic wheels on earth. Employing the types of Trinitarian geometry made famous by Chancellor Thierry of Chartres, multiple geometrical design plans were developed and superimposed one upon the other in constructing the final cosmic wheel outline. The final wheel, then, signified the mystery of an ordered diversity subsumed in divine oneness.

At Chartres, for example, above the labyrinth floor representing the tortuous pilgrimage route in this life to the holy city of Jerusalem, the great cosmic west wheel shows the heavenly city of Revelation with Christ at the center surrounded by the Apostles and the angels. The west wheel has been analyzed as being geometrically structured from five different superimposed designs. Elaborating upon studies by John James, Painton Cowen points out that one of these designs is

> built up on two units measured . . . in Roman feet of 29.6 cm; one of 3 feet and another of 10 feet, which reduces to ⅔ and ⅓ to give 6⅔ and 3⅓ feet (an expansion of the number 3, and a division by 3, being a neat echo of Thierry's preoccupation with the geometric configuration of the Trinity).[25]

The geometrical problem Dante calls attention to is logically insoluble. Through his analogy, however, he undoubtedly reminded his contemporaries of similar problems in theological-geometry that had been, by contrast, brilliantly solved. For the "proof" of the geometry resided not only in the magnificent tracery of the greatest earthly wheel windows, but in the flying buttresses, the vaulted roofs, the harmoniously divided nave aisles and the balanced cruciform plans of many European "temples." In a period of widespread disease, political upheaval and early death, these constructs of divine geometry expressed the collective aspirations of village, town and city; for as iconographic constructs, they both embodied the form of the universe and also served as communal centers, hospitals, religious houses and pilgrimage sites. Dante's wheel icons in the *Commedia*, like the overall cosmic figural design of the poem, demonstrate that the poet owed a debt to the largely unknown geometers, glaziers, stone masons, sculptors, artisans and master builders of the cathedrals.

At the conclusion of the *Purgatorio* and the *Paradiso*, the deepest spiritual realities overwhelm certain of Dante's human powers by degrees, in accordance with the stage reached in the pilgrimage. At the same time, the poet's faculties are enlightened. Before Beatrice in the Earthly Paradise, Dante at first falls vanquished by past sin. His mind, though later illumined, still also seems spiritually "ingombra" or incumbered; he claims to capture in words only a shadow of the living light manifest in the garden (*Purg.* 31.139–

45). Before the transforming icons of Godhead, the poet suffers a nearly total failure of memory and speech. His logical reason is confounded. But having seemingly reached the outermost limits of his spiritual capacities, Dante is remarkably "smitten," and he finally experiences Beatific Vision.

Unexpectedly and miraculously, Dante's mind is struck by a jolting "flash" of apprehension. The poet's intuitive reason, within the frame of its human powers, is suddenly illumined through the gift of grace and instantaneously and effortlessly turned toward its end in God, and he gains transfiguring mystical insight into the Divine.[26] "My mind," the poet concisely writes, "was smitten by a flash wherein its wish came to it" (*Par.* 33.140–41: "mia mente fu percossa/ da un fulgore in che sua voglia venne"). Yet even as his immaterial mind is illumined and moved, Dante experiences the loss of his lesser and now unnecessary power to receive visual images from external reality. His words are brief and dramatic: "Here power failed the lofty phantasy" (*Par.* 33.142: "A l'alta fantasia qui mancò possa").

Virgil, speaking of ordinary apprehension in which the image-receiving power is retained, had explained this movement of the mind to Dante in *Purgatorio*:

> Vostra apprensiva da esser verace
> tragge intenzione, e dentro a voi la spiega,
> sì che l'animo ad essa volger face;
> e se, rivolto, inver' di lei si piega,
> quel piegare è amor, quell' è natura
> che per piacer di novo in voi si lega.
> Poi, come 'l foco movesi in altura
> per la sua forma ch'è nata a salire
> là dove più in sua matera dura,
> così l'animo preso entra in disire,
> ch'è moto spiritale, e mai non posa
> fin che la cosa amata il fa gioire.
>
> (18.22–33)

> Your faculty of apprehension draws an
> image from a real existence and displays
> it within you, so that it makes the mind turn toward it
> And if, being turned, the mind inclines toward it,
> that inclination is love; that inclination is nature,
> which is bound in you anew in pleasure.
> Then, even as fire moves upward by reason of

> its form, whose nature is to ascend to where
> it lasts longest in its matter
> So the enamoured mind falls captive to desire,
> which is a spiritual movement, and never rests
> until the object of its love makes it rejoice.

While the perfection of Godhead overpowers Dante's lower faculties, the poem is not radically undermined in its epistemology or aesthetically "fragmented" in any essential way by the inescapable human failures of its narrator. Dante never presents himself, in the manner of some Reformation and many modern artists, as composing his work from his own autonomous subjectivity. His rich subjectivity is self-evident, but it is a subjectivity depicted in medieval fashion as being divinely guided from without, in symmetry with his individual choice and desire, into wider conformity with the external cosmos and "true" universal history. Through divine external intervention as well as through interior volition, Dante's faltering and limited human subjectivity repeatedly subsumes initial fragmentary impressions and apprehensions in ever more virtuous unifying experiences and images. Dante's first experiences, even during Beatific Vision, are constantly being transcended. The complete range of the poet's always changing human perceptions and apprehensions reside in the language of the poem, language replete with echoes of the past and prefigurations of the future.

It is from the divinely directed universal nature of the poet's spiritually fulfilling and deeply experienced actions, even more than from the poet's individual and slow but finally enlightened human understanding of what transpires, that Dante is joined *in figura*—and by inference the reader and all persons might be as well—to the underlying form and movement of external reality. And it is primarily through reenactment of the Exodus, the Redemption and the Transfiguration that the poem is "grounded," not by modern "referents," but by medieval historical, typological bonds in "true" historical events recorded in Books of God represented as accessible to the connatural knowledge of Dante and his readers. The Bible, initially signified in the procession in the Earthly Paradise and then in the fulfilled personages of the heavenly rose, is accordingly present at those first and last wondrous moments when Dante gazes into the eyes of his lady. The "volume" of the Cosmos, progressively unveiled to Dante during his twofold journey and then largely synthesized and reflected in Beatrice's eyes at the edge of the stellar sphere, is brilliantly and completely "ingathered" in the very icons of Godhead to which the poet, following the gaze of his lady, lifts his own eyes in the Empyrean.

Though in the light of Infinite Being the leaves of the Book of the World, the spheres and the immaterial cosmos appear as "si squaderna" or scattered (*Par.* 33.87), the poem itself, from a human viewpoint, divulges the ordered twofold, universal biblical-pilgrimage path through lower mazes to holy centers in the ascending hierarchy of creation. And though the words of Scripture are said to be sometimes thrust aside or behind (*Par.* 29.88–89), and though these words—as Beatrice declares—condescend to our "assigning foot and hand to God with other meaning" (*Par.* 4.44–45: "e piedi e mano/ attribuisce a Dio, e altro intende"), still these words are represented as pointing to "true" universal history, reenacted by Dante, in accordance with the reader's human objective capacity to understand. "Were not the Scripture over you," the Divine Eagle of Justice announces to Dante in the sphere of Jupiter, "there were marvelous ground for questioning" (*Par.* 19.83–84: se la Scrittura sovra voi non fosse,/ da dubitar sarebbe a maraviglia").

Having looked into the luminous source of creation, Dante, impelled by the external power of divine love in harmony with his own desire and will, is moved for the last time. His movement is profoundly spiritual. It is a transcendent interior imitation of the circular wheeling of the sparkling angels about that point of divine brightness at the center of the immaterial angelic temple bordering the stars. It is the penultimate interior reenactment of the spiritual and physical circular whirling of the scintillating theologians about the sun, of the steady rotation of the planets and spheres in the temple of the physical universe, of even the lowly foreshadowing processional movements of figured terrestial celebrants in the most sacred pilgrimage temples of this world. Dante is at last turned in concord with the universe:

> ma già volgeva il mio disio e 'l *velle*,
> sì come rota ch'igualmente è mossa,
> l'amor che move il sole e l'altre stelle.

(Par. 33.143–145)

> But already my desire and will were revolved—
> even as a wheel that moves equally—by the
> Love that moves the sun and the other stars.

19. Plain glass window, western facade of San Pietro, Assisi (ca. 1268). A moving universe signified by a three-dimensional floral wheel of light is nested within an outer luminous ring and rotates about a still point at the center. *Photograph by the author.*

20. Upper Church facade, San Francisco, Assisi (ca. 1232). In this gracefully intricate stained glass window, an interplay of central petals, stars within circles, fused spoke-petal icons and circles joined by wavering bands all turn together, wheel within concentric wheel, about the changeless center of the hub.*

*This earthly wheel, like the heavenly wheels described by Dante in *Paradiso* 33, carries figural associations with Ezekiel's biblical vision of the four creatures in a flaming wheel. Icons of the four evangelists, antitypes of the four creatures seen by Ezekiel, stand at the four corners of this Italian window that joins the earthly and the divine through its figurism. *Photograph by the author.*

21. Moses before the burning bush. Detail from lancet window in the
Chapel of St. Peregrinus, St. Denis. In *De Administratione,* Abbot Suger
discussed the details of this Moses and Exodus window appropriately
situated in the apsidal chapel of St. Peregrine, the saint of the pilgrims.
Photograph by the author.

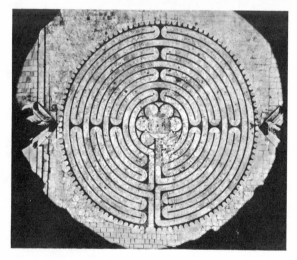

22. The 12.88-meter stone labyrinth floor at Chartres, dating from at
least the thirteenth century, forms a great circle across the lower nave
under the west facade wheel window. Medieval pilgrims are believed to
have negotiated the labyrinth on their knees, acting out *in figura* an
Exodus pilgrimage of conversion through the maze of this world to a
central station, a rosette signifying Jerusalem. (Photographed from
above.)

84

23. The central of these three floral wheels on the western facade of San Pietro, Assisi (ca. 1268) revolves with seemingly clockwise and counterclockwise motions in an Italian elaboration of French designs. Worldly motion and change, at times associated with the wheel of Fortune, were traditionally emphasized in the exterior design of circular windows; heavenly realms of light and immortality were emphasized in the interior iconographic design. Through their perfect circles, church wheel windows—whether primitive or elaborate—shared in signifying the created universe. *Photograph by the author.*

24. Spoked wheel window (ca. 1163), west facade of the Santa Maria Maggiore, Assisi. This primitive "rota" window overlooks the Piazza Vescovado where St. Francis renounced worldly goods and allegorically accepted Lady Poverty, as recorded in *Paradiso* 11. Even the most ornate of later iconographic circular designs have their origins in the simple oculus or round window of early Provençal and northern Italian Romanesque architecture.*

* According to local legend, St. Clare (the follower of St. Francis) stood holding a monstrance in the spiritual eye of an early thirteenth century round window, an open window without spokes or radii still extant at San Damiano outside the city, thus putting the Saracen forces of Frederic II to flight. Like Beatrice, the legendary St. Clare exercised her spiritual power from a perfect circle that beamed heavenly light. *Photograph by the author.*

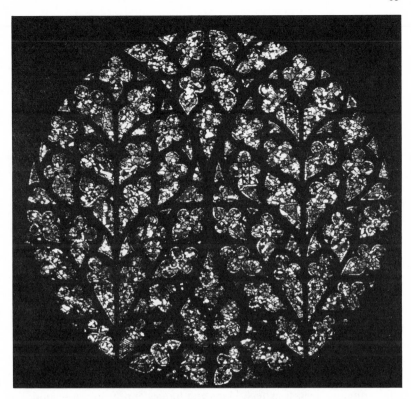

25. The south transept wheel-rose of Lincoln cathedral (ca. 1210, restored), in the manner of Dante's icons of Godhead in *Paradiso* 33, "ingathers" the leaves of created being within the all-encompassing volume of a perfect, circular cosmos. The recurring living leaves in the cosmic volume, in *vesica piscis* form, merge in a luminous juxtaposition of large leaf designs, intermediate leaf designs and thousands of tiny leaf-shaped glass fragments. The window, referred to in a poem of the thirteenth century as one of the two "oculi" of the church, was constructed under Bishop of Lincoln Robert Grosseteste, the formulator of scientific-metaphysical optical theories and the teacher of Roger Bacon. *Photograph by Painton Cowan.*

26. North wheel (ca. 1285, restored) at Notre Dame, Paris. Beyond the
Virgin and the surrounding Hebrew prophets at the center of this
extraordinarily delicate wheel, kings and judges appear in the second
circle and high priests in the outermost circles. The window's intricate
tracery, filled with approximately 700 panes and an estimated 50,000
pieces of glass, was developed from metaphysical-geometrical, 16-point
star-within-star designs.

In *Paradiso* 31, Dante gazes upward at the wheel-rose of the heavenly
city, moving his eyes up, down and then around in a circle. *Photograph
by the author.*

27. Santa Chiara, Assisi, exterior west facade (ca. 1257–1265). The trinal wheels, in both their number and motion, suggest the whirling wheels seen by Dante during a stage of the Beatific Vision. Circular layered stonework, arched radii and stained glass combine to create the effect of depth and movement. *Photograph by the author.*

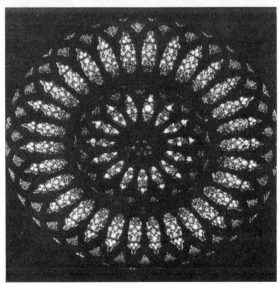

28. Santa Chiara, interior. Viewed from within, the wheel shows forth a dynamic cosmos represented as a seemingly three-dimensional vortex of light revolving about a single luminous point. *Photograph by Painton Cowan.*

THREE

The Medieval World Book Remembered

On the Form of Spenser's *The Faerie Queene*

"Where is that happy land of Faery," quips Spenser in the prologue to the second book of *The Faerie Queene*. And in a rhetorical reply that has both puzzled and delighted generations of commentators and has led to unproductive searches for extended allusions to the "new philosophy" in the poem, Spenser proclaims with mock seriousness that "Faerie lond" can be found by certain "signs" just as surely as the newly discovered regions of the earth:[1]

> dayly . . . through hardy enterprize,
> Many great Regions are discouered,
> Which to late age were neuer mentioned.
> Who euer heard of th' Indian *Peru*?
> Or who in venturous vessell measured
> The *Amazons* huge riuer now found trew?
> Of fruitfullest *Virginia* who did euer vew?
>
> (Prologue 2.2)

The poet then raises seemingly provocative questions about the nature of the cosmos.

> should witlesse man so much misweene
> That nothing is, but that which he hath seene?
> What if within the Moones faire shining spheare?
> What if in euery other starre vnseene

Of other wordes he happily should heare?
He wonder would much more; yet such to some appeare.
                                                    (Prologue 2.3)

Like the lands and strange inhabitants of the new continent and the celestial worlds within the moon and stars, "this famous antique history" of faeryland, the poet insists, is not the "painted forgery" of an "idle braine," but rather "matter of just memory,/ Sith none, that breatheth living aire, does know" (Prologue 2.1).

Is the Elizabethan Spenser anticipating the Romantics by implying that the justly remembered "truths" of his fictive faeryland rest upon the truths unveiled by the creative imagination?

Hardly. In his poem and letter to Sir Walter Raleigh of 23 January 1589, Spenser makes clear that the highest truths of virtue and knowledge are discovered by right reason.[2] And in the House of Alma episode in book 2 of *The Faerie Queene*, the poet discloses imagination or "Phantasie" as a largely visual associative power that, unregulated by reason, leads to madness.

Neither does Spenser allude to the new world Indians or to the sphere of the moon to make an essentially medieval argument for the supposed historical truth of the literal sense. Throughout *The Faerie Queene*, the poet constantly introduces action, images and references that reveal the literal sense as a beautiful lie. In the prologue to book 1, Spenser's supposed "proofs" for the reality of faeryland are suspect to say the least. It has long been recognized that the poet's allusion to the "witlesse" men who disbelieve in a world within the moon probably draws upon a fantastic episode in Lodovico Ariosto's *Orlando Furioso*: the journey of Astolfe on a mythical beast, a hippogriff, to the moon where he discovers the hero Orlando's lost wits. In writing of the "*Amazons* huge riuer" along with "th' Indian *Peru*," the poet ambiguously implies the existence of the mythical female warriors; but it is doubtful that Spenser as an informed Elizabethan actually believed that Francesco de Oreliana's reported meeting with a female tribe in the Brazilian jungles confirmed the "truth" of myths about the Amazons.

Aware of both factual and fanciful evidence about the new world and its Indians, Spenser treats this evidence with the same light and casual tone that he reserves for the depiction of a whimsical, unregulated imagination or Fancy. For the poet presents "Fancy, like a louely boy" (3.12.7) jauntily pacing through the "idle aire" of Busyrane's house in the gaudy apparel of an American Indian:

His garment neither was of silke nor say,
  But painted plumes, in goodly order dight,
  Like as the sunburnt *Indians* do aray
  Their tawney bodies, in their proudest plight:
  As those same plumes, so seemd he vaine and light,
  That by his gate might easily appeare;
  For still he far'd as dancing in delight,
  And in his hand a windy fan did beare,
That in the idle aire he mou'd still here and there.

(3.12.8)*

In this bold, direct emblematic representation, Fancy is associated with artifice. This personified figure is dressed up in outward "guise" like a new world Indian, but he most directly suggests a ballet performer wearing traditional painted plumes in an Elizabethan court show. A surface, festive exuberance infuses Spenser's depiction; there is a sense of energy, emotive release, and delight in pretense that characterizes both court disguisings and much of the outward emblematic fable of *The Faerie Queene*.

A contrasting emblem of "Phantasie," so exaggerated as to be superficially amusing, appears in the House of Alma episode. "Phantasie" is there represented as a suffering, melancholic man

Of swarth complexion, and of crabbed hew,
That him full of melancholy did show;
Bent hollow beetle browes, sharpe staring eyes,
That mad or foolish seemd; one by his vew
Mote deeme him borne with ill disposed skyes,
When oblique *Saturne* sate in the house of agonyes

(2.9.52)

Spenser clearly views the power of a largely visual imagination unregulated by right reason—an imagination that can be too light or too heavy—as disruptive to the balance of individual human faculties. And when the poet makes claims about the relation of faeryland to this world that are based upon "truths" of imagination so extravagant as to be outrageous, then those claims need to be carefully examined.

There can be no doubt that Spenser imaginatively conceived of faeryland as comparable to regions of the earth, that he was indeed conscious of the changing face of sixteenth century geographical

---

* References are to book, canto and stanza.

cosmography, and that he incorporated America—and in another passage India, too—into the antique land of faery. But did he really expect readers to believe that the antique faeryland realm, remembered only by the poet, existed as a historical fact, that *"Elfin"* once was actually monarch over "all that now *America* men call" (2.10.72)?

Spenser, of course, simply is not serious. As William Nelson has perceptively observed,[3] the poet is following a distinguished array of "enlightened" Renaissance writers who mocked the medieval convention, illustrated in Dante's letter to Can Grande della Scala, of pretending that the literal sense is historically true. By Spenser's time the mocking of the pretense had itself become a convention, having been used by François Rabelais in *Gargantua and Pantagurel,* Ariosto in *Orlando Furioso,* Matteo Boiardo in *Orlando Innamorato,* Miguel de Cervantes in *Don Quixote,* and Sir Thomas More in *Utopia.* Spenser similarly, in the prologue to book 2, pretends through indirect statement and an appeal to both empirical and imaginary geographical-cosmographical "evidence" that faeryland can literally be found; but in the rest of the poem and in his letter to Sir Walter Raleigh, he leaves no doubt that faeryland in its literal sense is a fiction. Yet in mentioning signs that point to faeryland, Spenser as an allegorist is inviting readers to pierce beyond the outward visual show and fable to the serious ideological meaning beneath. The truth of faeryland is the truth of its immaterial ideological and spiritual dimension. Unlike false Courtesy which, the poet writes in the prologue to book 6, is visually enticing and "Fashioned to please the eies of them, that pas," true courtesy as a form of spirituality lies in the rational comprehension of virtue:

> vertues seat is deep within the mynd,
> And not in outward shows, but inward thoughts defynd.
>
> (Prologue 6.5)

The structured universe of Spenser's faeryland, though open to varied emblematic representations, could have been effectively signified by a traditional cosmographical icon for an ordered universe: a dot at the center of a circle. This particular figure of the assumed perfect immaterial form of the earth and the cosmos was used even by Spenser's friend and teacher Gabriel Harvey. On the title page of his personal copy of *The Surveye of the World, or Situation of the earth,* Harvey penned this figure in his own hand.[4]

The Surveye of the World, an unillustrated cosmographical work supposedly written by Dionise Alexandrine and "englished" in 1572 by Thomas Twine, contains an opening section on the iconographic "generall division of the Earth into three partes" following traditional medieval T-and-O conceptions. The Mare Internum, or Mediterranean Sea, is described as having the shape of an upright T in the lower half of a flat, generally oval land mass that is enclosed "almost rounde with the Ocean Sea like a great ilande." "Asie" occupies the upper half of the circle orientated toward the East; "Europe," the lower half or northwestern quarter; and "*Libes,* or *Aphrica,*" the lower right or southwestern quarter.[5] In *The Surveye of the World,* as in other medieval world icons, unchanging abstract ideas symbolized in geometrical figures and numerical divisions can again be seen to impose structure upon the mutable accidental forms of physical nature. And in an analogous fashion, such ideas expressed through geometrical and numerically divided emblems were used by Spenser to impress form upon *The Faerie Queene.*

Illustrated or written iconographic representations of medieval T-and-O earth forms were available in the sixteenth century in a voluminous body of works: in old and new pilgrimage tracts; in new works of cosmography by William Cuningham, Ortelius, Jan Jansson and others which contained both recent empirical materials and descriptions of the T-and-O earth icons of the ancients; and in standard T-and-O delineations such as the *Mappa Mundi: Compasse and Cyrcuit of the worlde* (ca. 1535) actually published in the sixteenth century.[6] So common were the T-and-O renderings that, according to cartographical bibliographer Marcel Destombes, some 1,106 detailed projections and some 660 simple projections survive just in manuscripts dating largely from the thirteenth through the fifteenth century.[7]

The chronicles of John Stow, Raphael Holinshed, Richard Grafton and others provided lists of kings, heroes, nobles and Apostles that incorporated medieval myths and much of the medieval iconographic outlook, because these chronicles were often copied from earlier sources. At court through chivalric tilts, fights at barriers, battles melange, and masques and spectacles, the iconography of the medieval world was indirectly passed on through the design of scenery and costumes and through the speeches of knights and performers.

Unquestionably, the new geography of Gerhard Mercator and Abraham Ortelius was in the ascendant in the sixteenth century. Gabriel Harvey himself had in his library, along with the medieval *Surveye of the World,* the Ptolemaic *La Geographia* (1548) which was a far better empirical guide to world geography than medieval T-and-O icons.[8] But it was precisely this "new" empirical geography, rediscovered in Ptolemaic texts and then augmented through exploration, that Spenser largely ignored.

Following eclectic Renaissance neo-Platonic and neo-Aristotelian views intermeshed with medieval iconography, Spenser invented and "disposed" *The Faerie Queene* around abstract ideas of virtue and order thought to be necessary to the education of a gentleman and presumed to govern both the little world of the person, the microcosm, and the greater world, the macrocosm. Although Spenser's imaginative delight in surface action occasionally distracts from didactic purposes, he is generally consistent in the way he decorously "disposes" the sensory veil of his fictive literal sense—with its myriad visual emblems, disparate narrative action and multiferious character-types—as a pleasurable means of revealing the "dark conceit" of his underlying structure of ideas. Spenser's friend Sir Phillip Sidney in *The Defence of Poesie* tersely outlined this traditional Renaissance method of composing an "allegory of the poets" in declaring that versifiers "shal use the narration but as an imaginative groundplat of a profitable invention."[9]

"Grounded" as it is in abstractions believed to underlie both microcosm and macrocosm, *The Faerie Queene*—as S. K. Heninger has convincingly shown—is derived from "the same cosmic patterns" and "the same poetics" as Spenser's *The Shepherdes Calender* and *The Fowre Hymes* and so is a "literary microcosm" that "reproduces the structure of the cosmos."[10] In illuminating critical studies, Heninger, A. Kent Hieatt, Alastair Fowler, Jane Aptekar and others have demonstrated how the form and content of Spenser's verse reflect the cyclical movements of the spheres; the divisions and numerology of the hours, days, seasons and zodiac signs; and the microcosmic-macrocosmic iconography of sixteenth century emblem books.[11] Yet one immediate area of absorbing Elizabethan cosmological concern has not been carefully examined: the degree to which *The Faerie Queene* incorporates *both* the old and new conceptions of the structure and iconography of the physical earth, and the iconography of earthly pilgrimage stations, within the context of wider cosmic patterns.

Because the point has never clearly been advanced, it should be emphasized that *The Faerie Queene* is a great heroic literary projection in a later century—a projection with a literal sense now removed to an imaginative faeryland realm—of the passing Book of the World as reinterpreted in eclectic fashion, with delight and dry wit but also with didactic seriousness, by an "enlightened" Renaissance artist of the Reformation.[12] With its profuse emblems of knights, giants, dwarfs, magicians, dragons, satyrs, beasts, amazons, castles, bowers, caves, holy mountains, and diverse classical, chivalric, biblical and hermetic figures, the poem in structure and content is an iconographic literary analogue for medieval-Renaissance composite verbal and pictorial representations of the entire earth.[13] From an imaginative distance and with imaginative alterations, the figures and form of Spenser's faeryland generally reflect the medieval world iconographic vision as rendered in cosmographical tracts, psalters, travel books, altar icons, architectural structures, and in the designs of Renaissance court theatrical spectacles and staged combats.

Just as the encompassing and demarking iconographic geometrical designs—the crosses, circles within circles, central and other points—on *mappaemundi* signify the underlying and constant immaterial substantial forms of a world that is subject, like the plenitude of emblematic figures it contains, to material and other accidental changes, so too the subsuming core emblems of *The Faerie Queene* point to spiritual forms that transcend lesser emblems of mortality and mutability. Moreover, the intermingled clusters of emblematic figures on *mappaemundi*, arranged in relation to the formative geometric and demarking icons and mostly depicted in action, are counterparts to the intermeshed groups of faeryland emblematic figures. Throughout the intervolved narratives of Spenser's epic, these faeryland figures are arranged in relation to core emblems, thus giving ideological-spiritual form to the work. In later books it is these core emblems that, together with emblematic character types, are most clearly analogous to medieval world book iconography. But in the first two books, narrative elements and associated emblems reflect those of biblical-pilgrimage accounts and stations and those of crusading materials.

Setting many of the fantastic character-types of medieval myth and chivalric romance in motion within his copious poem, Spenser transforms the terrors and marvels of a remembered "antique" medieval world into a selfconsciously artificial fable, one often displaying a lightness in tone educed in part from Italian epic romances. The poet, though didactically earnest, constantly modulates his narrative voice from the serious to the playful and, frequently, to the mocking. Terrible struggles involving giants and amazons are given antic touches; processions of monsters and allegorical figures in troops are presented as obvious "disguisings"; and depictions of partly human creatures are exaggerated to an extent that makes the character-types unmistakably fictitious.

Like Spenser's faeryland, the medieval iconographic world—as described in the largely fictitious travel accounts of the fourteenth century *Book of Sir John Maundeville* (ca. 1365)—contains "folk of dyverse shap."[14] Though most likely composed in France by Jean de Bourgogne and Jean d'Outremeuse, this book purports to reveal the "true" marvels seen by the supposed "British" Maundeville who leaves St. Albans in England in 1332. "Litylle folk as dwerfes," the author calling himself Maundeville writes, are found on the islands beyond India. On other islands near the African realm of Prester John, Maundeville claims that there live "grete geauntes of xxviii, fote longe or xxx fote long" (p. 205). Maundeville becomes incredulous, however, in reporting that "men sayden . . . that in an yle beyond . . . were geantes of gretters sature, summe of xlv fote or of l. fote long." Honest suspicion wins the day, for the author adds that "I sayh, none of tho"; Maundeville holds to the existence of moderate giants of no greater stature than "xxx fote" (p. 206).

In *The Faerie Queene* central figures of virtue or reason are, of course, usually of comely appearance: the featured male and female knights; the pagan gods in their temples, shrines or gardens; and the ladies of virtue or holiness. Minor character-types assisting the central figures often have most curious shapes: the dwarf carrying Una's bag (1.1.6), the "Faunes and Satyres" having "forheads with rough hornes" who encounter Una (1.6.16), and the holy hermit in rustic weeds who spiritually heals Timias and Serena (6.5.38). The author Maundeville had written without skepticism on the existence of "folk" with animal feet who are "stronge and myghty and swift renneres, for their taken wylde bestes with rennyng" (p. 148). Spenser, too, comments in a similar vein upon the woodland savage who, without "armes or weapon" and "naked without needfull vestiments," was "swift as any Bucke in chace" (6.4.4–7).

But in depicting another "wilde and saluage man" who attempts to rape Amoret in a wood (4.7.5), the poet goes beyond Maundeville and other travel writers in combining grotesque features to form an extreme of ludicrous ugliness. Maundeville insists that on islands near "Inde" there are persons with "lippe aboue the mouth so gret that when their slepen in the sonne, their keueren alle the face with that lippe" (p. 147). On another island not far from these umbrella-lip persons, Maundeville asserts that there lives another famous group having "grete eres and longe that hangen doun to here knees" (p. 148). Spenser, with some but not with pronounced allegorical purpose, presents a comparable visual representation of the "saluage man" who attacks Amoret: "His neather lip was not like man nor beast,/ But like a wide deep poke, downe hanging low" (4.7.6). Of the "saluage man's" monstrous ears, the poet writes:

> And downe both sides two wide long eares did glow,
> And raught downe to his waste, when up he stood,
> More great than th' eares of Elephants by *Indus* flood.
>
> (4.7.6)

The man's mouth is said to "gape/ With hughe great teeth, like to a tusked Boare" (4.7.5); and the man's body is depicted as "All ouergrowne with haire, that could awape/ An hardy hart" (4.7.5). A horrible partly animal shape is thus given to this allegorical figure of Lust; but in this case, Spenser also uses exaggeration to parody the medieval tradition of associating grotesque human features with the features of animals.

Educated or well-placed Elizabethans—Sidney, the Earl of Leicester and Harvey among them—would have immediately recognized all or most of the medieval stories about giants, dwarfs, savages and comparable figures as fiction. But then, just as now, it was the very fantastical nature of these wildly tall tales that appealed to the imagination and that in the sixteenth century provided images for Italian writers of romances, for the designers and authors of court spectacles and "staged" combats, and for the English court poets fascinated by this "antique" world.

The medieval world iconographic order, however, was disintegrating. Popular emblem books produced in the sixteenth and seventeenth centuries—many containing new emblems "made up" by author-inventors Andrea Alciati, Francis Quarles, George Wither and others—show a fragmented variety of designs that are often unassimilated into the larger medieval iconographic framework.

As a British poet of the Reformation, Spenser apparently did not believe that spiritual truths could be learned from the supposed "essences" of relics and pilgrimage "stations," yet he retained an aesthetic attachment to the iconographic order of the medieval world and to pilgrimage traditions. He drew upon and used medieval icons while "making up" his own comparable but original emblems. He placed narrative action in an imaginative faeryland of just memory, invented a selfconsciously fictive literal sense that in the prologue to book 2 he briefly pretended was historically true, and then proceeded to manipulate character-types with considerable distanced amusement.

Emblems for the diversity of sensory creation, dispersed in *The*

Faerie Queene and other works within containing ideational-geometric icons, are related by correspondence to some all-sustaining figure or image at a thematic center or "core." On the circular T-and-O icons of the earth, this core is the point or cross at the "middle," representing the city of Jerusalem and of the Son; in European and British cathedrals, the axial crossing of nave and transept where the high altar originally stood, holding the host and, on occasion, icons of the earth. In Dante's *Commedia*, the poet travels to this center: three intermingling circles of light and human form at the spiritual font of the universe. And in *The Faerie Queene*, the central type is Gloriana in her faeryland city, Cleopolis, which mirrors an earthly and heavenly Jerusalem.

A crusading Red Cross Knight who will become St. George wanders through dispersed iconographic landscapes in book 1. The knight becomes lost in a labyrinth of error, slays a dragon that is compared to Nile slime, encounters a false hermit, fights Saracens, journeys to a holy mountain of revelation, gazes from its summit upon the New Jerusalem, and then goes on to a castle of Eden associated with an ultimate allegorical "East." In book 2, a Palmer accompanies the knight Guyon on a journey past Fortunate Isles to a bower of excess. Dispersed but formal pilgrimage themes fade from the later books, but chivalric male and female knights continue on quests—over straight paths, meandering byways, or through labyrinths—to temples, hermitages, houses and gardens similar to those in comprehensive descriptions or drawings of the iconographic world.

Around the thematic and subsuming center of Gloriana in faeryland Cleopolis, a number of lesser but corresponding core emblems—those, for example, of the House of Alma, the Temple of Venus, the Garden of Adonis, the Temple of Isis, the "glassy globe" of Merlin—are placed in the midst of, or are otherwise related to, emblems of circles, compasses or wheels. And very possibly with the realization that *The Faerie Queene* would never be completed, Spenser adds to book 6 the famous description of the circular dance of virtuous nymphs on Ireland's Mt. Acidale, placing himself into the scene in the persona and guise of Colin Clout playing to dancers. As has frequently been pointed out, this allusion to Colin—who here dons pastoral garb—hints at the termination of martial themes even as it carries the reader back in a circular pattern to complementary references in the prologue to book 1. There Spenser in his persona as narrator writes of removing his previously assumed "maske" of "Shepherds weeds," appropriate to past pastoral activities, in order to sing in his new epic of knights and ladies and chivalric deeds.

James Nohrnberg has called attention to a number of "evidences of the terminal character" of book 6,[15] notably in the comparatively disengaged view of narrative quest action and in the withdrawal and embowering of characters such as Sir Tristram, Priscilla and Serena. Yet there are also evidences that the actions and discoveries of certain central figures will necessarily continue. Spenser's circular pattern of allusion in itself precludes an absolutely final termination of the work. While in this last completed book a chaste nymph said to be the "handmayd" of Gloriana appears on Mt. Acidale, the Faerie Queene herself is absent and by implication may yet someday follow the example of her servant and become manifest. And although the key figure in the book, the Knight of Courtesy Calidore, finally captures the Blatent Beast of Rumor, the beast escapes. Unlike the history of other knights in the poem, moreover, the history of the knight Calidore in book 6 is brought up to the present of the narrative, and the text suggests that his quests and adventures will continue.

For in one lower dimension of meaning and abstraction, Spenser's airy fable in all six books embodies thematic and structural patterns and circular emblems that can have no end. The patterns and emblems point to the life of the human being, a being of spirit transcending this world, but also a being in this world who is constantly moving between extremes of fall and regeneration, continence and incontinence, error and right choice, sin and holiness. It is this theme of change and mortality in the lower realms of creation that Spenser addresses also in *Two Cantos of Mutabilitie*, a work apparently produced apart from *The Faerie Queene*.[16]

Dante had introduced Virgil's moving speech on love at canto 17 of the *Purgatorio*, as near as possible to the "middle" of the three-canticle poem as established by a count of cantos. In *The Faerie Queene*, Spenser's core emblems and statements on the central theme of love, critics have observed, are similarly but more casually placed by a count of cantos at the approximate middle of the completed six books. Core emblems are neatly paired. The Garden of Adonis gives expression to cosmic love in the sixth canto of book 3, a volume dedicated to wide conceptions of spiritual Chastity. The Temple of Venus stands as an emblem of earthly love between couples and appears in the seventh canto of book 4, a book on the subject of Friendship. Through virtuous emblematic female figures introduced into core and other episodes—Belphoebe, Venus and Britomart in book 3, and again Venus and Britomart in books 4 and 5—Spenser discloses the diverse virtues of love that are subsumed in the ultimate, central type of Gloriana in Cleopolis.

Other paired emblems in paired books, enfolding middle books 3 and 4, offer examples of those virtues of Right Reason and Holiness that are necessarily conjoined with love in Gloriana. Nested on either side of the middle volumes, book 2 on Temperance presents the House of Alma in canto 10 as an emblem of the rational moral order in the human being, the family, the body politic, and the cosmos; book 5 on Justice presents the Temple of Isis in canto 7 as an emblem of the rational judicial ordering of microcosm and macrocosm. Framing books 1 and 6 complete the nest of volumes, with the emblematic House of Holiness in canto 10 of book 1 depicting individual Holiness, and the emblematic Hermitage of spiritual Courtesy in canto 6 of book 2 illustrating collective spiritual holiness.

Numerous other paired or ideologically interrelated core emblems might readily be mentioned. Emblems of vice, for example, contrast with emblems of virtue: the House of Lucifera stands in emblematic opposition to the House of Holiness; the Bower of Bliss contrasts with the Garden of Adonis. Because it is constructed from networks of corresponding ideas of virtue and opposing ideas of vice, the poem can be seen simultaneously to have various interwoven structural patterns. Most obvious is the ideological pattern based upon the differing virtues necessary to the private and public person. The first three books deal with Holiness, Temperance and Chastity, respectively, revealing the private virtues; the last three books on Friendship, Justice and Courtesy address the public virtues.

On the highest metaphysical plane of abstract meaning, this invention of ideas embraces conceptions that transcend the physical realm of motion and time. The ideas are presumably static and eternal; and Spenser sought to veil them in sensuous core emblems placed at thematic centers throughout his poem to impose an eternal order upon transient being. Subsuming all emblems of virtuous female figures, the ultimate type of Gloriana suggests— even to some degree in name—the resplendent, unchanging ideological form of public virtue beyond the material, a form that nevertheless reflects or "mirrors" the supposed essence of earthly Queen Elizabeth. And in the subsuming type of the magnificent Prince Arthur, an emblem of unified, ideal private virtue is presented, complementing but still requiring total fulfillment in the all-encompassing form of the ruling Gloriana.

Although Spenser completed only six of the 12 projected books, this invention of a literary idealist, with its internal circular structural patterns and partial thematic closure in book 6, leaves no overriding critical impression of being unfinished. The complex underlying structure and surface diversity may indeed at times cause some confusion for readers accustomed to dominating narrative design, but certainly not a sharp sense of loss because six projected books are lacking. In his letter of 1589 to Sir Walter Raleigh, Spenser remarks upon the possibility of composing as many as 24 books, the "first twelve" on the "privat Moral Virtues" represented in Arthur "before he was king." "These first twelve books: which if I find to be well accepted," Spenser writes, "I may be perhaps encouraged to frame the other part of Politick Virtues in his person, after that he came to be king."[17] Spenser's ideological invention, however, allowed him to contract or expand his poem without fatal structural damage. One can imagine a *Faerie Queene* in three books, or four, or five, or even ten. In each case, the work as an allegory would be either less or more interrelated and subsumed through core emblems, one theme and figure within the other. One can also imagine it being expanded, following Spenser's own speculations, to a poem of 24 books. But in its present state, *The Faerie Queene* exists in six books as an extraordinarily varied linguistic-emblematic creation, rich in textures and shadings of meaning, with a self-contained and strong didactic content and structure.

The planned but unrealized 12-book form to reveal the "privat Moral Virtues" derives in part from Spenser's conceptions of the 12 Aristotelian virtues, the 12-book divisions of the classical epic, and the patterned 12-part cosmos divided in zodiac signs, months, and day-and-night hours. The poem's 12 projected books and faeryland regions, though, each presumably with new planned "sets" of knights and different iconographic landscapes, are analogous in number to the 12 regions frequently ascribed to the medieval Book of the World, each region inhabited or controlled by certain knights or holy men who were listed in chronicles and tracts as successors respectively of antique classical or biblical heroes, and of Christ's 12 disciples. The 12-part cosmic pattern is stressed on many world icons by images, surrounding circular renderings of the earth, showing the 12 signs of the zodiac related to seasonal change, and the 12 wind zones related to climatic change.

THE TEMPLES OF AN IMAGINATIVE FAERYLAND

As early as 1644 the English knight Sir Kenelyn Digby insisted, in a general fashion without making refined philosophical distinctions, that Spenser as an ideological poet was above all a philosophical idealist. "Surveying his works," Digby writes, "you shall finde him a constant disciple of *Platoes* School."[18] In a remarkable but categorical seventeenth century "critical" tract, *Observations on the 22. Stanza in the 9th. Canto of the 2d. Book of Spencers Faery Queen*, Digby offers a line-by-line reading of the meanings to be found in Spenser's passage on the cosmic icons and numbers of the House of Alma. Although the specifics of the interpretation can readily be questioned, this early ideological "critic" properly emphasizes the traditional kinds of microcosmic-macrocosmic correspondences that many Renaissance readers would have discerned both in the poem and in the existing universe. This widely traveled and individualistic nobleman, a naval commander and a public proponent of the new philosophy, displays a fascination with the ideational-geometric forms of the medieval world vision.

Commenting on the hierarchical numerical structure of the House of Alma "Proportion'd equally by seven and nine," Digby observes that the poet

> meanes the influences of the superior substances (which governe the inferiour) into the two differing parts or Man; to wit, of the *Starres* (the most powerfull of which, are the seven Planets, into the body: and of the Angels divided into nine Hierarchies or Orders) into his soul (p. 16).

Digby, in quoting the line about the House "Frame" that "seemed partly Circular, and part Triangular," writes that the poet "meanes the mind and body of Man; the first being by him compared to a Circle, and the latter to a Triangle." The "Quadrate" that was "twixt them both," he continues, "meaneth the foure principall humors in mans Bodie, Choler, Blood, Phleme and Melancholy" (pp. 6, 15).

In discussing the correspondences supposedly relating humans, the world and God, Digby advances the sort of ideological interpretation that doubtless influenced medieval cartographers in their placement of Jerusalem, the City of God, as a point at the center of T-and-O icons. "As God hath neither beginning nor ending . . .," writes Digby of Spenser's passage on the circular part of Alma's House, "God is compared to a Circle." He adds as well that "mans soul is a Circle, whose circumference is limited by the true center of it, which is onely God. For as a circumference doth in all parts alike respect that indivisible Point, . . . so all the interiour actions of mans soul ought to have no other respective Point to direct themselves unto, but God." Digby then states that Spenser's circle icon also signifies the "great world": "And if you take *all together*," he writes, "Man is a little world, an exact type of the great world, and of God himself" (p. 7).

References to the circular form of the cosmos and the earth were, of course, common in biblical literature and cosmographical works. Gabriel Harvey's copy of *The Surveye of the World* contained a passage describing the earth as "being compassed almost rounde with the Ocean Sea like a greate ilande."[19] The revisionary *The Cosmographical Glasse* (1559) by William Cuningham also included an allusion to the T-and-O icons of "ancient Geographers" who asserted that the earth was "invironed, and compassed" by "the mightye Ocean seas, seemeth as it were an Island."[20]

In *The Book of Sir John Maundeville*, the travel account cited in recent scholarship as actually having been read by Spenser,[21] the alleged "British" author associates the exact middle of the earth, said to be marked by a small stone "compas" in the Temple of the Holy Sepulchre in Jerusalem, with Joseph of Aramathea, the supposed founder of the English Church. "British" Maundeville states that the stone is at the spot where "Joseph of Aramathie leyde the body of oure lord where he had taken Him down of the croys, and there he wassched the woundes of oure lord, and that compas saye men is the myddes of the world." Maundeville writes of going upward over the globe on an Exodus pilgrimage to the earth's center and highest point at Jerusalem and then down the other side of the globe on a journey deep into Asia. Maundeville notes that "in goynge from Scotland or from Englond toward Jerusalem men gon upward alweys. For oure land," he continues with the English perspective that colors many passages in the book, "is in the lowe partie of the earthe toward the west, and the lond of Prestre Johnis the lowe partie of the erthe toward the est." Maundeville insists that he wished to go all the way East to the Terrestrial Paradise, which he describes at length on the basis of what "wise men say"; but he modestly confesses, "I was not there. It is far beyond; and I repent not going there, but I was not worthy" (p. 220).

Maundeville necessarily locates Jerusalem at a geographic center because cosmography had to be made consistent with Psalm 74.12 which avowed that God "wrought salvation in the midst of the earth." And in the midst of Jerusalem, of course, rose the round Temple of the Holy Sepulchre which in turn contained the round, stone microcosmic compass that precisely marked the earth's middle. Most arresting is the fact that Maundeville was aware that the circular form of the Holy Sepulchre was repeated in circular temples elsewhere in the world, temples that in their design and religious significance were lesser types of the "true" Jerusalem temple. He notes that the Egyptians constructed to their god "Fenix" "a temple made round after the shappe of the temple of Jerusalem." He assumes that the worship of the dying and resurrecting bird-god is a pagan allegorical veil for the higher Christian worship of the Son. "A man may well lykene that bryd unto God," he writes, "because that there nys no god but one, and also that oure Lord aroos from deth to lyue the thridde day" (p. 34).

Giving a strong British cast to his comments on the Holy Sepulchre, Maundeville observes that at the site of this Jerusalem temple, "Seynte Elyne," the alleged British mother of Constantine, discovered the tomb of Christ and found the "true cross." He then associates the center of the temple, marked by the "compass" of Joseph, with the compass-form of the earth and the cosmos: "Be ther ymagyned a figure that hath a gret compas, and aboute the poynt of the gret compas (that is clept the center) be made another litille compas. . . . Now thanne, be the gret compas represented for the firmament, and the litille compas represented for the erthe" (p. 59).

In *The Faerie Queene*, through ideological-emblematic correspondence, circular allegorical "core" emblems in central books 3 and 4—most notably the emblematic Temple of Venus and Garden of Adonis—signify different qualities of love that are unified and subsumed in the all-embracing core emblem of Cleopolis, the faeryland city that mirrors the earthly and heavenly Jerusalem. Consequently, the Temple and the Garden are themselves also depicted as directly corresponding to the holy center that is Jerusalem.

"Right in the midst" of the Temple of Venus, Spenser writes, paraphrasing Psalm 74 with its allusion to the "middle" geographic location of the Holy City, "the Goddesse selfe did stand/ Upon an altar" (4.10.39). The goddess Venus, signifying physical love and generation, appears enshrined on a shimmering altar that, like the central glasslike tower of faeryland Cleopolis, is "Pure in aspect, and like to christall glasse" (4.10.39). The temple contains "an hundred marble pillors round," and "An hundred Altars round about were set" (4.10.37–38). Like the geocosm of the earth itself, the temple is "seated in an Island strong" where it is discovered by the knight Busyrane "Within the compasse of that Islands space" (4.10.6, 21). At the center of the temple on the circular island, the great goddess "*Venus*, Queene of beautie and of grace" (4.10.44) influences with her look

> . . . all things . . ., that nurish vitall blood,
> Soon as with fury thou doest them inspire,
> In generation seeke to quench their inward fire.
>
> So all the world by thee at first was made,
> And dayly yet thou doest the same repayre
>
> (4.10.46–47)

"Right in the middest of that Paradise," writes Spenser of the Garden of Adonis that also corresponds to Jerusalem, rises a mount with a summit bower. Within that bower Venus, now signifying physical fecundity and love in union with higher heavenly love, "possessth" Adonis, the god who dies and is resurrected in accord with the regular changes of the seasons (3.6.46). "All be he subject to mortality," Spenser explains of Adonis,

> Yet is eterne in mutabilitie,
> And by succession made perpetuall,
> Transformed oft, and chaunged diuerslie:
> For him the Father of all formes they call
>
> (3.6.47)

Further, in an an allegorical reference that joins Adonis, the "Father of all formes" with an emblem for the eternal human soul, Spenser notes that in the bower Adonis's "true loue faire *Psyche* with him plays" (3.6.50).

In a garden below the bower, an "Old *Genius*" with a "double nature," both eternal and mutable, clothes the eternal substantial forms of "naked babes" (3.6.31–32), sending them on a journey through life that is represented as circular. After being clothed, the babes are said to go

> . . . into the chungefull world againe,
> Till thither they returne, where first they grew,
> So like a wheele around they runne from old to new.
>
> (3.6.33)

But the mutability of the babes, as they turn round in life like a wheel, is said to be only an "outward fashion." "The substance is eterne," Spenser adds, "and bideth so" (3.6.37–38).

The emblem of a compass is employed to identify yet another circular center corresponding to great Cleopolis in book 3. Here, the figure Paridell asserts that antique British Troynouant, in the manner of Gloriana's capital city, was constructed "huge" in "scope" by Aeneas's descendent Brute "to be the compasse of his kingdomes seat" (3.9.46). Like the city of Lincoln which was also built by Brute, Troynouant is "renowmed far away" and attracts travelers "from East and West" who seek it out as the goal of their "endlong" journeys. But both Lincoln and Troynouant are said to be exceeded in splendor by the Faerie Queene's capital. One "Cannot two fairer Cities find this day," Paridell continues, "Except *Cleopolis*" (3.9.51).

THE TOWER OF GLASS

The supreme center of the faeryland world, the seat of Gloriana's power and the synthesizing fulfillment of all virtuous faeryland cities, is a shimmering metropolis distinguished by a mysterious, soaring "towre of glass" called Panthea. It is a "bright towre, all built of christall cleene," that "seemed the brightest thing, that was." The metropolis itself—"*Cleopolis*, the fairest citie was that might be seene" (1.10.58)—is enclosed by a "golden wall" (2.10.72). The Red Cross Knight, during a heavenly vision on the summit of the Mount of Holiness in book 1, states that "great *Cleopolis* . . ./ In which the fairest *Faerie Queene* doth dwell" (1.10.58) is itself excelled only by the corresponding "New Jerusalem," the heavenly celestial city where "blessed Angels to and fro descend/ From highest heauen" (1.10.56). Only the "bright Angels towre" of the spiritually transcendent New Jerusalem, Red Cross continues, "dims that towre of glas" of Cleopolis (1.10.58).

Had *The Faerie Queene* been completed following Spenser's outline in the letter to Raleigh, it would have been in glittering Cleopolis that the Faerie Queene would have received her knights and sent them out on their individual quests. Very possibly Cleopolis, like the island Temple of Venus, would have been depicted as an island center of crystal, a center surrounded by the "glassy See" spanned by the "bridge of bras" mentioned in the faeryland chronicles in book 2 (2.10.73). For the bridge over that sea, echoing with the sound of "heavens thunder" and so associated with celestial realms, is recorded in the chronicles as having been constructed just after Cleopolis's wall of gold and tower of glass.

The bridge, though given no exact faeryland location in the chronicles, appears another imaginative city addition upon which Spenser could have elaborated in describing Gloriana's feast.

In his letter to Raleigh, Spenser does not discuss the final, planned relationship of Arthur and Gloriana; it seems likely, however, that at the end of the poem this greatest of knights would have come to the shimmering city, in Spenser's words, "to be king." Cleopolis, then, would have been the site of Arthur's assumption of monarchical power probably through marriage to Gloriana—the allegorical union of Magnificence and Glory.

Spenser undoubtedly conceived of the faeryland city that transcends all earthly places under the influence of passages from Revelation 21.2–31. These verses describe the descent of the heavenly city, the New Jerusalem, resplendent in "pure gold, like to transparent glass." Yet just as transcendent Gloriana is analogous to and "mirrors" the true essence of earthly Queen Elizabeth, so too that bright faeryland city with its tower of glass reflects past and contemporaneous seats of English royal authority, such as Windsor and London. But because Spenser was writing of "antique" faeryland realms, he turned in particular for similes in his early books, commentators have noted,[22] to the root "antique" source and center of English religious and political power: the town presently called Glastonbury in southwest England, the supposed burial place of Arthur in misty lowlands beneath a pyramidal mount or "Tor." By tradition this is the site of the mythical Isle of Avalon where, according to legends, faeries roamed and ancient Celtic warriors lay entombed.

While the town now called Glastonbury has been seen by commentators to be reflected in Cleopolis, Spenser's indebtedness to the details of its local pilgrimage legends and traditions, topographical features, and even its prominent and symbolically significant sixteenth century name have escaped notice. Overlooked as well is the earthly analogue for the central architectural building of faeryland: Gloriana's tower of glass.

In "Somerset-shire" near Avalon, John Stow writes in the 1580 edition of his *Chronicles*, Arthur aided by the good sorcerer Merlin "kept the order of the round table" at "*Camelot*" moving it at times to "*Carleon*" and "*Winchester*."[23] In this same region, Stow reports in the 1570 edition, "*Mordred* was slayne, and Arthure wounded unto death. He was buried in the Ile of *Avalon*, now called Glastonbury."[24] In the 1565, 1570 and 1580 editions of the *Chronicles*, all dedicated to the Earl of Leicester, Stow states that the bones of Arthur were discovered in 1191 in "a goodly olde sepulture about whiche there stode two pyllers . . . upon the sepulture was a crosse of leade layde, whereon was written, here lieth the noble king of Brytons *Arthur*, buried, in the Ile of Avalon."[25]

The Isle of Avalon at Glastonbury is also the place where Joseph of Arimathea was said to have come from Jerusalem and to have left the red cross of Christianity and the relics of the passion. Thus Glastonbury—the actual historical site of a first century Near Eastern–style anchorite community and a later famed medieval abbey—through correspondence with the Holy City of the East became the British "New Jerusalem" and the earliest sacred British center of medieval pilgrimage. The fifth century bard Melgram in a Latin poem had observed that Joseph brought to England white and silver cruets containing the blood and sweat of Jesus.[26] Thomas Malory in the eleventh century *Morte Arthur* had written generally of the Holy Grail and then of Joseph. Then in mid-thirteenth century additions to William of Malmesbury's *De Antiquitate*, an anonymous author wrote, first, of Joseph's arrival in England; next, of the hermit Walwam's questioning of Launcelot about "the mystery of a certain well, the water of which frequently changes its taste and colour"; and finally of "the vessel there called the Holy Grail."[27] It was Spenser in *The Faerie Queene* who recorded the legend, current in his own period, that Joseph of Arimathea had carried the Grail of the last supper from Jerusalem to England:

> Yet true it is . . .
> Hither came Joseph of Arimathy,
> Who brought with him the holy grayle, (they say)
> And preacht the truth, but since it greatly did decay.
>
> (2.10.53)

According to the elaborated legend apparently indebted in part to the Malmsbury text and current in the eighteenth century, Joseph buried the Grail at the foot of Glastonbury Tor, at ancient "Chalcselle" or Chalice Hill in a holy well that seasonally flows with red waters.

"Glastonbury is ye holyest erth of england," wrote the anonymous author of the poetic *lyfe of Joseph of Armathia*, published by Richard Pynson in 1520, in an open attempt to attract pilgrims to the British New Jerusalem. The author explains how heaven and earth were joined when

> . . . Jhesu the mighty
> He sent to Joseph the aungell gabryell
> Which had hym as the wrytyng doth specify
> Of our ladyes assumpsyn to bylde a chapell[28]

The angel Gabriel, according to medieval tradition, descended from heaven alighting and speaking with Joseph on the peak of Glastonbury Tor. There in very ancient times a stone church was built and dedicated to the archangel. Destroyed by an earthquake in 1275 and then rebuilt about 1290 only to fall again into ruin, the partially reconstructed remains of the church in Spenser's time consisted of a 70-foot-high stone tower that stood commandingly uplifted, rising on the Tor summit above the usual swirling morning mists of the lowlands and silhouetted by the region's frequently shifting patches and beams of bright sunlight.[29]

Drawings of the tower, together with pyramidal illustrations of the labeled "Tor," appear on Christopher Saxton's map of Somersetshire in 1575, part of this cartographer's series of maps of England. The tower and Tor are illustrated in the same fashion on maps of the area by John Speed (1610) and Joannis Blaeu (1648). Most striking is the fact that the drawn tower and Tor are depicted on all of these maps next to the inscribed name "Glassenbury." Saxton spells the name in this manner; Blaeu and Speed add a final "e."[30]

At ancient "Glassenbury" some nine miles from the western English coastline of the Atlantic Ocean, where streams are raised and lowered by tidal currents and the moisture and sunlight cause curious optical effects, the cone-shaped Tor dominates the landscape for many miles around. In a labyrinth of nested terraces encircling the summit tower, the Tor rises to a height of 520 feet above the moors and flatlands. Celts of the Iron Age lived in this region and possibly used the Tor maze for pagan religious rituals. In the Christian era after the original anchorite establishment transformed into a large monastic community, one having obvious traditional ties with communities and sites in the Holy Land, medieval pilgrims at "Glassenbury" passed over a chain of pilgrimage stations. These began near and led through the abbey, including stops for relics of the Exodus and Passion and, in the thirteenth and later centuries, a stop for the tomb of King Arthur. The pilgrims then ascended the pathways of the Tor labyrinth to their pilgrimage goal: the tower "station" surmounting this Isle of Glass.

Tradition holds that it was here in the region of Avalon, Isabelle Rathbone points out, where Arthur received his magic sword Excalibur from the Lady of the Lake. The king then returned to the area to be treated for a fatal wound, and finally was transported by faery ladies on a barge to his resting place on Avalon Isle at the foot of "Glassenbury" Tor. For in medieval romance, as Rathbone has shown, Avalon was the traditional haunt of the faery queen and her court, the faeryland realm where Queen Morgan le Fay kept

Ogier the Dane for 200 years before releasing him to the normal world.[31]

In prehistoric times Glastonbury was one among a number of southwestern British islands enveloped by the waters of the nearby Atlantic Ocean, the others being the Tors of Meare, Wedmore, Altheney and Beckery. When the waters receded in the Neolithic period, the ocean floor around the Tors pushed upward and was covered by a shrub forest. Then the land about the Tors sank to near sea level and was washed by ocean tidal flows. Marshlands and lagoons formed; the Tors still served as islands but were now inhabited by ancient peoples. John Hankin has observed that these islands were called "fortunate" by John Leland when in 1582 he quoted Geoffrey of Monmouth's description of Avalon.[32] Thus Glastonbury, popularly believed to mean "City of Glass" from the possible Celtic derivation of its name *Yns-witrin*, was associated with legends about islands and the sea. Among the Saxon, Norman and Celtic kings buried there was King Edgar, founder of the first powerful British navy and the historical favorite of sixteenth century navigational theorist John Dee.[33]

With its tower of glass, Cleopolis mirrors London and Windsor and even Arthur's seat at Colchester, but Spenser in his text does not stress such comparisons. When the poet describes the faeryland court and palace, for example, of the virtuous "souerayne Lady Queene" Marcella (5.9.20), as one among many analogues for Elizabeth's court and royal government on earth, he makes no attempt to use similes pointing to London or some other royal seat. Marcella's "stately pallace" with its "many towres, and tarras mounted hye,/ And all their tops bright glistering with gold" (5.9.21) is outwardly just a "pompous show" that must be balanced by the interior restraint and justice of the faeryland queen within.

Rather, beyond Windsor or London or other British locales, Avalon, the Isle of Glass, was depicted in chronicles and romances as the "antique" font of British Christianity and the supposed site of the greatest tales of English knightly chivalry. In *The Faerie Queene*, the ancient Isle becomes through general analogy a thematic center, corresponding to the earthly and heavenly New Jerusalem, for the faeryland city of Cleopolis. And the antique faeryland tower of glass—an image derived both from biblical reference and British cosmography—is directly comparable to the earthly antique tower that rises over the mists of Avalon, high above Arthur's tomb, at the summit and center of the "Glassenbury" Tor pilgrimage maze.

MERLIN'S "GLASSIE GLOBE"

Spenser was never to write of the projected "feast of Gloriana" and of her likely marriage to Arthur at her "kingdomes seat" Cleopolis. The great faeryland city, like Gloriana herself, remains always there at the ideological-emblematic center of the poem as the subsuming, ideal capital to which all lesser virtuous seats of power correspond. But with Spenser's more or less permanent removal to Ireland beginning in 1580, the poet's direct references to the city disappear from the last three books to be replaced by increasing allusions to Irish locales and to lesser core emblems. Gone too from the later books are most of the dispersed narrative crusading and pilgrimage allusions particularly evident in books 1 and 2, allusions in part suggested by chivalric pageants, masques and festivities at the London Inner Temple and the London Elizabethan court. Nevertheless, Spenser, using correspondences, held to the poem's basic ideological design.

In book 3, the poet therefore introduces as a lesser core emblem the miniature "glassie globe" of Merlin (3.2.21), an occult mirror of both the poem and external universe that brilliantly encapsulates events, persons and places in microcosmic pictures. Britomart, the female Knight of Chastity and a surrogate for Gloriana, is inspired to a burning but virtuous love for Arthegal, the Knight of Justice and a surrogate for Arthur, after she sees images in Merlin's globe. This love underscores and corresponds to Arthur's love for Gloriana, with both pairs of virtuous figures apparently destined for wedded union in Cleopolis. The fascinating microcosmic "looking glasse" of Merlin (3.2.18) functions as a magical visual index to the central "invention" of the poem—the eventual union of Chastity and Justice, of Glory and Magnificence—even as it reflects the cosmography of the imagined faeryland and of the actual cosmos. "Who wonders not," writes Spenser of this miraculous device, "that reades so wonderous worke?" (3.2.20). In an episode motivating pivotal thematic action, Britomart sees in Merlin's globe a miniature image of Arthegal moving through a strange emblematic landscape, his face displayed like the sun rising from the east.

> Eftsoones there was presented to her eye
>   A comely knight, all arm'd in complete wize,
>   Through whose bright ventayle lifted vp on hye
>   His manly face, that did his foes agrize,

> And friends to termes of gentle truce entize,
> Lookt foorth, as *Phoebus* face out of the east,
> Betwixt two shadie mountaines doth arize
>
> (3.2.24)

The female knight, enraptured by the sight but doubtful about the unknown locale in which her lover's shadow appears, consults Merlin on the emblematic-cosmological issue of "under what coast of heaven the man did dwell," whether "beyond the *Africk Ismaell*,/ Or th' Indian *Peru* he were" (3.3.6). These references to the new cosmography, it will be recalled, echo the familiar passage in the prologue to book 2, the passage identifying "th' Indian *Peru*" as among the "Many great Regions" discovered "dayly . . . through hardy enterprize." In answering, Merlin emphasizes a primary poetic theme by simply assuring Britomart that her knight will return from distant realms "to this his native soyle" (3.3.27). Yet from the shadow in the globe and from conversations with Merlin, Britomart learns that her progeny by Arthegal will rule an empire embracing all of faeryland and all of the actual earth.

Merlin's microcosmic "glassie globe," the extraordinary product of "South-wales" "deepe science, and hell-dreaded might" (3.2.18), is obviously indebted to Platonic world conceptions in *Phaedrus* 225D and to magical glasses in Ptolemaic and literary mythology; but the seer's glass most closely resembles, with certain distinctions, the "glasses" of sixteenth century cosmographers revealed in published works. In dedicating his book *The Cosmographical Glasse* to the Earl of Leicester, for example, William Cuningham writes, "I . . . have devised this mirrour, or Cosmographical Glasse" to reflect "the heavens with her planets and starres, th' Earthe with her beautifull Regions, and the Seas with her merueilous increase" (Aii). Cuningham adds that in his mirror "we may behold, not one or two personages, but the heavens" and the rest of the cosmos. He does identify, however, a wide range of curious beings: "dragons," the "Chrocodile"; the strange folk of "Africke"; the odd inhabitants of "Asia" including "Pygmeans," "spirites" and "Anthopophagi"; and the Indians of the New World (folio 185–87). He even notes how, by looking upon the constant "increase" of the sea upon the earth's shorelines, "she shal not (if men be diligent)" using his "Glasse," "creape into any of these places" (Aii).

Cuningham anticipates the words of Spenser when, in an expository dialogue in his work between the scholar Spoudaeus and the teacher Philonicus, the scholar speaks traditionally of "Cosmographie" as that "arte whiche doe set forth, and describe the universall worlde" (fol. 5). The teacher then adds that "what so ever is betwixt the seate of the almighty governour of all lyving creatures, and the center of the earth: is called the worlde. And is compared to a round ball and globe" (fol. 9).

Merlin's "glassie globe" has the same range of reflected vision as Cuningham's "Glasse" but now offers "perfect sight."

> It vertue had, to shew in perfect sight,
>> What euer thing was in the world contaynd,
>> Betwixt the lowest earth and heauens hight
>
> (3.2.19)

Taking its form from the "universal world," the sorcerer's mirror "round and hollow shaped was,/ Like to the world it selfe, and seem'd a world of glas" (3.2.19).

One magical feature of the glass is unique. The seer's device focuses, not only upon the cosmos, but upon whatever "to the looker appertayned." The magic mirror had originally been invented as a spy glass for King Ryence, so that "neuer foes his kingdome might inuade,/ But he it knew at home before he hard/ Tydings thereof" (3.2.21). Merlin's glass can also magically disclose what "frend had faynd" as well as what "foe had wrought" (3.2.19). Gaining insight and knowledge from the visions in the glass, Merlin then uses magic to attain power over evil beings and nature. The seer controls "stubborn feends" that are "to his seruice bound," compelling them to labor incessantly on an unfinished wall "in compas to compile" his underground seat of power (3.3.10, 14). His spells also affect the physical world and "hostes of men":

> For he by words could call out of the sky
>> Both Sunne and Moone, and make them him obay:
>> The land to sea, and sea to maineland dry,
>> And darkesome night he eke could turne to day:
>> Huge hostes of men he could alone dismay
>
> (3.3.12)

The microcosmic "glassie globe that *Merlin* made" emerges as a supreme magical cosmographical glass that wondrously alters according to the user's need. Spenser wrote of this globe at a time when magical and scientific experimentation had yet to be sharply distinguished, when Theophrastus Paracelsus, Johann Kepler, Tycho Brahe, John Dee and Nicolaus Copernicus unavoidably confused the ciphers and metaphysics of magicians with the mathematics and scientific logic of the new philosophers. But Spenser, adopting a posture of amused detachment toward Merlin and his glass, reveals again a dominating impulse to be playfully imaginative in his surface representations of cosmography. On this surface level, the poet delights in the imaginative variety of old and new systems, in the mythic magical devices and actions comparable to those in fictive chivalric romances and in masquing spectacles.

In his persona as narrator, Spenser distances himself from Merlin by making this virtuous seer crabbed and distracted in manner. The sorcerer is depicted smiling "softly" in irony and then bursting "forth in laughter" when Britomart and her nurse Glauce seek to deceive him by approaching in disguise (3.3.17–19). After prophesying, Merlin falls into a "suddein fit, and half extatick stoure" that instills fear in the pair (3.3.50). "Goe to see that dreadfull place" where Merlin dwells, Spenser commands the reader, adding with offhanded insouciance, "if thou euer that same way/ To trauell." "Lay thine eare" against the ground to hear the "ghastly noise" of "yron chaines," "rombling" cauldrons, and groaning and pained spirits, Spenser continues with mock serious-ness. "It will stonne thy feeble braines" (3.3.8–9).

Spenser also distances his *literary* mirror of the cosmos—his poem—from the similar but also different artifact within an artifact that is Merlin's mirror. Both creations, through their visual images, suggest ideas concerned with the unifying power of love and possibly of works of art as well. But Spenser's poem is not an occult device that has magical properties. It is a product of six-teenth century rhetorical theory and supposed right reason. How-ever imaginative its surfaces and textures, the poem seeks to reveal in a metaphysical rather than a magical fashion the abstract "truths" of reality.[34]

THE WHEEL ROSE OF ACIDALE

A circular green and sacred hill, rather than the underground compass of Merlin's seat or the magic of his circular glass, gives a considerable measure of thematic and ideological coherence to Spenser's poem. Lacking a final scene in the faeryland city and tower that mirrors the sacred green mount and the tower at English Glassenbury, Spenser sets a lesser scene containing ele-ments of closure on the hill of Acidale.[35] This hill on an "open plaine," "round about . . . bordered with a wood" (6.10.6), is surmounted and given order by circle within circle of dancing virgins who all move around the axial figure of a maiden. The Hill has served as a nursery for Florimell, a figure of beauty. And as a former "soueraine" seat of Venus where the goddess both enjoyed "play and sport" and once held her "royall court" (6.10.9), Acidale is another emblematic font and center of the power of love. In its allegorical essence, Acidale both reflects and has components of spiritual identity with other seats of love's power, most prominently the island Temple of Venus, the Garden of Adonis, and the all-subsuming city of Cleopolis with its analogue in the nested, circular terraces of Glassenbury Tor.

Bonds of correspondence are cemented by the allegorical figures present on Acidale. Although Venus is absent because she finds this sacred site unfit for her full majesty (6.10.9), the outer ring of dancing virgins

> Are *Venus* Damzels, all within her fee,
> But differing in honour and degree:
> They all are Graces, which on her depend
>
> (6.10.21)

Gloriana too is missing but is represented by the maiden at the middle of the dance, a surrogate whom the poet claims he will praise until some future time when the Faerie Queene's "glory shall be farre displayd" (6.10.28).

Emblematic details are carefully developed in a fashion that leads to revelatory associations. On the summit of the hill, the Knight of Courtesy, Calidore, comes unexpectedly upon an unknown shepherd piping to "An hundred naked maidens lilly white/ . . . dauncing in delight" (6.10.11). The knight observes that "All they without were raunged in a ring/ And daunced round" (6.10.12). Once again a "compasse" emblem, corresponding with those at other seats of love, is introduced. The knight sees that an outer moving "compasse" of maidens encloses like a garland an inner moving circle of three ladies:

> . . . but in the midst of them
> Three other Ladies did both daunce and sing,
> The whilest the rest them round about did hemme,
> And like a girlond did in compasse stemme:
>
> (6.10.12)

Calidore then gazes upon the innermost figure:

And in the middest of those same three, was placed
Another Damzell, as a precious gemme,
   Amidst a ring most richly well enchaced,
That with her goodly presence all the rest much graced.

(6.10.12)

And suddenly, cosmic correspondences are revealed as the
dancers are compared, not only to a garland of flowers and to a
ring framing a precious stone, but also to the cyclical movement of
the heavenly bodies. "Looke," exclaims the narrator, "how the
Crowne, which *Ariadne* wore" has been transported to the skies
where it serves as an "ornament" to the stars "which round about
her move in order excellent" (6.10.13). The central virgin is said to
be similarly "Crownd" but "with a rosie girlond . . ./ . . . as the
crew/ About her daunst" (6.10.14).

As Calidore continues to gaze in wonder, this strange and
evanescent scene

. . . vanisht all away out of his sight,
And cleane were gone, which way he neuer knew;
All saue the shepheard

(6.10.18)

But even before this magical disappearance, the narrator has
begun to lift the imagistic veil to disclose the immaterial abstract
ideas that give meaning to these fictional sensuous surfaces.

The three Graces in the inner ring are emblematic, the shepherd
explains, of that spiritual love expressed through refining social
arts: those of "curtesie" and "Civility" (6.10.23). The "Hand-
maides of *Venus*" in the outer ring are Graces emblematic of a
wider, elemental love (6.10.15). It is the central maiden, however,
who is the most meaningful. The shepherd is said to have prac-
ticed his art by performing for her alone. This fourth Grace "made
him pipe so merrily, as never none" (6.10.15); therefore, she has
been seen to embody in some measure that engendering Grace of
Art that James Nohrnberg has traced to classical myths about
Charis, the wife of the artisan Hephaestus.[36] Earlier in the April
eclogue of the *Shepherd's Calender*, a song of Colin's had placed the
Graces in the company of the pagan Muses. Now on Mt. Acidale,
where beautiful Florimell was nursed, a preeminent Grace nurses
the shepherd's art through inspiration. This may suggest, as
Nohrnberg has maintained by reference to the Garden of Adonis, a
neo-Platonic interpretation: "that Plotinine extension of contem-

plation into the promulgation of forms" (p. 659).

The shepherd in fact identifies this fourth Grace as "Firme Chastity," the subsuming and transcendent form of spiritual love in which "many Graces gathered are" (6.10.27). The central virgin has accordingly been found to assimilate that most bountiful grace associated in book 6 with the surrogate figure Serena: providential "heavenly grace" that conjoins with other graces in an allegorical hypostasis of love (6.8.37).[37]

The remarkable core female figure crowned with a "rosie girland" and the lily-white nymphs who circle her in the manner of stars about crowned Ariadne emerge in this last completed book as a Reformation poet's striking blending of neo-Platonic and Christian conceptions and myths with the transmuted iconography of the dynamic medieval wheel windows that honored the Virgin Mary. Within the central changeless floral medallions of medieval wheel windows—medallions that were the fulfilled types of the rose designs at the hub of circular labyrinth floors below—the crowned Virgin appeared as the chaste font of nurturing love, and the infant Son she held represented the divine font of bountiful grace. Around the Virgin, virtuous allegorical figures appeared amid emblematic stars and white lillies of spiritual purity, wheeling in a universal dance of love that signified the movement of the created cosmos. In Spenser's Reformation wheel dance, removed to an earthly hill, circling virgins move in correspondence with the stars and the cosmos.

Gazing upon this earthly wheel is a shepherd engaged in his lyric art—a shepherd who, it is now very clear, is Spenser in the persona he had assumed in the *Shepherd's Calender*: that of "Poore Colin Clout" (6.10.16). Having taken up again the pastoral "maske" of "lowly Shephards weeds" that he announced, in the prologue to book 1, he would discard; and having profusely introduced pastoral themes into the later books written in Ireland, Spenser in the guise of Colin on the green Irish hill of Acidale, the last of the central core emblems of love, bursts out in emotive song in final praise of Gloriana:

> Sunne of the world, great glory of the sky,
>   That all the earth doest lighten with thy rayes,
>   Great *Gloriana*, greatest Maiesty,
>   Pardon thy shepheard, mongst so many layes,
>   As he hath sung of thee in all his dayes,
>   To make one minime of thy poore handmayd,
>   And underneath thy feete to place her prayse,

That when thy glory shall be farre displayd
To future age of her this mention may be made.

(6.10.28)

118

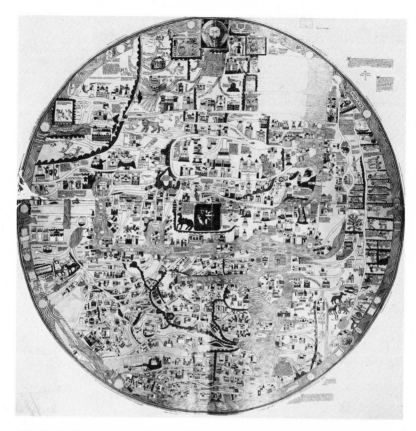

29. Ebstorf mappamundi (ca. 1235–1284) discloses the head and hands
of the Son, the First Parents in Eden (top left of center), Jerusalem
(center), the Sinai regions and the Exodus route across the Red Sea
(above and right of center), "Babylon" in Egypt (lower oval within the
Nile river line, right) and a plethora of temples, curious beasts and
strange figures like those appearing in Spenser's *The Faerie Queene*.
A satyr, giants and dwarfs are depicted at the outer right rim;
Amazons, St. George and the dragon are among the figures at the outer
left rim.

This map is believed to have been produced to accompany the
cosmographical-historical-mythological work *Otia Imperiala* (ca. 1211) by
Gervaise of Tilbury, a British teacher of canon law in Bologna. The
Epstorf map has been seen as influencing the form of the Hereford
mappamundi (ca. 1285). The two world icons, with earthly Jerusalem at
their centers, hung as altarpieces in Ebstorf Cathedral in Hanover and
Hereford Cathedral in England, respectively. *Courtesy of the New York
Public Library.*

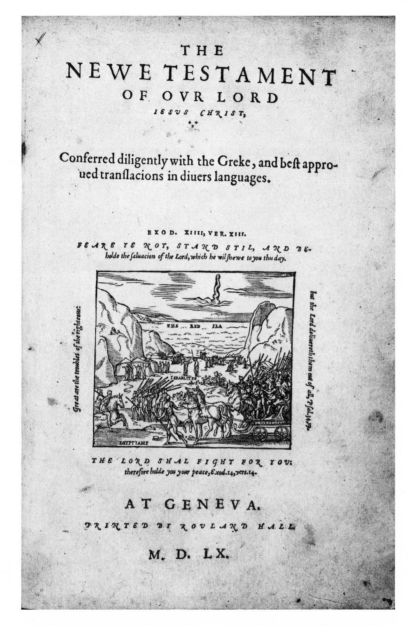

THE
NEWE TESTAMENT
OF OVR LORD
IESVS CHRIST,

Conferred diligently with the Greke, and beft appro-
ued tranflacions in diuers languages.

EXOD. XIIII, VER. XIII.

FEARE YE NOT, STAND STIL, AND BE-
holde the faluacion of the Lord, which he wil fhewe to you this day.

THE LORD SHAL FIGHT FOR YOV:
therefore holde you your peace, Exod.14, vers.14.

AT GENEVA.

PRINTED BY ROVLAND HALL

M. D. LX.

30. So important was the Exodus as a type that it was illustrated on both the Old and New Testament frontispiece pages in the Geneva Bible of 1560. Spenser stressed the Exodus as a central theme of book 1 of *The Faerie Queene,* and Milton introduced the biblical episode *in figura* into book 12 of *Paradise Lost. Courtesy of the Huntington Library.*

31. The Reformation divine Thomas Fuller denounces the Crusades in
The Historie of the Holy Warre (1636). Like Milton in *Paradise Lost*
3.469–96, he mocks Christians who made long pilgrimages to Jerusalem.
Fuller retains, however, the Reformation writer's absorption in details
of Holy Land places and events; his work's frontispiece illustrates the
traditional association of the "Temple of the Sepulchre" and the
European cathedral, an association evident in cathedral figurism.
Courtesy of the Huntington Library.

121

32. Ground plans of some early British temples that take their iconographic form from Constantine's Temple of the Holy Sepulchre in Jerusalem, the church believed to be the fulfillment of earlier holy temples. The round temple design was particularly popular throughout Britain and Europe before the construction, beginning in the twelfth century, of the "new" cruciform Gothic cathedrals. Spenser was influenced by the circular designs in his poetic description of faeryland temples.

Top, left to right: Temple Bruer, Lincolnshire (main church); Temple Bruer, Lincolnshire (crypt); Old Temple, London; Church of the Holy Sepulchre, Northhampton; Ludlow Castle, Salop. *Right center:* Parish Church, West Thurrock, Essex. *Bottom, left to right:* Templars Church, western heights of Dover; Hospitaller Church, Little Maplestead, Essex; New Temple, London; Church of St. John, Clerkenwell; Church of the Holy Sepulchre, Cambridge. *From a report to the Order of St. John. Courtesy of the Order's museum and library, St. John's Gate, Clerkenwell.*

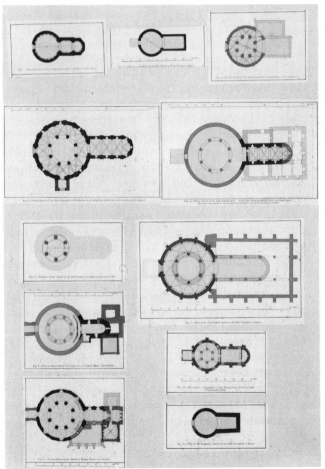

FOUR

The Reformation Journey of Red Cross

Mirrored Paths from Egypt to Jerusalem

In counterpoint to the cyclical and circular emblems that signify thematic cores functioning in *The Faerie Queene* as goals of spiritual pilgrimage or discovery, Spenser introduces the emblematic "dispersed" and wandering Exodus-like journey of the Red Cross Knight in book 1. Red Cross's journey draws imaginatively upon conflated British and Near Eastern pilgrimage traditions along with materials from chivalric romance. Two interrelated narrative motifs dominate the book: first, the Red Cross Knight's gaining of the faith, hope and charity of Holiness, and of a regenerated spiritual self-identity, during repeated falls and spiritual conversions on the Exodus-like pathway to a faeryland Eden; and second, Red Cross's development as a new kind of universal crusading knight and future pilgrim, one who marries the Una of faith and serves the spiritually luminous Gloriana.

Commentators have neglected the fact that a pronounced ideological problem of Spenser, as an English Reformation poet of chivalry, was that the loyalty of both the Roman Catholic Red Cross Knights Templar and White Cross Knights Hospitallers to the British Crown had been suspect. The members of the two orders had sworn allegiance to the Pope in Rome and to their respective Roman Grand Masters in Jerusalem. The Temple Church of the Red Cross Knights in London had been outside the ordinary political and religious jurisdiction of the British monarchy, with appointments to the Temple Church being made by the knights themselves with the approval of the Jerusalem Grand Master.[1]

When the English Red Cross Knights were disbanded by the crown in 1309 and their property eventually transferred to the Knights Hospitallers, control merely shifted from one band of Roman Knights to another. In 1540 Parliament, under pressure from Henry VIII, took possession of the lands and houses of the Hospitallers and terminated the order in Britain. Yet the order's wider fame, and that of their fortress and hospital headquarters on the Mediterranean island of Malta, reached new heights in the summer and fall of 1565 when they turned back, against huge odds, the assault of the Saracen Turks of Sultan Soliman I. This great battle, regarded throughout Europe as an extension of the Crusades with Christians once again poised against the encroaching infidel, in fact ended the incursion of the Saracens into the West.[2]

Spenser's creation of the faeryland Red Cross Knight can be seen too as a poetic Reformation response to the actual contemporaneous making of presumably pernicious Roman Red Cross Knights loyal to the Pope. In 1575, the Protestant pilgrim Leonhart Rauwolff recounted with distaste how this Roman ceremony was conducted in Jerusalem's Temple of the Holy Sepulchre. According to Rauwolff, a Franciscan "Guardian" gave the official initiation speech:

> At the Command of God, and the See of *Rome*, and for the Encrease of the Church of *Rome*, I create you N. N. now a Member of the *Roman* Church, a Knight. . . . And further he adds, That in the room of his Holiness the *Pope* of *Rome*, he doth Absolve him of all his Sins: And that he doth also give him leave, and command him, by the Oath he hath taken to his Holiness the Pope, to wear the usual red Cross (as a Sign where he may be known) publickly in his Coat of Arms, and on his Clothes.[3]

Rauwolff is here writing of the Roman Red Cross Knights of the Sepulchre, an order whose initiation rituals were widely described in sixteenth century pilgrim texts and in editions of Ortelius's *Theatrum Orbis*. Rauwolff considers the group venal and corrupt, and he contemptuously rejects an offer to join. He has harsh views as well about the former "Knights *Templars* of Jerusalem" who, having been "invented by His Holiness the Pope," engaged in religious devotions comparable to those of Spenser's faeryland magician Archiamago. Rauwolff notes:

> This Order is more Secular than Divine, . . . for they need not so say Mass, nor perform any other Devotion; but when they have heard Mass, and said so many *Pater-Nosters* and *Ave Maries*, they have sufficiently discharged their Office (p. 360).

Sixteenth century English pilgrim Faynes Moryson, who like Rauwolff was asked in Jerusalem to join the Roman Red Cross Knights, faced a chivalric choice parallel to those of knightly figures in *The Faerie Queene*. Moryson had opportunities to become a member of the Red Cross Knights of the Sepulchre who were loyal to the Pope, or the international Knights of the Garter, with their red cross empressa and patron St. George, who were loyal to the Crown of England. In Jerusalem, Moryson vigorously refused the offer to become a Roman knight, speaking out forthrightly to the Guardian Friars in the Holy City, whom he thought similar to the friars in England, on the burning political-religious issue of the day:

> I professed, that if I were worthy of that title, I might not crave it, nor receive it offered, in respect of the oath imposing militarie duties upon me. . . . I should be tied thereby, to hate and prosecute all of the reformed Religion, which many of my friends and kinsmen professed.[4]

Viewing the friars as both mercenary and untrustworthy, the Englishman adds that these clerics in Jerusalem "as they in England . . . asking nothing for diet, yet under the title of gift of almes, expect more than the most greedy Host" (p. 35).

Some years later, Moryson was daubed a Knight of the Garter by King James, and the English monarch bestowed upon him the Red Cross impressa of St. George and the Garter collar with a pendant image of the saint.

Spenser's epic absolutely demanded the creation of a new kind of Red Cross Knight, one who swore allegiance to the faith and person of the "true" Faerie Queene rather than to the Emperor of the West who wore the triple crown. The epic further demanded that this new Red Cross Knight receive a spiritual education in a true religious "house" and "hospital" different from the old houses and hospitals of the Roman Red Cross and White Cross Knights. The new Red Cross Knight would be required to engage in individual chivalric battle for his faeryland queen, just as loyal British knights in iconographic disguise fought at Whitehall in staged combats in honor of Elizabeth. And the new Red Cross Knight would necessarily fight in faeryland locales and landscapes comparable to those leading to the corresponding earthly British and Holy Land "New Jerusalem." But now the ancient British New Jerusalem of antique Avalon, a seat of authority of the Tudor monarchy's supposed ancestor Arthur and his British knights, would become a primary analogue for the antique faeryland city of

Cleopolis, the seat of power for Gloriana and her Order of Maiden-hood Knights. Cleopolis and its earthly British analogue Avalon would correspond to or suggest a number of other seats of knight-hood: the old Red Cross Knights headquarters in the Temple at Jerusalem and in the British Inner Temple at London, and the headquarters of the successors of the Red Cross Knights—the Knights of the Garter—in the castle supposedly first constructed in part by Arthur at Windsor. As a supposed descendent of Arthur, Henry VII, according to Elias Ashmole who compared Henry to biblical King David, also at this castle "built a Temple to our Lord and Saviour, . . . (together with an Hospital)."[5] And in Spenser's poem, the allegorical journey of the Red Cross Knight would mirror, through simile, merged elements of the British and Exodus pilgrimages to the British and Holy Land "New Jerusalem," the last regularly associated with Eden. Although *The Faerie Queene* has yet to be examined in the light of these two intermingled pilgrim-age traditions, they afford insight into the poet's character-types, themes and dispersed narrative design.

In writing of the Red Cross Knight's Exodus-like spiritual jour-ney, Spenser associates both Red Cross and Near Eastern and Exodus locales with the dragon-slaying knight St. George, the patron of Elizabeth's Order of the Garter and the supposed one-time pilgrim to Jerusalem. "George," writes Jacobus de Voragine, "comes from *gero*, pilgrim, *gir*, precious, and *ys*, counsellor: for he was a pilgrim in his contempt for the world. . . ." Voragine identi-fies both Near Eastern and African sites as the possible places where George killed the dragon, settling finally for "Lybia"; the pilgrims and cosmographers, however, gave weight to the view that the dragon was killed on the Holy Land pilgrimage route, possibly at ancient "Berytus,"—modern Beirut.[6]

In Gabriel Harvey's copy of *The Surveye of the World*, the south-eastern shoulder of the Mare Interum, an area near Egypt and the Holy Land, is labeled "Brachium S. Georgi," for the English translator notes that he will include the names of places "whereby they are knowne by all travailers at this day. . . ."[7] And the earlier, anonymously written *Mappa Mundi* also calls attention to the name St. George, noting that the "Maremedian" or Mediterranean Sea extends from the "Gulfe of S. George" in the east to the "porte of Nessembre in the West," and emphasizing that at the "mydle" of the earth "there Jerusalem standeth. . . ."

To end the Exodus-like journey of the Red Cross Knight, Spenser draws upon the traditional pilgrimage theme of an Eden far in the east as the final often inaccessible station of spiritual travel. Jerusalem, it has been noted, represented for medieval pilgrims a typological fulfillment of the foreshadowing Terrestial Paradise, with the Cross of Christ, the "Second Adam," said to have been made from the wood of the Tree of Life, and the skull of the "First Adam" said to have been buried in a cave beneath Golgotha. But maps and pilgrimage tracts located the original Eden beyond Jerusalem somewhere in the east. In the words of the author of *Mappa Mundi*, the garden is "towarde Orient," where "no earthly man that may come . . . but god or his angels lede him and gyde him thyther."[8] Maps showing Eden in the Arabian deserts east of Jerusalem appeared in the Bishops Bibles of 1574 and 1575 and in the Geneva Bible of 1560. An additional illustration depicting Adam surrounded by friendly animals in Eden was published in the Bishops Bible of 1575. Before critically examining the journey of the Red Cross Knight in the light of Spenser's special sixteenth century British Reformation perspective, such essential but neglected biblical materials along with popular printed texts and the merged English and Holy Land pilgrimage traditions should be briefly reviewed.

As a learned moral and religious allegorist, Spenser, simply by looking into the printed English Bibles of the sixteenth century, would have become deeply aware of the details of the biblical Israelites' Exodus journey to Jerusalem over a well-known route with carefully designated holy sites. The sixteenth century Geneva and Bishops Bibles included illustrated maps showing the meandering line and the 42 pilgrimage stations of the Exodus leading to the Holy City, the stations first mentioned in the twelfth century by Fetellus and Anonymous Pilgrim VI (Pseudo-Beda). In the Geneva Bibles, an emblematic illustration of an Exodus scene was even printed as a frontispiece for the title pages of both the Old and the New Testaments: Egyptians with their chariots on the shores of the Red Sea with a pillar-shaped cloud in the background on the further shore. In the Geneva Bible of 1560, printed by Rouland Hall, and the Bishops Bible of 1575 and the Geneva Bible of 1576, both printed in London by Richarde Jugge and Christopher Barker, respectively, maps with only minor variations in design all contain an Exodus line that passes by illustrated Mt. Sinai and its monastery, always listed as station 12, and then moves on to the last numbered stations which point in the general direction of Jerusalem.[9]

In book 2 it is the Knight of Temperance, Guyon—accompanied by a Palmer with staff and beads—whose intricately plotted allegorical adventures lead to emblematic centers. Although these centers lack the general sequential narrative ordering of book 1, they are again analogous to certain Exodus themes, events and places. Unlike Red Cross who experiences sudden, recurrent falls from and recoveries of faith, Guyon is engaged in often turbulent allegorical actions, aimed at unveiling a basic classical "mean" of temperate virtue that complements actual faith. The chivalric actions of this knight accordingly end, not in a spiritual marriage in an exalted Castle of Eden, but rather in a false but "daintie Paradise" (2.12.58) where the witch Arcrasia has transformed men into "seeming" beasts, where the barren pleasures of this faeryland type of Circe are antithetical to those in the spiritually fecund Garden of Adonis. Still, the Palmer—whose very name signifies a pilgrim following in the footsteps of Moses and the Israelites— guides, instructs and enlightens Guyon in episodes that add religious dimension to the classical values being disclosed.

As C. P. Brand has demonstrated, the mysterious buoyant Idle Lake over which Guyon and the Palmer sail in the wandering ship of Phaedria is in part a poetic adaptation of Tasso's description in *Gerusalemme Liberata* of the "acque bituminose" of the Dead Sea, the lake that in Tasso's epic surrounds the island of the witch Armida.[10] For centuries Palmers reported that bitumen in this sea buoyed up human bodies and heavy objects, causing them to float lightly on the surface. In Spenser's faeryland the Idle Lake similarly supports Pyrocles, who continues to burn with inward sensual fires even after he has thrown himself upon the lake's waters (2.6.46). In the very next canto, Guyon looks upon a door to Hell in the cave of Mamon and confronts temptations of wealth and power. The temptations are parallel to those stressed in biblical and pilgrimage accounts of the Dead Sea region, the traditional mouth of Hell and the site of the cities of Sodom and Gomorrah. Later when Guyon visits the House of Alma, he moves through an allegorical structure with a frame that will be seen to resemble those of the most holy pilgrimage temples. And in canto 12 Guyon's companion the Palmer uses his staff, said to be of the same wood as the healing "rod of Mercury" (2.12.41), to change Arcrasia's victims from seeming beasts into men. In employing this "mighty staffe, that could all charmes defeat" (2.12.11), a staff of "wondrous powre" (2.11.8) that causes trembling in those who behold it, the Palmer resembles Moses holding up his rod in the wilderness to overcome the enemies of the Almighty.

Exodus themes are even more pronounced in book 1 on Holiness. Specific Holy Land sites, personages and objects of special significance to Spenser in this first book are in fact mentioned in the fourteenth century pilgrimage narrative of the Englishman Thomas Brygg, an equerry or chaplain to the English knight Thomas Swynburne. Brygg journeyed first to Egypt where he commented on sights made famous by a centuries-old tradition: the numerous "Saracens"; the Nile River "descending, as it is said from the terrestrial paradise"; the strange and dangerous beasts including "water monsters called crocodiles, bigger and also longer than men." He next traveled over the "desert of Arabia" to the monastery of St. Catherine "situated in a valley at the foot of Mount Sinai." Here resided, he observes, 100 Greek monks who were said to protect the body of the saint in the monastery. Brygg then climbed to the summit of the mountain where "there is a church, where Moses received from God the Tables of the Testament." Continuing his pilgrimage by moving again over the desert of Arabia, Brygg arrived at Jerusalem and there remarked upon many of the traditional pilgrimage stations. Foremost among them was "the Holy Sepulchre of our Lord Jesus Christ," described as being at the very "middle" of a large church. Then "descending through the chapel of St. Helena" in this church, he came to "a crypt under the mount called Calvary, where was found the Cross of Christ by Blessed Helena." Outside the church in the environs of Jerusalem, Brygg mentions and marks in his manuscript with a cross a "crypt where Christ asked God the Father, and sweated drops of blood trickling down to the ground." He visited also the "Pool of Siloe, where Christ gave sight to the man blind from his birth." Traveling on "toward the river Jordan," Brygg notes that he arrived at "the said river, in which Christ was baptized by Blessed John the Baptist." The final stage of Brygg's journey came with his movement from Jerusalem to Berytus, the seaport city with a station and chapel commemorating St. George's defeat of the dragon. Brygg comments that it was at the "chapel, where St. George killed the dragon, where we finished our pilgrimage to the Holy Land in honour of the Omnipotent God, to whom be honour and glory for ever world without end. Amen."[11]

In the early sixteenth century before the ravaging and dissolution of Glastonbury Abbey in 1539 by Henry VIII, pilgrims who were unable or unwilling to make the long journey taken by Brygg could act out at least certain elements of a Holy Land pilgrimage at the English Isle of Glass. But now, as in Spenser's *The Faerie Queene*, the pilgrims or travelers encountered sacred sites that called attention to past English personages and episodes as well as to traditional Holy Land stations, persons and events. St. George and St. Michael, the two figures who fought the dragon of evil, were especially venerated at Glastonbury. Pilgrims were quartered on High Street at a hospice appropriately named the St. George and Pilgrim Inn, a structure erected about 1475, replacing a Hospitium and Abbots Inn, and still in use today.[12] Pilgrims making their "round" in the late fifteenth and early sixteenth centuries walked south from the inn and then turned left and moved toward the east, along the main mile-long pilgrimage chain. The pathway led first past a holy tree on Glastonbury Abbey grounds, then through the abbey itself, next over part of Chalcselle Hill with its miraculous well, and finally up the pathways and terraces of Glastonbury Tor to the summit tower, the place where by tradition St. Michael had addressed Joseph of Arimathea.

At the first stop near the western perimeter of the abbey property, pilgrims saw the tree that was associated with English church founder Joseph of Arimathea, and which therefore became a living emblem of the renewal of spiritual life. The anonymous author of *the lyfe of Joseph of Armathia*, in identifying the pilgrimage sites of Glastonbury, comments:

> A walnut tree . . . there dooth stande
> In the holy grounde called the cemetory
> Harde by ye place where kyne Arthur was founde
> South fro Josephs chapell it is walled in rounde
> It bereth no leaves tyll the day of saynt Barnabe.[13]

At nearby "werall" hill, the author continues, are "hawthornes" that miraculously "bere grene leaves at Christmas." According to the author, Joseph was a "gostly physician" engaged in the renewal of souls; thus, the wondrous blossoming trees signified the spiritual power of this holy man. A frontispiece etching, showing a blossoming tree growing from the body of Joseph, appears in the anonymously written *treatyse . . . of Pylate of Joseph of Armathy*, published in London by Wynkyn de Worde (ca. 1510). Pilgrim legends elaborated in the seventeenth century affirmed that Joseph's staff flowered when the holy man struck it into the ground on "werall" hill.

Passing eastward through the abbey grounds, pilgrims visited the remains of the chapel of St. Dunstan, entered the Abbey Church at the St. Mary's or Lady Chapel that was also called the St. Joseph Chapel, and then walked down a long colonnaded hall called "The Galilee." In the Abbey Church proper at the foot of the main altar, pilgrims made an important stop at the tomb of Arthur. Stops were also made in the church at a host of chapels, including the Chapel of the Holy Sepulchre.

An astonishing array of relics housed in the Abbey Church recalled sites and past events on the Holy Land Exodus and Redemption pilgrimage routes. On the Exodus pathway over the Sinai deserts, for example, religious travelers regularly stopped at the alleged places where Moses parted the Red Sea with his rod, where manna fell from heaven, where Moses struck water from a rock, and where Moses erected an altar near Mt. Sinai. At British Avalon pilgrims apparently remembered such events when venerating fragments of manna, the rod of Moses, and pieces of Moses' altar.[14]

Along with visiting and praying at the abbey's Chapel of the Holy Sepulchre close to the tomb of Arthur, British pilgrims could look upon relics presumably chipped away from two stations—Golgotha and Christ's tomb—within the actual Jerusalem Church of the Holy Sepulchre: namely, eight portions of Mt. Calvary, earth from where the Cross stood, a stone from the hole where the Cross was fixed and pieces of Christ's sepulchre. A plethora of other Redemption relics allegedly from Jerusalem were also displayed in the abbey, including part of the table of the Last Supper, a piece of the pillar of the scourging, the Lord's hair, two sponges from which the Lord drank, one of the nails of the Cross, pieces of the true Cross and much more. This distressingly literal collection was augmented by British holy objects, some recognized as relics and others of undetermined status: the remains of St. Dunstan, Joseph of Aramathea and Guinevere; St. Helena's arm; and the Blessed Virgin's crystal cross given to Arthur.[15]

However disquieting to modern sensibility, the Holy Land relics graphically illustrate how a collective attempt was made somehow to transport the physical being and spiritual essence of Near Eastern objects to a new location to stimulate religious experience. But British and Celtic materials now were merged with Holy Land pilgrimage objects associated with, among other occurrences, the Exodus events on Mt. Sinai and the Redemption events at Jerusalem. "Here are preserved the human remains of many saints," writes William of Malmesbury of the abbey and its relics, "nor is there any space in the building that is free of their ashes. . . . Rightly, therefore, it is called the heavenly sanctuary on earth, of so large a number of saints it is the repository."[16]

Outside the abbey and its grounds, in the valley to the east separating Chalcselle Hill from "Glassenbury" Tor, pilgrims halted to bathe in or drink from the sacred well of spiritual renewal, a well said in chronicles to have been visited by SS. Patrick, Bridget, Aldhelm and Dunstan.[17] Continuing eastward, pilgrims ascended the narrow pathway leading up the Tor and then either climbed directly or threaded the labyrinth of terraces to St. Michael's tower on the peak.

From the summit persons in earlier centuries, like persons today, could look out over moorlands that are often illuminated by pyramidal rays of sunlight piercing massive, swiftly moving storm clouds, the effect of unsettled Atlantic coastal weather patterns. At the tower of St. Michael, pilgrims could gaze upward into this dramatic Avalon sky from which, tradition held, the great archangel Gabriel descended to Joseph. They could look to the west past distant Tors, in the direction of the supposed Fortunate Isles, to see the sometimes visible Atlantic Ocean glinting through mists or flashing in beams of clear sunlight. And they could gaze down at Chalcselle Hill and toward the huge abbey where the Tudors' supposed ancestor, King Arthur, lay buried and, according to local legends, would rise again in time of England's trial.

Geoffrey Ashe, in an essay on the Tor labyrinth, has rightly associated this British pilgrimage mount with Dante's Mount of Purgatory.[18] Dante, after all, had placed the Garden of Eden, a fulfilled antitype of Jerusalem, at the summit and center of ring within ring of nested terraces rising one above the other but joined by an ascending pilgrimage path. And Dante's Eden is uplifted on an otherworldly pilgrimage mountain that is, in turn, the fulfillment of both Mt. Sinai and Mt. Sion. Given the relics and shrines on the English Avalon pilgrimage chain that point, not only to local saints and Celtic legends, but also to Near Eastern holy objects and sites; and recognizing too that "Glassenbury" Tor functioned as a mount of purgation for pilgrims who wished to turn their souls from sin to grace, it is clear that the Avalon chain and Tor, developed by an anchorite community, served as a British counterpart to the mountains of Exodus and Redemption on the Holy Land route to the earthly New Jerusalem.

AN "AEGYPTIAN VALE" AND "WASTFULL DESERTS"

In book 1 of *The Faerie Queene*, Exodus and Redemption pilgrimage themes are obviously interwoven with many other allegorical meanings. Implied political references to Mary Stuart and to Phillip II of Spain, for example, arise from the evil activities of cunning Duessa and proud Orgoglio, respectively, in cantos 7 and 8. In the pilgrimage disguises and unholy magical practices of the false

Archiamago, religious and pilgrimage motifs blend with the sorcery and spells of chivalric romance and Celtic folklore. But the Exodus and Redemption themes are pervasive and, through both ideological invention and related actions and emblems, they provide a general narrative structure for the book.

One of these key themes is Red Cross's redemption in book 1 through the blood of Christ. Blood becomes a recurrent image; for the blood Spenser associates with Original Sin, and with the Old Testament events of the Exodus—the crossing of the Red Sea and the receiving of the Law on Mt. Sinai—points through simile to the fulfilling New Testament event of the spilling of Christ's blood in Jerusalem.

The Red Cross Knight, of course, even wears the emblem of the Crusaders and of the Redemption:

> But on his brest a bloudie Crosse he bore,
>   The deare remembrance of his dying Lord,
>   For whose sweete sake that glorious badge he wore,
>   And dead a liuing euer him ador'd:
>   Upon his shield the like was also scor'd,
>   For soueraine hope, which in his helpe he had:
>   Right faithfull true he was in deede and word[19]
>
>   (1.1.2)

After Red Cross and his lady Una, in the traditional fashion of erring pilgrims, "wander to and fro in wayes unknowne" in a dark wood; and after they continue on an emblematic way of error by taking a "beaten" path that they believe is "like to lead" through the usual pilgrimage "labyrinth," the pair encounters a great dragon, half woman but with a long tail or "train" of error, that Red Cross challenges in combat (1.1.11). The dragon leaps "fierce upon" the bloody cross of the knight's shield wrapping its long train about Red Cross. But when Una is identified with the true religion and Church by her cry, "Add faith unto your force" (1.1.19), Red Cross heeds his lady's advice and so acquires the spiritual strength necessary for victory. The knight is now able to strangle this dragon of gross materiality, a creature that coarsely "vomits" poisonous substances and evil books just as the Nile gives birth to deformed beings:[20]

> As when old father *Nilus* gins to swell
>   With timely pride aboue the *Aegyptian* vale,
>   His fattie waues do fertile slime outwell,
>   . . . .

But when his later spring gins to auale,
Huge heapes of mudd he leaues, wherein there breed
Ten thousand kindes of creatures, partly male
And partly female of his fruitfull seed;
Such ugly monstrous shapes elswhere may no man reed.

(1.1.21)

Underlying this analogy and the general action is the traditional patristic conception of worldly Egypt and its parent river as grotesquely physical, excessively fertile, proud and sinful.

The erratic and often confused movement of Red Cross is, in general, away from this worldly infidel realm of sensuality and sin toward eventual spiritual regeneration. In a precipitous series of Reformation spiritual "ups and downs" that anticipate those of the character-type Christian in John Bunyan's *Pilgrim's Progress*, Red Cross repeatedly falls into a spiritual condition close to despair but again and again is resurrected through faith in the blood of the Cross. On his journey, Red Cross meets evil pilgrimage types: the false hermit, the false Christian knight, the false pilgrim, and a number of false infidel Saracen knights. At an important juncture, he is spiritually healed at the House of Holiness, a faeryland hospice on a path of conversion and redemption that mirrors actual pilgrimage monastic establishments such as those at the base of Mt. Sinai and of Glassenbury Tor. In the last three cantos Red Cross follows a centuries-old pattern of spiritual travel embodied both in Holy Land and English pilgrimage practice and in Dante's *Commedia*. He ascends a Mount of Holiness. He learns the way to a heavenly city reflecting the earthly Jerusalem, and he finally arrives at a site associated with the Earthly Paradise. For in these last three cantos, Red Cross, though still subject to spiritual falls, does triumph spiritually. He defeats a dragon of evil and marries Una at a Castle of Eden. And he pledges to follow a pilgrimage pathway to a celestial New Jerusalem that in *The Faerie Queene* is analogous both to earthly Jerusalem and to Gloriana's Cleopolis.

But first Red Cross must turn away from emblematic sites and figures that suggest the physical and the deceitful: the earthly slime of the "Aegyptian vale," the fecund mud of the proud Nile itself, and the treacherous crocodile on the Nile's bank. And following his defeat of the dragon in canto 1, he must overcome temptation in the evil House of Lucifera, the antithesis of the House of Holiness.

Like the structures for which the Israelites made brick in worldly

Egypt, as recounted in the biblical Exodus, the House of Lucifera is constructed of "squared bricke,/ Which cunningly was without morter laid" (1.4.4). This emblematic house of the seven deadly sins rests upon a "weake foundation" on a "sandie hill, that still did flit/ And fall away." Its false physical foundation and falsely laid walls are, in the manner of emblems of worldly Egypt, "bravely garnished" with false, external "golden foile" (1.4.4–5). Within the house amid a proud display of gold and "pretious stone" (1.4.8), vain Lucifera sits paradoxically on high—"for lowly she did hate"— holding a "mirrhour bright" and so revealing her self-love (1.4.10). Her person like her throne rests upon error, for beneath her feet "was layne/ A dreadfull Dragon with an hideous trayne" (1.4.10).

In the house's "commune hall" before Lucifera and Duessa, Red Cross meets and prepares to fight a "Sarazin" knight. Antithetical emblems are defiantly raised: the shield of the Christian knight with its "bloody cross" opposing the Sarazin's "heathnish shield, wherein with letters red,/ Was writt *Sansjoy*" (1.4.38). In a terrible combat compared in simile to a battle between a virtuous "Gryfon" and an evil "dragon" (1.5.8), Red Cross gains the advantage, though he suffers a wound. At this moment as the Christian Knight is about to slay his enemy, *Sansjoy* vanishes in a dark cloud. Red Cross is left with the "heatheish shield" as a prize; but his wounds provide an opportunity for Duessa, the divisive opposite to Una of the true faith, to display a mock grief analogous to that of a deceitful denizen of Egypt:

> As when a wearie traveller, that strayes
>> By muddy shore of broad seven-mouthed Nile,
>> Unweeting of the perillous wandring wayes,
>> Doth meete a cruell craftie Crocodile,
>> Which in false griefe hyding his harmefull guile,
>> Doth weepe full sore
>
> (1.5.18)

A range of pilgrimage figures appear in following cantos—a seeming anchorite, a lion of the desert, a dusty pilgrim and a number of Saracen knights—but the inner nature of the figures is not always immediately recognizable. Amid the blur and whirl of fast-paced action, the art of Spenser's narrative rests in part upon the stage-by-stage progressive revelation of concealed identities. There are moments of suspense and of mild, detached humour as the virtuous characters gradually become aware of who is a true friend or enemy. Then after a build-up of emblematic details, an "unveiling" of true natures occurs with an allegorical-didactic "naming" of figures and episodes.

When Red Cross, for example, first comes upon an aging anchorite who has knowledge of a faeryland "wastfull wildernesse" (1.1.32), this seemingly "Sober" and "sagely sad" hermit wears the garb of a true religious solitary:

> . . . in long blacke weedes yclad,
> His feete all bare, his beard all hoarie gray,
> And by his belt his booke he hanging had
>
> (1.1.29)

This aged sire's "shew" of simplicity and performance of spiritual exercises are rendered in such a spiritual light that the figure begins to emerge as perhaps truly holy. Even the sire's "little lowly Hermitage" seems a very sacred place with its

> . . . holy Chappell edifyde,
> Wherein the Hermite dewly wont to say
> His holy things each morne and euentyde:
> Thereby a Christall streame did gently play,
> Which from a sacred fountaine welled forth alway.
>
> (1.1.34)

But at night when the hermit conjures up dreams that trouble the sleeping Red Cross Knight, it becomes clear that this religious solitary is evil. The anchorite is fully identified only when a spirit, ordered by the hermit to the cave of Morpheus, announces that he has been by "*Archiamago* sent" (1.1.43). Wickedness has been graphically disclosed to readers; but Red Cross, at this stage of his spiritual development, journeys on the next day without becoming completely aware of the identity of his malicious host.

Ironically but significantly, it is a lion of the desert—a creature interpreted in strained fashion as representing pride, or the Church of England, or even Henry VIII—that quickly discerns the essential virtue or vice of characters and events. Yet the lion is another emblem drawn from stories of pilgrimage and of the desert fathers,[21] stories that show how even the most ferocious beasts recognize and protect holy persons of the true Church. In Spenser's allegory, Una's relationship with the lion points essentially to the controlling spiritual power of the Church upon wild but noble animal nature.

Separated from Red Cross and journeying "Farre from all peoples prease, as in exile,/ In wildernesse and wastfull deserts"

(1.3.3), Una, like the holy solitaries, faces the lion in a patterned recapitulation of such an encounter in pilgrimage-anchorite tradition. In its structured action, the meeting parallels Dante's sudden confrontation with a lion in *Inferno* 1 and pilgrimage accounts of meetings with lions on Holy Land pathways. In the *Inferno*, however, Dante is close to spiritual death at the time of his encounter, and he is driven backward and downward.[22] Una, by contrast, is spiritually pure. Like St. Mark and other anchorite fathers, she gains the lion's protection.

The patterned episode in Spenser's poem is conventional. There is the lion's sudden appearance and rush forward as if to devour a victim:

> A ramping Lyon rushed suddainly,
> Hunting full greedie after saluage blood;
> Soone as the royall virgin he did spy,
> With gaping mouth at her ran greedily,
> To haue attonce devour'd her tender corse:
>
> (1.3.5)

Next, the lion recognizes the innate virtue of the supposed victim and, amazed, grows meek:

> But to the pray when as he drew more ny,
> His bloudie rage asswaged with remorse,
> And with the sight amazd, forgat his furious forse.
>
> (1.3.5)

The lion becomes docile and acts as guardian:

> The Lyon would not leave her desolate,
>   But with her went along, as a strong gard
>   Of her chast person, and a faithfull mate
>
> (1.3.9)

Later when Una is captured and menaced by the pernicious Kirkrapine, the church robber of Rome, the lion swiftly recognizes, attacks and kills the unholy thief. The noble beast finally dies defending Una against the Saracen *Sansloy*.

The Reformation pilgrimage of Una through a faeryland world obviously revises Roman traditions of historical pilgrimage in the actual world. Spenser persistently employs in new ways, and yet persistently attacks or mocks, Roman character-types and archetypal Roman pilgrimage events. When in a later episode Una, now accompanied by the "salvage" knight Satrayne, hurries to-

ward a distant "wearie wight" to learn the "newes," Spenser
places the traditional and often recounted meeting of pilgrims on
desert pathways in transformed Reformation perspective.[23] The
"wight" acts strangely:

> But he them spying, gan to turne aside,
> For feare as seemd, or for some feigned losse;
> More greedy they of newes, fast toward him do crosse.
>
> (1.6.34)

So unanticipated is Una's and Satrayne's sighting of this "spy-
ing" figure that they lack the detachment and time to penetrate a
surface and deceitful "guise." They rush on toward the figure,
deluded by a "greedy" desire for news, in a parody of a true
emblematic "crosse" or crossing. Yet in the next stanza the narrator unmasks the "wight" as a fatigued, dusty pilgrim whose action
and condition, though suggesting misguided religious fervor, also
signify an underlying foolishness.

> A silly man, in simple weedes forworne,
> And soild with dust of the long dried way;
> His sandales were with toilesome trauell torne,
> And face all tand with scorching sunny ray,
> As he had traveild many a sommers day,
> Through boyling sands of *Arabie* and *Ynde*;
> His wearie limbes upon: and eke behind,
> His scrip did hang, in which his needments he did bind.
>
> (1.6.35)

In telling a fallacious tale about Red Cross's alleged death at the
hands of a Saracen knight, this silly pilgrim is at last partially
unveiled as a still-unknown figure of evil. The pilgrim remains
something of a mysterious stranger until, in the final stanza of
canto 6, the narrator decisively unshrouds this cunning stranger,
exposing

> . . . that false *Pilgrim*, which that leasing told,
> Being in deed old *Archimage*
>
> (1.6.48)

A HOUSE OF HOLINESS

In a decisive episode within the House of Holiness at the foot of
the Mount of Holiness, Red Cross receives spiritual instruction

from virtuous ladies in preparation for his mountaintop meeting with the hermit Contemplation. At last he is transformed into the new religious-military knight loyal to Una and Gloriana, a knight who on the mountain conclusively learns that he will someday become St. George of England.

It is Una of the true faith who, observing Red Cross's "feeble" and "decayed plight" (1.10.2), leads him to the "auntient house . . ./, Renowmd throughout the world for sacred lore" (1.10.3). Like the monastery of St. Catherine—originally called the monastery of St. Mary—at the base of Mt. Sinai, and like the early Holy Land pilgrimage hospices established by Paula and other Roman matrons, the faeryland House of Holiness exists because of the spiritual beneficence of holy ladies: Charissa, the "chiefest foundoresse" of the house; Mercie, the "Patronesse" of the faeryland house's religious "order" (1.10.44); and heavenly Caelia, the directing "Ladie of the place" (1.10.8).

During a harrowing education that quickly propels the knight to spiritual heights and then to spiritual despair, Red Cross meets a series of allegorical female figures who personify the theological and other virtues. Very generally, these women are comparable to those attending Dante in the Eden of the *Purgatorio*. But while Dante in Eden becomes spiritually contrite and confesses his sins, he does not, like the Red Cross Knight, fall so dramatically that he considers suicide. In the *Purgatorio*, the Florentine poet makes a steady spiritual ascent by acting out a sequence of typological episodes, an ascent marked by setbacks but not radical reversals. In Eden, Dante sees the three virgins representing the theological virtues moving toward him as a group. In the House of Holiness, Red Cross receives only one theological sister, Fidelia, and then suffers from painful guilt and despair before he is eventually restored by the second and third sisters, Speranza and Charissa. It is characteristic of the knight's new Reformation religious education that the last sister Charissa represents, not the spirituality of virginity, but rather of virtuous fecundity in marriage and has been of "late in child-bed" (1.10.29). As a final step in Red Cross's renewal through Reformation religious values, the knight is tended by the aged dame Mercie who gives lessons in Good Works and controls the "holy Hospitall" (1.10.36) of the house.

This faeryland hospital is a Reformation counterpart to the great monastic hospitals, particularly those founded by the Knights Hospitallers at Jerusalem and in Europe, for the spiritual and physical care of crusaders and pilgrims. The Knights Hospitallers' houses of hospitality were organized under the control of a specially appointed brother who supervised a staff in charitable and medical activities. So, too, the faeryland hospital is operated by a "Guardian and Steward" Patience (1.10.37) who supervises six "beadsmen" in designated activities derived from the period of the Crusades: feeding persons, clothing persons, attending to the sick and dying, aiding or ransoming prisoners of "Turkes and Sarazins," burying the dead and overseeing orphans of the dead (1.10.40). Even in England and Ireland until 1540 certain of these charitable activities were carried on by the Knights Hospitallers in their houses of hospitality, with infirmaries attached, at the Clerkenwell Priory, London, and the Kilhamnin Priory, Dublin.[24]

The special treatment of the new Red Cross Knight in the faeryland hospital appears an imaginative reaction to the supposed care of Protestant patients at the old Roman establishments. Englishman Faynes Moryson's comments in 1595, for instance, on the aid given to Protestants at the famed holy hospital in Jerusalem is nothing less than sinister. Moryson's outward courtesy toward the Italian guardians and friars seems to have been inspired by fear.

"We beheld upon the wall in the chamber where we lodged," he writes, "the names of Henry Bacon and Andrew Verseline," two English gentlemen who had recently been "treated" with fatal results by the friars. "The names," he continues, "were written there upon the foureteenth of August 1595, and lay before us, both sleeping and waking, warning us like so many prodigies or visions to take heed to our steps."

Dangers supposedly existed for reformed English at the hospital, according to Moryson, because "these Italian Friars, (according to the Papists manner,) . . . first make the sicke confesse their sinnes, and receive the Lords Supper, before they suffer Physitian or Apothecary to come to them, or any kitchin physicke to be given them." Moryson explains how two Englishmen and two "Flemmings" were wounded in a dispute while drinking at Bethlehem. All four men refused to confess to the friars, and so, Moryson adds, "It was apparent to the Friars, that they were of the reformed Religion, (whom they terme heretickes)." The friars "began to neglect them"; and "within eight daies space" all died except Roger Bacon who passed away only "a very few days after." Moryson, deeply unsettled by the supposed deviousness of these Italian-speaking friars with their seeming pretense of hospitality, gives the most terrible overtone of evil to the hospitalization of the Protestant patients.

Moryson observes that Englishman Roger Bacon, "seeing his life to depend upon the friars care of him, shewed a Novice Friar long bracelets of peeces of gold twined about his arme. . . . I know not whether the hope of this booty made him die sooner. . . ." And Moryson secretly muses that in one respect the English patients in this "holy" hospital may actually have received "too much care, namely by poison (as some suspect): for the Friars have one of their order, who is skilfull in physicke, and hath a chamber furnished with cooling waters, sirops, and other medicines most fit for that countrey. . . ."[25]

During the spiritual transformation of Red Cross into an ideal Reformation knight, the first sister Fidelia comes to him bearing dramatically contrasting emblems of life and death, emblems that inspire the knight's violent changes in spiritual condition. In her right hand she carries a sacramental cup of gold "With wine and water fild up to the hight,/ In which a Serpent did himselfe enfold" (1.10.13); in her left hand, she holds a "sacred Booke, with bloud ywrit" and so associated with the regenerating blood of Christ. Fidelia lectures from the book with "words to kill/ And raise againe to life the hart, that she did thrill" (1.10.19).

The meanings of the emblems are well known. In the Gospel of John 3.14–15, it has been noted, Moses' lifting up of the brass serpent in the wilderness is said to be the lifting up of Christ. And Paul in 2 Corinthians 3.5, writing of the Bible, observes that "the letter killeth, but the Spirit giveth life." The Geneva Bible, moreover, glosses "the letter" as meaning "the Law of Moses" in the Old Testament, and the "Spirit" as referring to "the vertue of God it selfe, in renewing, justifying and saving of men" in the New Testament. Accordingly, both Fidelia's cup with its wine and water and serpent, and her book with its words written in blood that kill and give life, are emblems pointing to the Redemption of humankind in Jerusalem as recorded in the Gospels.

Listening to Fidelia and aware of the "lore" of her sisters, Red Cross grows "to such perfection of all heavenly grace,/ That wretched world he gan for to abhore" (1.10.21). Then he experiences a sudden spiritual fall and, in torment of soul, considers suicide:

> And prickt with anguish of his sinnes so sore,
> That he desirde to end his wretched dayes:
> So much the dart of sinfull guilt the soule dismayes.

> (1.10.21)

Red Cross is aided by the second sister Speranza, who has "Upon her arme a siluer anchor" of hope. She seeks to teach the knight "how to take assured hold/ Upon her siluer anchor, as was meet," but Red Cross continues to suffer from "distressed doubtfull agonie," "Desdeining life, desiring leaue to die" (1.10.16–22).

Una, finding her knight in this condition, accepts the help of heavenly Caelia who sends Red Cross to that curious allegorical holy hospital where he is treated for a "grieued conscience." The Guardian Patience "bleeds" the knightly patient using a leech (1.10.23); "salves and med'cines" are applied to attack a "festring sore . . . twixt the marow and the skin" (1.10.24–25). And a "streight diet" is prescribed along with "fasting every day" to bring down the "swelling of his woundes" (1.10.23–26). Then the hospital attendants open the "festring sore" and "pluck it out with pincers" (1.10.26), an allegorical operation resulting in an allegorically "cured conscience" (1.10.29).

Only after this spiritual hospitalization is Red Cross ready to meet the third sister, the "wondrous beauty" Charissa, who instructs him in "love and righteousnesse" (1.10.30–33). Released to the care of dame Mercie, the last of the feminine lecturers, and to further allegorical hospital attendants, Red Cross accepts instruction in Good Works and learns of "godly worke of Almes and charitee" (1.10.45). His education at the House of Holiness completed, the knight then follows Mercie over a "painfull" path "Forth to an hill, that was both steepe and hy," and so begins his ascent of the Mount of Holiness (1.10.46).

THE FAERYLAND MOUNTAIN OF GOD

On the peak of the sacred Mount of Holiness, the elderly hermit Contemplation in his "Hermitage" near a summit "chappell" (1.10.46) reveals to Red Cross, who has been a "man of earth," the true pilgrimage pathway to a transcendant heavenly goal: the New Jerusalem of the Prophets. "And wash thy hands with guilt of bloudy field," declaims Contemplation of evil earthly battles, "For bloud can naught but sin, and wars but sorrowes yield" (1.10.60). Contemplation directs the knight toward an eternal city:

> Then seeke this path, that I do thee presage,
> Which after all to heauen shall thee send;

> Then peaceably thy painefull pilgrimage
> To yonder same *Hierusalem* do bend,
> Where is for thee ordained a blessed end:
>
> (1.10.61)

The event is a blending, as critics have suggested, of the man of earth's natural vision and a heavenly vision.[26] This event is replete with references to purgation, regeneration and spiritual ascent drawn selectively from biblical Exodus and Redemption materials, conflated with elements from chivalric romance. For Red Cross has need of an Exodus-like conversion of his soul in preparation for his redemptive marriage to Una.

The mountain calls to the narrator's mind Moses' crossing of the Red Sea, an emblem of baptism. The holy mount is

> Such one, as that same mighty man of God,
> That bloud-red billowes like a walled front
> On either side disparted with his rod,
>
> (1.10.53)

This mountain, moreover, is like the one on which Moses in receiving the Law

> Dwelt fortie dayes upon; where writ in stone
> With bloudy letters by the hand of God,
> The bitter doome of death and balefull mone
> He did receiue, whiles flashing fire about him shone.
>
> (1.10.53)

From the mountain's summit, Red Cross views the New Jerusalem, the recognized analogue for both a faeryland city and the earthly city of the Cross. Contemplation declares:

> . . . *Hierusalem* that is,
> The new *Hierusalem*, that God has built
> For those to dwell in, that are chosen his,
> His chosen people purg'd from sinfull guilt,
> With pretious bloud, which cruelly was spilt
> On cursed tree, of that unspotted lam
>
> (1.10.57)

Red Cross quickly confesses that this heavenly city "does far surpas" even that "fairest Citie" Cleopolis with its "towre of glas" (1.10.58).

With eyes "dazed" by the "passing brightnesse" of spiritual revelation and with his "feeble sence" enlightened by visionary experience (1.10.67), the Red Cross Knight "At last . . . himselfe he gan to find" (1.10.68). Red Cross has not known his future identity throughout most of book 1. In his journey of renewal, he has had to wander "inward" into error, has had to suffer falls and spiritual ascents. For Red Cross thoroughout most of book 1, contrary to some critical opinion, does not allegorically represent St. George. Only in canto 10 after Red Cross is spiritually transformed in the House of Holiness and spiritually enlightened on the Mount of Holiness, only then does the guiding hermit Contemplation announce that the knight *shall* in the future become St. George of England:

> For thou emongst those Saints, whom thou doest see,
> Shalt be a Saint, and thine owne nations frend
> And Patrone: thou Saint *George* shalt called bee,
> Saint *George* of mery England, the signe of victoree.
>
> (1.10.61)

In an imaginative collage of materials typical of Spenser, themes of romance and courtly love now conjoin with pilgrimage and crusading motifs. When Red Cross exclaims, "O! let me not . . . then turne againe/ Backe to the world" (1.10.63) and speaks of abandoning "deeds of armes" and "Ladies loue" (1.10.62), Contemplation insists that Red Cross in effect retain his courtly dedication and crusading zeal until the time is right for heavenly pilgrimage. "That may not be," admonishes Contemplation when Red Cross expresses his desire to go directly on "that last long voiage fare" to a heavenly city. "Ne maist thou yit," Contemplation continues, "Forgo that royall maides bequeathed care" (1.10.63). Red Cross promises to serve Gloriana and to "abett" Una's "cause disconsolate" (1.10.64). Only then will the knight "backe returne unto this place,/ To walke this way in Pilgrims poore estate" in an otherworldly journey (1.10.64).

In the meantime, before ascending the heavenly pathway, Red Cross will go forward in faeryland as a new kind of converted knight and spiritual crusader, a faeryland pilgrim in arms, toward union with Una in the Castle of Eden. And for three days he will do battle with the most terrible of dragons and so prove his spiritual loyalty both to Una and Gloriana. "Striue your excellent selfe to excell," Una calls to Red Cross as he prepares to meet the dragon,

> That shall ye euermore renowmed make
> Aboue all knights on earth, that batteill undertake.
>
> (1.11.2)

THE CASTLE OF EDEN

The mythic theme of a journey of return to a transcendent Jerusalem and Eden in the spiritual East dominates the conclusion of the first book. "Behold I see the haven nigh at hand," the narrator exclaims in the book's final canto, as if preparing for a landing after a long sea voyage. Although this expanded trope is the conventional one used through the centuries by epic writers including Dante, here it carries particular thematic weight. "*Phoebus*," the narrator relates, is just about to raise "his flaming creast" in the East over Castle Eden and its environs. The "fayre virgin" Una is described as about to be "landed . . ., now at her journeyes end" (1.12.1–2). And in Castle Eden the King of Eden himself later proclaims to Red Cross: "Now safe ye seised have the shore,/ And well arrived are" (1.12.17).

In climactic faeryland episodes, the thematic Exodus-like pilgrimage of return coalesces with chivalric themes of desperate combat against evil and triumphant marriage to faith. During intervals in Red Cross's spiritually essential, three-day fight with the dragon, the knight is restored by holy substances identified with biblical sites and ancient pilgrimage stations. Then Red Cross, victorious over the dragon, is greeted by the King and Queen of Eden, escorted into Castle Eden and there wedded in festive solemnity to Una. This chivalric marriage—celebrated with music, dance, speeches and floral displays—carries the ritual and iconographic significations of court tiltyard and masquing spectacles that occurred year after year at Elizabeth's court. Elizabeth presided as the mythic queen of an imaginary world, as leading nobles fought staged battles. At Westminster in 1558, the Earl of Leicester, the Duke of Norfolk and the Earl of Sussex were among the challengers in such a "Just, Tournament, and fight at Barrier." In 1571 Thomas Cecil won a prize in barriers combat. And in 1580 at an evening "Tournament on horsebacke" at Westminster celebrating the Chief Marshall of France's investiture into the Order of the Garter, Spenser's literary friend Philip Sidney joined with the Earle of Arundell, "calling himself Callophisus," in a fight before the queen and her court seated on the "North side of the Tarrace." Illuminated by torches and "beset with Lords, Ladies, and Persons of Qualitie, sumptuously apparelled," the terrace was said to have the semblance of "rather a Theater Celestiall, than a Pallace or earthly building."[27]

According to a pamphlet entitled "Triumph shewed before the

Queene's Majestie," Elizabeth observed a most unusual staged battle in 1581 from a wood-and-canvas "Castle of Beauty," a castle defended by knights in the unlikely guise of Adam and Eve "as they were in Paradise." The Queen there received homage as "divine Beautie, whose beames shine like the sun, . . . the light of the world, the marvell of men, the mirrour of nature." On the first day after speeches, musical interludes, and the throwing of "floures and such fansies" against the castle walls, Philip Sidney and three other knights, attired as "Sons of Desire," attempted to storm the castle out of love for the monarch. Sidney and his group ran at tilt "six courses" against defenders led by Adam and Eve, played by Thomas Parrat and Master Cook. On the second day the contestants battled in a general "tournie" in which "they lashed it out lustilie, and fought couragiouslie, as if the Greeks and Trojans had dealth their deadlie dole." The Triumph ended when Sidney and his companions acknowledged "Vertue (which stands for the gard of this fortresse) to be too strong for the strongest Desire." They offered an olive branch to the queen and announced themselves "slaves to this fortresse for ever, which title they will beare in their foreheads." Elizabeth, as the theatrical world's queen, was then extolled for exerting the spiritual powers that permit humankind to be "restored againe to paradise," to an Edenic "garden" where "vertues grow as thicke as leaves. . . ."[28]

In faeryland outside the castle of the King and Queen of Eden, Red Cross, before he can pay comparable homage to this mythic pair, must also throw himself into combat. His opponent is the most colossal and crassly material of dragons, a monster that in

> . . . largenesse measured much land
> And made wide shadow under his huge wast
> As mountaine doth the valley overcast.
>
> (1.11.8)

The beast—covered with "brasen scales" that "Like plated coate of steele, so couched neare,/ That nought mote perce . . ."—charges with its gigantic "flaggy wings" hovering over the knight (1.11.9). During desperate fighting, Red Cross plunges a spear into flesh beneath the creature's "left wing, than broad displayd" (1.11.20); but striking next with his sword, the knight cannot penetrate the scales. By evening Red Cross is close to defeat—"Faint, wearie, sore, emboyled, grieued"—suffering what "never man such mischiefes did torment;/ Death better were . . ." (1.11.28).

Driven backward and then overthrown at the first day's end, Red Cross falls into the "siluer flood" of a "springing well." The healing powers of this *"well of life"* (1.11.29), the narrator asserts, are greater than those of waters famed both in medical lore and classical writings: those of "English *Bath*" and the "german *Spau*" that were physically restorative, those of Boeotian *"Cephise"* that could magically turn the fleece of a sheep white in color, and those of the River *"Hebrus"* that carried the severed but still-singing head of Orpheus. In accentuating the well's spiritual powers, the narrator divulges that in efficacy it exceeds even the waters of "Silo," the pool mentioned in John 9.7, located on the Jerusalem pilgrimage ring just outside the figured Eden of the walled Holy City. The well is also more powerful, the narrator adds, than the *"Jordan,"* the river cited in 2 Kings 5.14 where pilgrims bathed before entrance into the earthly Jerusalem (1.11.30).

So potent are the emblematic waters that on the next day Red Cross fights with hands "baptized" by "holy water dew/ Wherein he fell" (1.11.36). The knight thus spiritually benefits as did many generations of pilgrims who considered their immersion in the waters of Silo and the Jordan a rite of baptism and spiritual rebirth. "For unto life the dead it could restore," the narrator sings of the faeryland waters, "And guilt of sinfull crimes cleane wash away;/ Those that with sicknesse were infected sore/ It could recure . . ." (1.11.30).

In the context of pilgrimage traditions, however, it is obvious that Red Cross is still engaged in physical and spiritual struggle, still in need of spiritual rebirth at a holy site suggesting stations located outside a walled city that figures Eden. On the second evening after unsuccessful combat with the monster, Red Cross is restored in the presence of Una, this time by an emblematic object of even greater power than the well: a *"tree of life"* that is said to be a reminder of "the crime of our first fathers fall" (1.11.46–47). Red Cross, still vulnerable as a man of earth, had earlier on this second day

> . . . recoyled backward, in the mire
> His nigh forwearied feeble feet did slide,
> And downe he fell, with dread of shame sore terrifide.
>
> (1.11.45)

At the place of this second fall, the tree of life, standing near a tree of "good and ill," trickles a curative "Balme" that gives life and allows persons to "reare againe/ The sencelesse corse appointed for the grave" (1.11.48).

As has been noted through citations of pilgrim accounts, it was at the New Jerusalem of Constantine that the restoring blood of

Christ trickled down from the wooden cross upon the skull of the first Adam, which was supposedly buried in a cave beneath Golgotha.[29] The blood flowed on a cross, rediscovered by Helena, said to have been made from a tree in Eden. And at the English New Jerusalem of "Glassenbury," the flowering trees of Joseph of Arimathea, of course, recalled to pilgrims in a more general way the redeeming power of the cross.

On the third day Red Cross, having gained in spiritual force, lunges forward and runs his sword through the mouth of the dragon. Now it is the monster's turn to come crashing down like "a huge rockie clift,/ Whose false foundation waves have washt away." In death the fallen creature lies "like an heaped mountaine" at the feet of the knight (1.11.54).

When trumpets sound and the "auncient Lord and aged Queene" march forth with court and people from Castle Eden to honor Red Cross and nearby Una, their entrance reflects the formal outdoor processions of costumed figures that frequently preceded court masques. First come "tall yong men" carrying "laurell brunches" of triumph which are placed before the knight (1.12.5–6). Children follow singing a "joyous lay" with "well attuned notes" (1.12.7). Next in line "comely virgins" holding "sweet Timbrels" move "dancing on a row" (1.12.6). Last come the Lord and Queen "Arrayd in antique robes" and surrounded by "sage and sober Peres, all grauely gownd" (1.12.5).

After Red Cross returns with the celebrants to Castle Eden and there enjoys a fine but temperate feast, a final dazzling entrance by Una into the hall marks the beginning of a faeryland indoor masque of Hymen. Una comes "As bright as doth the morning starre appeare/ Out of the East, with flaming lockes bedight . . ." (1.12.21). She enters as a "blazing Brightnesse" of heavenly beauty, her white garment more wondrous than woven "silke and silver" (1.12.22).

There are the usual Spenserian allegorical complications. Archiamago, disguised as a messenger, attempts to halt the marriage and advance the claims of false Duessa; but his plot and guise are exposed by Una in a last demonstration of spiritual "revelation." And because Red Cross has promised to serve "six yeares in warlike wize" under Gloriana, after taking his wedding vows he must go away from Castle Eden for that "terme." But he leaves no doubt that he will return to his spiritual-allegorical home with Una (1.12.18–19).

Thus the long, wandering, Exodus-like journey of the faeryland Red Cross Knight over worldly paths to a union with faith, in a place associated with Eden, reaches its apotheosis. The knight has wedded one who, as the Lord of Eden explains, is the "onely daughter" and an "heyre apparaunt" of his kingdom that embraces all the earth (1.12.20). But Una also has a "heavenly beautie" and "heavenly lineaments" that cause Red Cross to "wonder much at her celestial sight" (1.12.22–23). For the future St. George is now married to a future imperial ruler of the world in whom temporal and spiritual power are joined—a type for Gloriana herself.

33. A virtuous lion guards St. Mark in this illustration from the
Bishop's Bible of 1574. The apostle was said to have tamed this wild
beast in the deserts of Egypt. In book 1 of *The Faerie Queene*, Spenser
depicts a lion guarding Una, drawing upon medieval traditions about
St. Mark and desert anchorites who were protected by wild beasts.
Courtesy of the Huntington Library.

150

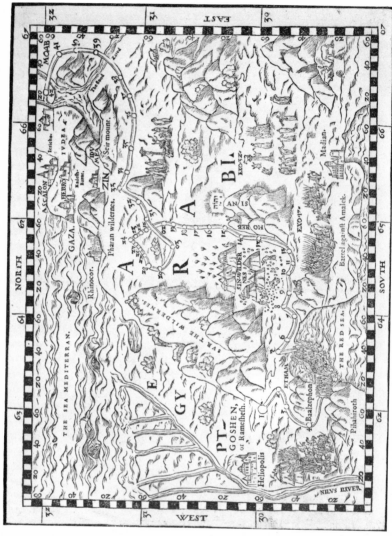

34. The ancient 42 stations of the Exodus that influenced Dante and Spenser. These pilgrimage stops, older than Jerusalem's stations of the Cross, are illustrated here in the Geneva Bible of 1560. *Courtesy of the Huntington Library.*

35. The pilgrimage stations of the Exodus, drawn by Hondius, as they appear in Samuel Purchas's *Purchas his Pilgrimes*, book 1 (1625). *Courtesy of the Huntington Library.*

152

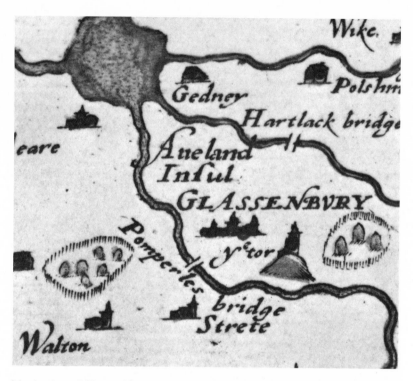

36. Ancient "Glassenbury" with "Ye tor" and its summit tower appear in this detail from Christopher Saxton's map of Somersetshire (1575). Also marked is "bridge Streete," the site of the St. George and Pilgrim Inn. *Courtesy of the New York Public Library.*

37. The terraced tor and tower at ancient "Glassenbury," the supposed site of mythical Avalon and the legendary haunt of the Faery Queen. The summit tower was a final goal of pilgrimage on the "Glassenbury" ring of stations. This site is a source for Gloriana's Cleopolis in *The Faerie Queene* and a British counterpart for terraced Mt. Sinai. *Photograph by the author.*

38. The alleged tomb of legendary King Arthur, the principal knight of Gloriana in *The Faerie Queene*. The tomb is a station on the "Glassenbury" pilgrimage chain. A manuscript of the *Historia Brittonum* (ca. 800) relates King Arthur's pilgrimage to Jerusalem and return to England. The supposed remains of the king and his queen, said to have been discovered in 1191 near the earliest chapel of Glastonbury Abbey, were placed here before the high altar of the Abbey Church in 1278. *Photograph by the author.*

FIVE

Alma, Allegory and the Mirrored Empire of Knights

Spenser's Changing Perspective on Universal History

In a neglected sixteenth century chronicle of knightly orders that were assumed to be precursors of Queen Elizabeth's Knights of the Garter, Gerard Legh tells of an unexpected meeting with Spenser's future patron Robert Dudley, Earl of Leicester, that highlights the consuming Elizabethan preoccupation with issues of medieval iconographic-cosmographic history. In this chronicle, *The Accedens of Armory* (1562), Legh also provides insight into those social and political forces that, together with rhetorical and biblical traditions, influenced Spenser's creation of the allegories of the Red Cross Knight and the House of Alma.

Attracted to the Inner Temple by news of the 1562 Christmas revels, Legh tells of wandering into the Temple Church and coming upon the Earl of Leicester masqued as the Grand Marshall of the Red Cross Knights Templar. The pair, though total strangers, quickly recognize their mutual interest in chivalric history. Leicester calls Legh a "lover of honour" and "gest of right." Speaking and acting as if in a chivalric romance, Leicester introduces the visitor to the Temple Church—with its circular nave, rectangular choir and triangulated nave floor plan—declaring it to be a knightly "House of Honor." He then leads Legh through the church to an inner so-called "office of Armes" where the visitor is introduced to "keepers" and shown "historical" records of knights and their orders. Next Legh is escorted to Leicester's "owne lodgeing" and listens to this masquing leader of the Red Cross Knights narrate a tale generally parallel to the "hinge" of book 1 of *The Faerie Queene*.[1]

Later in the evening, Legh accompanies Leicester to the revels in the Inner Temple banqueting hall. The visitor watches as the earl, now wearing gilt armor, announces himself as "the mighty Pala- philos, . . . High Constable Marshall of the Knights Templar, Patron of the honourable Order of Pegasus."[2] Leicester then per- forms in ceremonies as the patron and leader of a theatrical order of 24 knights, ruled by Elizabeth in the guise of Pallas Athena, with initiation rituals comparable to those actually followed by the queen's Knights of the Garter.

In his revels address to 24 masquers about to be inducted into the Pegasus-Templar order, Leicester speaks of the strengths and weaknesses of the allegorical House of Honor signified by the Temple Church and its knights and ladies. He also invokes the psychomachy theme that will be implicit in Spenser's Alma epi- sode. Leicester states that the "severall members, made create and conioyne one unseparable body, as the whole may support the partes." This "framing," he adds, forms a "buyldinge" that could grow weak "being devyded" but will prove invincible "being together."[3] Leicester then bestows upon the masquers Templar- Pegasus emblems corresponding to those given to members of Elizabeth's Garter order: the Mantle of Pallas, corresponding to the Mantle of the Garter; the Collar of Pallas with pendant Pegasus, corresponding to the Collar of the Garter with pendant St. George; and the sword of Justice, corresponding to the sword of St. George.

A chivalric tournament of costumed knights next appears to have been staged, possibly in traditional allegorical fashion with the Pegasus-Templar knights defending the House of their body politic against assault by discordant figures. Legh states only that the knights, after "sacrifice" in the Inner Temple Church, prepare for testing by "Tylt and Turney" and are further "masked." But even this reference to a suggested testing of knights who comprise a House, given wider contexts, stands as a thematic precursor to Spenser's later poetic creation of an allegorical battle involving the knights of the House of Alma.

These previously unheeded masquing activities of the Earl of Leicester give expression to the popular British Loyalist view, also advanced by Spenser, that power falls to Tudor monarchs by right of antique succession from chivalric orders and virtuous leaders. In Leicester's allegory, as in Spenser's *The Faerie Queene*, lines of authority flow back to rulers and knights who, like the early apostolic followers of Christ, will be seen to be associated with holy places and events at the earth's medieval spiritual center in the Holy Land. Cosmographic iconography and biblical typology become inextricably interwoven with chivalric, faeryland and Tudor historical myth and, in fact, serve as a supposedly authoritative basis for that myth.

Leicester's histrionic activities also lend support for the view, long held in Spenser commentary, that he is in the early books of *The Faerie Queene* one of the persons signified by Arthur, surrogates of Arthur such as Arthegal and, of course, the Red Cross Knight.[4] Acting and speaking as the masquing heir of crusading knights, this rumored physical lover of the queen—like the queen herself—would have been publicly identified with the revived order of British Red Cross Knights, the predecessors in theory of the Garter Order to which Leicester belonged and which Elizabeth ruled. Leicester remained a member of the Knights of the Garter and the Inner Temple while he was Spenser's patron. His Temple recitations and roles would have gained considerable notoriety in court circles, and they were fully recorded and available to Spenser in Legh's published work. It should come as no surprise, then, that sections of *The Faerie Queene*—the text of book 1 on the Red Cross Knight and Una, and passages in book 2 on the knight Guyon's tour of the House of Alma (2.9–10)—reflect the kinds of allegorical revels and tales that so delighted Leicester, the queen and court aristocrats. They reflect as well the medieval cosmographic-historical iconography that Spenser draws upon and lightly mocks.

Spenser's rendering of the antique historical materials, unlike Leicester's, will be seen to be sophisticated and wry. While employing old-fashioned chronicle stories and iconography to advance Tudor claims to universal imperial power over church and state, the poet cunningly parodies the stories' outlandish exaggerations while flippantly acknowledging the existence of contravening scientific historical and cosmographical literature. Spenser stands between two worlds of historical vision: the antique iconographic and the modern empirical. His poetic mirroring of revelry and universal chronicle history, given its edge of satire, marks a turn in sensibility from the medieval historical vision, vaguely foreshadowing particularly in the Alma episode, a new kind of epic history that will be explored in the next century by John Milton.

Spenser's microcosmic-macrocosmic House of Alma visited by Guyon and Arthur has structure, it will be recalled, consisting of a masculine circle poised on a seven-by-nine rectangle surmounting a feminine triangle:

> The frame thereof seemed partly circulare,
> And part triangulare; O worke divine!

The one imperfect, mortall, foeminine,
The 'other immortall, perfect, masculine;
And twixt them both a quadrate was the base,
Proportioned equally by seven and nine;
Nine was the circle sett in heavens place:
All which compacted made a goodly diapase.[5]

This odd faeryland residence is ruled by Alma, a representative of the soul, and filled with knights and ladies who signify spiritual excess or paucity or balance. An allegorical body politic embodying ideas of temperance, the House has been recognized as one among a number of core icons with circles that are subsumed by the ultimate faeryland city and chivalric society of Gloriana's Cleopolis.

Though conveying multiple meanings, Spenser's House specifically reflects the chivalric functions along with the circular iconographic design—with rectangular and triangular forms interposed—of that Inner Temple round church in London. For the London church, used for the ceremonies of first the original Knights Templar and later the Knights Hospitallers, is yet another early example of those houses of the soul, the round temples, built by these two crusading orders throughout Britain and Europe to correspond iconographically to the "ideal" form of Constantine's New Jerusalem of the Sepulchre. It was well known that "ye Temple" in London, as Thomas Dingley later reported, "belonged to the Order of the Knights Templars . . . their Ensigne was a Red Cross." To corroborate his identification of the "Ensigne," Dingley repeated the popular Elizabethan story that prone statues with legs crossed, placed on the Temple Church nave floor, covered the graves of Red Cross Knights "buried Cross legg'd as you may see."[6] The Temple round church had been consecrated in 1185 by Latin patriarch Heraclius of Jerusalem who traveled to England for this purpose. Until the destruction of the Templar order in 1320, the church remained under the control of the Templar Grand Master whose Crusader Kingdom headquarters was Jerusalem's temple area. The London church was subsequently governed and used by the Knights Hospitallers until, in the mid-sixteenth century, Henry VIII disbanded the British Hospitallers, seized the church and revived the rituals of the Red Cross Templars as a Reformation chivalric order. In the sixteenth century, the emblem of the Red Cross Knight's Inner Temple was the flying horse Pegasus, a device Legh in *The Accedens of Armory* interpreted allegorically as meaning "honour whose condition Sorares" (fol. 202).

In *The Faerie Queene*, the storehouse of universal history—a chamber of memory within Alma's apex circle—moreover, has a close but as yet unremarked forerunner in the round Temple Church's "office of Arms" described by Leicester. When Leicester shows off this inner office, he points out source documents—chronicles, histories, maps, genealogical materials, and records of coronations and triumphs—of a sort also contained in Spenser's faeryland chamber, documents essential to the preparation of old-fashioned cosmographic-iconographic histories. The literary devices of the patron here appear to have influenced the poet.

The Senior Warder, introduced by Leicester in the Inner Temple's office, is a type easily recognizable in the overseer of Spenser's cell. Leicester says of the temple office:

> The keper therof was his Caligate knight named deligence, wher ley comlye couched books of auncient geastes, deades of honour, chronicles of countres, and histories of sundry sortes, ther weare also, the orders of Coronacions, Creaceons; Dubbinges, . . . Orders of Robes Royall & honorable Triumphes, & Mornings, curiouslie hanged, and decked with mappes of sundrie countreis . . . (fol. 106).

Two allegorical helpers in the Temple Church assist the keeper "Deligence": "his pursevant Trustye, And his messenger (Swifte). Studiouslye keping these monuments from wormie wormes" (fol. 206). "Further within" the "office of Armes," one of the helpers places "afore" Gerald Legh and the Pegasus-Templar's "Herehaught Marshall" important historical volumes disclosing the ancestry of royal and aristocratic families: "foure legers of hudge volume, all of single cotes. . . . uppon a side borde laye straighte Pedegrees ascending. And Genealogies descending . . ." (fol. 206–07).

Spenser, direct and incisive, provides far sharper, more witty allegorical definition to his closely comparable action and character-types. In Spenser's poem a "ruinous" old "man of infinite remembrance" named Eumanestes, a man half blind but with a vigorous mind, replaces Leicester's Deligence as the overseer of ancient records. And if an allegorical helper called Swifte tends and delivers documents in Leicester's account, so too does a similar helper named Anameste in Spenser's. Writing of Eumanestes's assistant, Spenser comments:

> A litle boy did on him still attend,
> To reach, when euer he for ought did send:
> And oft when things were lost, or laid amis,
> That boy them sought, and vnto him did lend.

> Therefore he *Anamnestes* cleped is,
> And that old man *Eumanestes*, by their propertis.
>
> (2.9.58)

Even the "wormie wormes" that endanger records in Leicester's office of Arms have their counterparts in memory's cell, for Eumanestes's chamber is completely

> . . . hangd about with rolles,
> And old records from auncient times deriu'd,
> Some made in books, some in long parchment scrolles,
> That were all worme-eaten, and full of canker holes.
>
> (2.9.57)

Just as Spenser's allegorical House with its inhabitants and keepers can be seen to mirror an actual chivalric establishment, so too the furious assault upon the body politic of Alma can be seen to mirror a tiltyard battle of a kind mentioned, and very possibly staged, as part of the Inner Temple revels. In a tournament of this sort, grotesque figures of uncontrolled passion, dressed in tattered costumes and armed with crude weapons, would attack the defenders of a microcosmic-macrocosmic allegorical residence.

In *The Faerie Queene* one band of fighters masked like tournament knights in plumes and animal costumes, rush forward as allegorical representatives of "Foolish delights and fond abusions." This band—"Some like to hounds, some like to Apes, dismayd./ Some like to Puttockes, all in plumes arayd" (2.11.11) —unsuccessfully attempt to storm one of the five ports, signifying the human senses, of Alma's House. Another troop beseiging Alma appears as "Vile caytiue wretches, ragged, rude deformed,/ All threatning death." This group is "in straunge manner armd,/ Some with unweldy clubs, some with long speares,/ Some rusty kniues, some staues in fire warmd" (2.9.13).

When Spenser later narrates a faeryland tournament in book 4, he surprisingly portrays the noble Arthegal, with virtue temporarily suppressed, in a "wyld disguize" that carries more than a hint of the bizarre. "Secret wit," the poet acidly observes, is evident in the words *"Saluagesse sans finesse"* on Arthegal's shield; for in a display of excessive naturalness, the shield of the great knight is "ragged," his armour "like saluage weed,/ With woody mosse bedight," and his horse "With oaken leaues attrapt" (4.4.39).

It will be remembered too that, in a Whitehall tourney of 1582, Sir Philip Sidney masked as Desire—the name of the central figure

in Leicester's own allegorical tale—sought with his chivalric com-
patriots to storm a scenic Castle of Beauty harboring Elizabeth in
the guise of Beauty, a castle guarded by knights dressed as Adam
and Eve. And in a spectacle of chivalric strangeness held at the
French court just a few days before the St. Bartholomew's Day
Massacre of 1572, Catholic knights in the unlikely masquing garb
of Amazons fought in a tiltyard engagement against Protestant
Huguenot knights attired as Saracens. As part of the same festivities, the Huguenots wore curious costumes, representing demonic
rebel knights, and battled angelic Catholic knights who defended a
great circular scenic depiction of the heavens in the production
Paradis d' Amour. In the sixteenth century, tournaments based
upon seiges and battles described in Tasso's *Jerusalem Liberata* were
even staged at the French court.[7]

At the Inner Temple on the same evening as the revels witnessed by Legh, Leicester tells the story of the figure Desire, a
story that appears to have left its mark upon the themes, characters, action and iconographic structure of book 1 of *The Faerie
Queene*. The figure Desire, in Leicester's allegory, discovers his
future knightly identity as a member of the chivalric order governed by Pallas Athena. In the manner of Spenser's Red Cross
Knight, Desire goes on a spiritual journey to various allegorical
houses, defeats a terrible serpent in an extended battle, learns of
his role as a future knight, and then marries a virtuous allegorical
lady, a female surrogate for the ruler of his knightly order.[8]

Carrying the "shielde" of "Governaunce" and accompanied by
Dame "Grace," Desire like Red Cross is spiritually educated,
tempted and challenged in the houses before his marriage, in this
instance, to "Dame beautie." In a "House of Doctrine" comparable
to Spenser's House of Holiness, Desire meets a spiritual teacher
"Dame Conguitie" who, like Red Cross's instructress Caelia, receives Desire "with his companions. And them instructed in all the
orders of their house." Traveling on, Desire later sees Dame
Beauty within the House of Solace, but the house's guardian
"Daunger will not let him enter." After falling into a spiritual
depression close to despair—a depression like that which overcomes Red Cross—Desire is saved by the figure "Counsell" who
"bade him not despayre" but to seek "wisdome." Desire gains this
"wisdome" in a "pallace of Comfort" where he at last attains to the
"fellowshippe of Knighthoode, with Perfeuerance. There was he
armed, with hardines."

Now spiritually prepared, Desire fights a serpent with nine heads, one of which represents the evil of "doublenes" and the others "enemyes to knighthood . . .: "Disposition, Delay, Shame, Misreporte, Discomfort, Variance, Envye, Detraction." Victorious over his foe, Desire learns of his full entrance into the order of Pegasus-Templar knighthood. He then sacrifices "in the Princes Temple to the goddes Pallas, who to continue his honor, joyned him in mariage with ladye Bewtye, and satisfied his desire" (fol. 208–211).

Arresting indeed is the fact that Leicester's initial, abbreviated tale and Spenser's later fully developed poetic book, despite obvious differences, share basic allegorical components: the celebration of faeryland types shadowing Elizabeth and her knightly followers; the microcosmic-macrocosmic psychomachy topos involving representations of virtue and opposing "doubleness"; ideological structure based upon conceptually related core icons that signify holy or evil houses and sites; meanings arising from a figure's discovery of true identify with the help of wisdom and grace; and discursive narratives centered on the figure's spiritual journey to faeryland houses, defeat of a dragon beseiging a desired lady, and marriage to this lady who is an allegorical surrogate for the figure's sovereign. Not the least striking is the fact that the allegory is told by a patron, acting out the role of the Red Cross Knights' Marshall, who also conducts a tour through the allegorical "house" of the round Inner Temple Church with its inner chamber of historical records.

It is in his exposition of universal history in book 2 that Spenser breaks dramatically in tone and viewpoint with his patron. With mocking asides and considerable novel exaggeration, Spenser, writing of Guyon and Arthur in Alma's cell of memory, archly contrives to have them read from antique chronicles and so "prove" the legitimacy of both faeryland and British monarchies. Arthur discovers the volume *Briton moniments* with its capsule chronicle of England, and Guyon finds the amusing companion work *Antiquitie of Faerie lond* "In which when as he greedily did looke,/ Th' off-spring of Elues and Faries there he fond" (2.9.60).

The histories in book 2 have been scrutinized against actual early British chronologies; the bloody English narrative has been seen as counterbalancing the "perfect" faery history, with neither of the two annals satisfactory in itself, but with the pair manifesting a comprehensive historical outlook that encompasses both the actual and the ideal.[9] Yet such a reading fails to register Spenser's complex reactions to a now-fragmented Tudor myth of a wider universal history. It is this wider myth that remained a force in Elizabethan culture until the sixteenth and seventeenth centuries when new cosmographic-historical publications, particularly by Richard Hakluyt and Samuel Purchas, altered its form. Today the myth's broad outlines have to be pieced together from scattered materials. But by knowing the contours of the myth, it is possible to see how mischievously and subversively Spenser plays upon it.

Stimulated by concerns over the right of Tudor monarchs to rule an empire, sixteenth century "historians" and chroniclers—among them Polydore Vergil, Raphael Holinshed and Andrew of Wytoun—sought in partially completed works to combine antique iconography with "modern" empirical cosmographic history and so to develop, within essentially a medieval chronicle framework, a new "universal" world vision. It is rarely noted, for example, that Holinshed wrote his famous *Chronicles*, as he admitted in the dedication to the 1557 edition, on the assumption that they would be part of a "universall Cosmographie of the whole worlde" to be composed by a number of authors assigned to their tasks by the queen's printer Reginald Wolfe. Holinshed explains that various persons under Wolfe's direction were to write "certaine particular Histories of every knowen nation." But Holinshed adds that the project failed when God called Wolfe "to his mercie" and when the charts prepared by Wolfe "were not founde so complete as wee wished." Holinshed accordingly published only his own segment of the universal cosmography-history, a segment drawn largely from earlier chronicles of "Englande, Scotlande, and Ireland."[10]

The older, scattered and partial cosmographic histories that the Holinshed group wished to change and enlarge in general rested, of course, upon belief in the antique three-continent *mappaemundi* projections of the earth, and upon belief in the literal truth of details of Old and New Testament epochal narratives. In the antique chronicles, the stories and travels of classical heroes such as Odysseus and Aeneas were usually dealt with in part as fables, but in their main outlines as literally true.

Old Testament events leading to the New Testament Passion were duly recorded. Then after the Crucifixion of Christ in Jerusalem, the Apostles, as Eusebius declared in his *Ecclesiastical History*, "passed throughout the whole earth, and their wordes unto the endes of the worlde."[11] Eusebius and a range of medieval chroniclers explained how each apostle went to a different country, gathered together a group of disciples and established a special branch of the universal Church. According to sources already noted and also to Gerald Legh, Joseph of Arimathea substituted for the Apostle Phillip in making the famous trip from Jerusalem to England carrying Passion relics. In the Middle Ages, pilgrimage churches, frequently circular temples, were erected over the remains of the local apostle or of some saintly follower. These churches in Paris, Glassenbury, Rome, Compostella and other cities became national shrines and holy stations—some fulfilled "New Jerusalems"—on medieval world pilgrimage pathways leading always to the Holy City at the center of the earth. The world became a foreshadowing type of the Kingdom of God. At its navel was the "true" New Jerusalem, a supposed shimmering city of gold and gems that in the imagination of western artists seemed always to hover, far away and yet spiritually near, in the luminosity of the eastern sky at the point of the morning sunrise.

Thus the Tudor historical myth took form. The journeys of the Apostles and of later secular and religious leaders were seen as a fulfillment of the earlier journeys of both Old Testament figures and pagan heroes such as Trojan Aeneas. A political as well as a religious dimension accrued to the myth.

According to Eusebius in *The First Books of Ecclesiastical History*, the first and much-traveled Christian emperor Constantine was both an inspired political leader and a fulfilled type of Moses, and the emperor's army was a powerful military force and a fulfillment of the tribes of the Israelites seeking the promised land.[12] The emperor in his last years, Eusebius reports, went on a pilgrimage to the Holy Land and was officially baptized in the River Jordan. And Constantine, like St. George, became identified as the vanquisher of a dragon. The emperor's defeat of Roman forces outside the Eternal City, Eusebius notes in his *Life of Constantine*, was later acclaimed at Constantinople in a famed icon. "To declare his victory over those savage Tyrants that had oppressed and persecuted the church," Eusebius writes, Constantine placed on his imperial palace gate in the East his own "Picture or Statue . . . having the sign of the Crosse over the head thereof, with the figure of a wounded Dragon lying couchant underneath his feete."[13] Andrew of Wyntoun later wrote in his *Chronicle* that the emperor actually attacked a dragon near Rome, "brist it," and then enclosed it, faeryland style, in a wall of brass.[14]

Straining to "Anglicize" both this mighty imperial warrior and his mother, Raphael Holinshed in his *Chronicles* declares that the emperor "begot of a britishe woman, and borne of hir in Britayne (as our writers doe affirme,) and created certainely Emperour in

Britayne, doubtlesse made his native countrey partaker of his hygh glorie and renoune."[15] Constantine's mother, the "britishe woman," now becomes "Empresse Helen," discoverer of the "Sepulchre of our Lorde" and the true "Crosse," and the builder with her son of the new "temple" in Jerusalem (pp. 90–92).

Holinshed dramatically explains in the *Chronicles* how Constantine, on his deathbed, insured that his imperial power was passed on to the rightful successor. "Raising himselfe up in his bed, in the presence of his other sonnes and counsellours," the chronicler writes," . . . he set the crowne upon his sonnes head, and adorned him with other imperiall roabes and garments" (p. 89). Readers looking further into the *Chronicles* could see an illustration of this crown on the head of yet another supposed rightful successor to the emperor, King Arthur. Perhaps through oversight but more likely through a political desire to emphasize the line of power, the drawing of the crowned head labeled "Arthur" that appears on page 131 is a reprint of the same drawing labeled "Constantine" on page 90. The same drawing is reprinted a third time on page 138 as an illustration of a still later successor also named Constantine, an immediate relative of King Arthur. "After the death of Arthur," Holinshed comments, "his cousin Constantine . . . beganne his reigne ouer the Brytayns, in the yeare of our Lorde, 542" (p. 158).

Unusual visual support for British imperial claims was also provided by marginal drawings of Constantine and his crown in a copy of Polydore Vergil's *Works*, published in Basle in 1534. Penned sometime before 1550 by an unidentified reader, the drawings include those depicting Constantine wearing his crown, Constantine being baptized in the River Jordan, and an enlarged view of just the imperial crown. The reader's marginal comments and the text of Virgil's work identify the crown as the one passed on by the emperor to the kings of England.[16]

Constantine's imperial authority over church and state thus devolved, in the view of Loyalist British chroniclers, upon King Arthur and his blood relatives and then upon Tudor monarchs. In *The Defence of Constantine* (1621) Richard Crakenthorp echoes such sentiments and, in stressing the extent of imperial power, asserts that British Constantine "made glorious the true faith of Christ . . . from Great Brittaine, euen to the utmost borders of the Earth."[17]

Concentrating on the supposed imperial source of Queen Elizabeth's world authority, Loyalist author John Foxe, in dedicating to the queen his *Actes and Monuments of these latter and perillous dayes* (1563), goes so far as to compare himself to Constantine's biographer Eusebius. Foxe then insists in conventional Loyalist fashion that

Elizabeth, as ruler of church and state, is "followyng the steppes" of "Constantine the great and mightie Emperour, the sonne of Helene an Englyshe Woman of this youre Realme and countrie."[18] A memorable dedication page etching supports Foxe's claim. Queen Elizabeth is illustrated cradled within a huge and ornate letter "C," the first letter of the word "Constantine" that begins the dedication. The queen is shown holding the emblems of her spiritual and temporal authority: in her left hand, the earth with a cross at its apex; and in her right hand, a sword.

The Tudor historical myth allowed Loyalist supporters of Elizabeth to insist upon her relationship to the Apostles and to succeeding military-religious figures who preached and defended the Christian faith. For it is British-born Constantine who defeats the evil dragon of Rome, establishes the first Christian empire over East and West, builds "temples" at the holiest sites in the world, journeys to the Holy Land to be baptized in the River Jordan, and on his deathbed gives to his rightful successor what will become the British crown granting power over church and state. The British "Empresse" mother of Constantine, after constructing the walls of London and Colchester, goes on pilgrimage to the Holy Land, discovers the True Cross and the Holy Sepulchre, aids in the building of Holy Land "temples," and then follows the example of Joseph of Arimathea in carrying Passion relics back to the West.[19]

Loyalist authors, moreover, credited Constantine with establishing an order of Christian knights, supposed forerunners of Elizabeth's Knights of the Garter. In *The Institution, Laws & Ceremonies of the most Noble Order of the Garter*, Elias Ashmole discusses heraldic emblems and chivalric history and finds the Garter Order to be the culmination of ancient knightly groups including King Arthur's Knights of the Round Table, the Hospitallers, Templars and the Knights of the Holy Sepulchre. And like Spenser's faeryland lady knight Britomart whose origins are traced by Merlin to heroic warriors of "ancient Troian blood" (3.3.22), the Knights of the Garter are here associated with the alleged Knights of Troy and, in addition, with the Knights of Argoes and even the Knights of Moses. But Ashmole takes special note of the imperial predecessor of Elizabeth by identifying "The Order of the Constantinian Angelick Knights of *St. George*" as "the first Military Order in Christendom" that "took beginning from the Emperor *Constantine* the *Great*." Ashmole observes that the "Habit of this Angelick Order is *White*, on the left side whereof is sewed a Red or Crimson Velvet *Cross Flory*." Under the "Protection of the Blessed Virgin, and the patronage of *St. George*," Ashmole continues, the order was called

Angelical, because the Cross with this inscription, *In hoc Signo vinces*, was shewed from Heaven to that Emperor by an Angel; and thence they of the Family descended from him (among whom were the Great *Master* of the *Order*) took the name *de Angelis*.[20]

John Anstis's celebrated *Black Book* or *The Register of the Most Noble Order of the Garter*—an analogue to the imaginative, timeless "book of fame" in which Gloriana's faeryland knights wish to be "eternised" (1.10.59)—also cites Constantine's knights, together with Trojan, Mosaic and crusading orders, as forerunners of the Garter band.

Ignoring the bitter antagonisms that made certain members of the Garter Order mortal political and religious enemies, Anstis and Ashmole emphatically proclaim the unity and love of this international band of chivalric brothers. "Formerly all *Christendom* had been disquieted," Anstis writes, but "Heaven at last directed" the founding of the Order. The group's emblems and garments were in themselves said to kindle "Sparks of Charity." The "Design" of the Order, Anstis adds, "was to promote Virtue, to obtain Peace, to settle a lasting Friendship."[21]

Imaginatively as fascinated by old-fashioned chronicles as by antique world iconography, Spenser in *The Faerie Queene* mirrors, amalgamates, and sometimes diffracts important segments of the antique universal histories embracing the Trojans, the tribes of Israel, the Apostles, the rulers of the Roman Empire, the British leaders and kings, the chivalric orders of knights, and an assortment of giants, dwarfs, Amazons, faeries, dragons and grotesque creatures. And as a political-allegorical feature of his epic, Spenser introduces Gloriana's faeryland Knights of Maidenhead as a composite, ideal, allegorical reflection of Elizabeth's international Knights of the Garter. Gloriana's demonstrated rule over her antique Maidenhead Order with its own history fulfills in faeryland the Tudor claim that in the actual world, Elizabeth was a direct successor of a line of supposed knightly and biblical leaders extending back to Arthur and Constantine and even to Moses. Under the presumed patronage of the pilgrim-knight St. George, Elizabeth's Garter Knights met each year at "King Arthur's" Windsor Castle and then returned to their individual kingdoms presumably to fight against evil. As sovereign of this knightly band, Elizabeth thus acted out the myth that she ruled a world empire with political-religious origins in Holy Land sites and persons.

Spenser treats the old European universal historical myth, as he does much medieval iconography, with a satiric smile. He maps out in his poem the overall religious-political chronological outlines represented in the antique documents, outlines that he and other British Loyalists used to support the Tudors. But as with his narration of chivalric tales, Spenser remains distanced from and wryly critical of the old-fashioned universal chronicle sources. He finds them filled with amusing nonsense. His historical references, sweeping and frequently ironic, stimulate the imagination and disarm the mind more than they compel full rational assent.

In the House of Alma narrative, the opening "local" chronicle focuses on Britain. According to this narrative, the line of succession leading to Tudor rule in the imperfect actual world was established despite recurring periods of terrible political confusion and bloodshed. This chronicle acts as a foil for a subsequent and seemingly idealized, fanciful "universal" faery history with the chain of succession to foreshadowed Tudor power now uncontested and neatly set out, a history that nevertheless adroitly parodies wider chronicle conventions.

Guyon's human companion, Arthur, reads the tumultuous British history (2.10.5–68) compiled in largely matter-of-fact fashion from a merging of materials found in Geoffrey of Monmouth, Grafton, Stow, Holinshed and other chronicle writers. Guyon then reads the delightful faeryland history (2.10.70–76) with its light mockery of the wider chronologies of Eusebius, Polydore Vergil and patristic commentators. As depicted in the faery chronicles of book 2 and in the later prophecies of book 3, the parallel elfin and British empires are sufficiently close to permit certain human characters, such as Red Cross and Arthegal, to cross over from the earthly plane to the empire of the faeries.

The local British chronicle stored in the House of Alma covers only the period from the arrival of the first mariner on English shores to events following the crowning of the "second Constantine," the rightful successor of the first Christian emperor. This British history, as has been seen, is later extended to the time of the Tudors by Merlin's prophesies in book 3.

Into the English account, Spenser interjects—without apparent irony—fabulous chronicle tales about Trojan Brute's landing in Britain and defeat of local giants, but the poet exhibits a detached skepticism by attributing the story of Joseph of Arimathea and the Holy Grail in England simply to what "they say" (2.10.53). Quickly skimming over some 700 years of bloody and politically confused English history involving Brute's decendents, Spenser finally identifies the "*Britons* first crownd Soueraine" as "*Coyll*," the ruler who "gaue for wife his daughter bright,/ Faire Helena" to Constantius (2.10.58–59). The issue of this union is British-born Constantine, the initial Christian king of Britain and the Roman "Emperour" (2.10.60). Following Constantine's death, Britain is described as again engulfed in political turmoil that ends only when the "weary *Britons*" "by consent of Commons and of Peares,/ . . . crownd the second Constantine with ioyous teares" (2.10.61–62).

By mentioning the two houses of the British Parliament, Spenser makes an important political point. Lacking a direct imperial successor by blood, the "consent" of "Commons" and "Peares" is required before a new ruler is crowned. But no Pope or foreign monarch, emperor or governing body has authority over British imperial rule.

The chain of succession is further delineated when Merlin, prophesying to Britomart in book 3, declares that her future son by Arthegal will someday follow in the line of King Arthur to the throne. This son, Merlin fortells, will be victorious over a usurper and will then take the famous "crowne, that was his fathers right." He will "therewith crowne himselfe" (3.3.29). Though later descendents of Britomart and Arthegal will at times be displaced as British rulers, Merlin foresees the eventual establishment of the family's permanent political power through the efforts of a famed descendent coming from the "Ile/ Of *Mona*," a shadowed reference to Henry VII as the formal founder of the Tudor dynasty. This descendent will end contests of "ciuile armes"—an apparent allusion to the Wars of the Roses—and bring together "nations different afore" in "eternall union" and "sacred Peace" (3.3.48–49). He will someday be succeeded by "a royall virgin."

In his contrasting, whimsical faeryland history, Spenser greatly enlarges his perspective also to parody certain topos and patterns of classicized Hebraic-Christian chronicle history: the creation of humankind, the association of the First Parents in the Garden, the long genealogies of the First Parents' descendants, the journeys of certain descendents to all nations of the world, and the descendents' establishment of a universal authority in these nations. This mocking of chronicle tales having scriptural background is oblique and selective. It is tempered in its scriptural echoes in several ways: the faery history is obviously fictional; it is couched in neoclassical allusions; it lacks the overt or implied theological dimensions of chronicle accounts of Scripture; and the faeryland history contains no shadowing of such climactic biblical events as the Fall, Redemption and Last Judgement. Primarily ridiculed is the excessive literalism of the old chronicle histories, the often outrageous and unintentionally comic spinning-out of classical and other secular and scriptual texts into detailed stories presented as factual truth. But there still remains implicit in the scriptural resonances of Spenser's imaginative faery history an unexpected, glancing, mildly stinging Reformation satire of the biblical stories themselves.

Spenser replaces God the Supreme Creator with a faeryland Prometheus. In a departure from Scriptures and pagan myth, this faeryland neoclassical revolutionary creates the first faery, Elfe, from divisive constituents: the parts of beasts and the fire of heaven (2.10.70). Elfe, like the postlapsarian Adam, is said to wander through the world; but Spenser archly adds, in a very nonbiblical aside, that Elfe does so on "wearie feet" (2.10.71). The scriptural story of Eve's creation from Adam's rib is not included. The male faery simply comes upon an already created female faery, a counterpart for Eve, in the neo-Platonic "gardins of Ado-nis" (2.10.71), a faeryland type for Eden. Lightly playing upon the tautology of whether this "authour of all woman kind" is "either Spright,/ Or Angell," Elfe with some drollery is said to call her "*Fay*" (2.10.71).

Elfe and Fay become the First Parents of a "mighty people" whose central figures, in the manner of the Apostles, "all the world warrayd" (2.10.72). The brief identification of just some of Elfe and Fay's descendents—including Elfin, Elfinan, Elfinell, Elfar, Elfinor, Elficleos, Elferon, Oberon and Tanaquill—is extended sufficiently to gain the amused understanding of chronicle readers puzzled by genealogical lists containing many nearly identical names.

The First Parents' eldest son, Elfin, overcomes a much-discussed problem of sixteenth century chronicle writers: the issue of which descendent of the First Parents, if any, brought truth and authority to America before its recorded discovery. Elfin, it has been noted, gained and held power in "all that now America men call" (2.10.72). Another descendant, Elfinell, obtains power like Trojan Brute by killing giants, but these faeryland monsters are now so strange that they become objects of satire: "The one of which had two heades, th' other three" (2.10.73). The imaginative faery figures Elficleos, Elferon and Oberon shadow Tudor monarchs who were very concerned about their public representations: Henry VII, Prince Arthur and Henry VIII, respectively. But Spenser's light tone smooths the edge of mild historical satire, and the poet's chronologies safely point in expected Loyalist fashion to future peace and unity through Tudor rule.

By illustrating lines of succession to power, Spenser outwardly realizes in his poem—with mocking overtones—a great political, religious and chivalric dream of the Tudor monarchy, a dream unfulfilled in the actual sixteenth century world of fractious British and European politics. Spenser's poem is a selfconsciously composed universal epic, dependent primarily upon the medieval mythic view of history and cosmography, which presents an imagined vision of a world empire ordered by an international band of knights under the legitimate sovereign rule of a single Reformation monarch.

In book 1, Una, a type for Gloriana, has been observed to be the legitimate royal heir who

> . . . by descent from Royall lynage came
> Of ancient Kings and Queenes, that had of yore
> Their sceptters stretcht from East to Westerne shore,
> And all the world in their subiection held
>
> (1.1.5)

Bifurcated Duessa, the pretender to power and the antithesis of Una, is identified as

> . . . the sole daughter of an Emperour,
> He that the wide West under his rule has,
> And high hath set his throne, where *Tiberis* doth pas.
>
> (1.2.22)

But at the marriage of Una and Red Cross, Duessa is abandoned by her false imperial father and so, in the words of Archiamago, becomes the "wofull daughter and forsaken heire/ Of that great Emperour of all the West" (1.12.26).

Here in Spenser's poetic faeryland, the true heir to imperial world religious authority is virtuous Una, the bride of Red Cross of England. The corresponding female heir to world temporal authority is chaste Britomart, the future bride of Arthegal of England. And because both Una and Britomart are lesser emblematic types of the Faerie Queene, it is Gloriana who has final sovereignty over church and state in a faeryland world empire mirroring the earthly empire under "Empress" Elizabeth.

Spenser thus successfully navigates what in Britain could have been dangerous political-religious streams, imaginatively and emotively defending Tudor authority even as he satirizes the broader medieval chronicle conventions upon which that authority was

theoretically based. His poetry brilliantly reinforces Loyalist senti-
ment even as it marks a sharp turn against unquestioning acceptance of the popular Reformation political-religious myth of British
and world history.

*Onſtantine the greate
and mightie Emperour, the
ſonne of Helene an Englyſhe
woman of this youre Realme
and countrie (moſte Chriſtian
and renowmed Prynceſſe
Queene Elizabeth) after he
had pacified and eſtabliſhed
the churche of Chriſt, being
long before vnder perſecu-
tion, frō the tyme of our ſaui-
our Chriſt almoſt 400 yeres:
and comming in his progreſſe
at length to a citie called Cæ-
ſaria, (where Euſebius wry-
ter of the Eccleſiaſticall ſtory
was then placed Byſhop) required of the ſayde Euſebius
vpon his owne free motion, to
demaund and aſke of him what ſo euer he thought expediēt or neceſſary for the ſtate
and commoditie of his Churche, promiſing to graunt vnto him the ſame, whatſoeuer
he ſhould aſke. whiche Euſebius, if he had the required what terrene benefite ſoeuer
he would, either of poſſeſſions to be geuen, or of impoſitiōs to be releaſed, or any other
lyke &c. he had no doubt obtained his requeſt of that ſo lyberall, and ſo noble harted
Emperour. But the good and godly Byſhop, more nedy then gredy, more ſpiritually
geuen, then worldly minded, who had learned rather to take a litle, thē to aſke much,
ſetting all other reſpectes aſide, made this petition, onely to obtaine at his maieſties*

39. Queen Elizabeth's alleged imperial world authority, supposedly derived from the first Christian emperor, Constantine, and so extending over church and state, is strikingly illustrated on the dedicatory page of *Actes and Monuments* (1563) by John Foxe. Elizabeth is shown cradled within the letter "C" of the dedication's first word, "Constantine." In the House of Alma episode of *The Faerie Queene* (2.10), Spenser similarly traces the British monarchy's supposed imperial power to that exercised by Constantine. *Courtesy of the Huntington Library.*

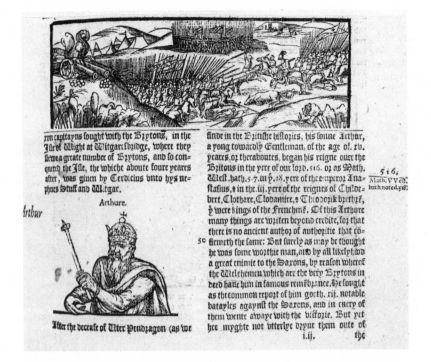

40. King Arthur as he appears in Raphael Holinshed's *Chronicles of Englande, Scotlande, and Ireland,* volume 1 (1957). An identical illustration labeled "Constantine" is found on page 90 of the *Chronicles,* visually reinforcing the Tudor claim that Arthur was in the line of succession from the emperor. *Courtesy of the Huntington Library.*

174

41. "Gloriana" and her knights. Queen Elizabeth (center, seated) reigns over the Knights of the Garter at this international order's annual banquet in St. George's Hall, Windsor Castle. Spenser "mirrored" Elizabeth and the order in creating Gloriana and her Knights of Maidenhead in *The Faerie Queene*. This drawing appears in Elias Ashmole's *The Institution, Laws & Ceremonies of the most Noble Order of the Garter* (1672). *Courtesy of the Huntington Library.*

42. Pendant of the Order of the Garter depicting St. George, patron of the order, slaying the dragon. In book 1 of Spenser's *The Faerie Queene*, the Red Cross Knight, before he battles and kills a dragon, is told by the hermit Contemplation that he "Saint *George* shalt called bee,/ Saint *George* of mery England" (1.10.61). *From Ashmole's* The Institution, Laws & Ceremonies. *Courtesy of the Huntington Library.*

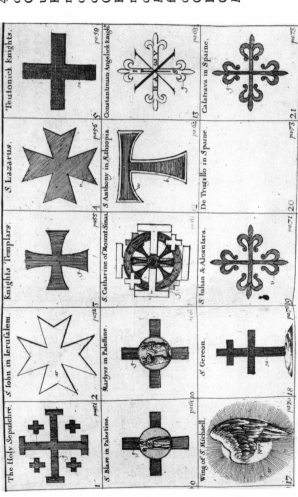

43. "Ensignes" of knightly orders—including the Red Cross Knights Templar (center, upper row) and the Angelic Knights of Constantine (far right, middle row)—in the line of chivalry supposedly culminating in the international Order of the Garter ruled by Elizabeth. Spenser accordingly made a Red Cross Knight, the central figure in book 1 of *The Faerie Queene*, one among the faeryland Reformation Knights of Maidenhead under empress Gloriana. *From Ashmole's The Institution, Laws & Ceremonies. Courtesy of the Huntington Library.*

SIX

Milton's Universal Epic and the Cosmographical-Historical Revolution

Inward Vision and Eyewitness Discovery

During his middle years in the 1640s and 1650s, John Milton selfconsciously developed, as a correlative to medieval biblical "historical" typology, a new Renaissance conception of how both history and geography might be most reliably presented. With incisive originality he used his new Renaissance historical-geographical conception to give unique images, tonalities, internal structures and multiple viewpoints to *Paradise Lost*, an epic created in imitation of supposedly "true" historical action.

In this his middle "empirical" phase, Milton was extremely active in jotting down plans for various future literary works and in composing reformist tracts and histories. He wrote at this time, among other pieces, outlines for a projected theatrical *sacra rappresentazione* "Adam Unparadiz'd" and for other planned biblical and British theatrical representations; the prose tracts *The Doctrine and Discipline of Divorce* (1643), *Areopagitica* (1644), and *Of Education* (1644); and early drafts of *A History of Britain* (published 1670) and *A Brief History of Moscovia* (published 1683). In these and other works Milton continued to depict biblical events within a general but increasingly blurred framework of traditional medieval foreshadowed and fulfilled "historical" typological epochs. At the same time there crystallized in Milton's writings—merged with

176

and sometimes taking prominence over typological patterns—a new view of historical and geographical reality at variance with the medieval outlook.

During this period, Milton expanded upon his classical and biblical Cambridge education, reading widely in the literature of global voyage and of educational and philosophical reform. He clearly turned against medieval iconographic geography. He rejected the medieval tradition of physical pilgrimage to Jerusalem. He scornfully pointed out the unreliability of medieval chronicle histories by Holinshed, Malmsbury, Bede and others. And largely under the influence of new views of "universal" history and geography propounded by Francis Bacon, Richard Hakluyt, Samuel Purchas, Samuel Hartlib and Abraham Ortelius, Milton came to believe that accurate history and geography might best be produced, not by depending upon the fictions of medieval chronicles and related medieval world iconography, but rather by studying authoritative eyewitness accounts by ancient and modern voyagers and travelers. Among these voyagers were moderns who, using the instruments of the new philosophy, had discovered new lands, new peoples and new worlds in space.

In becoming a "new" critical historian, Milton admired and was influenced by a number of earlier historians including those writing in Latin such as Polybius, Paulus Jovius and Sallust. Yet the poet, it will be seen, gained a publicly advocated and defined "method" as well as rich ancient and modern source materials for his new geography and history particularly from two voluminous source works: the three-folio collection of eyewitness English travel accounts published in 1589 by preacher Richard Hakluyt as *The Principal Navigations, Voyages, Traffiques, and Discoveries of the English Nation, made by Sea or Over-Land to Remote and Farthest Distant Quarters of the Earth, At any Time within the Compasse of these 1,600 years* and additions to these folios published in following years by Hakluyt's friend and literary heir, the preacher Samuel Purchas.[1] In 1613 Purchas brought out over 700 travel accounts, most of them bequeathed to him by Hakluyt, under the title *Purchas his Pilgrimage, Or Relations Of The World And The Religions Observed In All Ages And places discovered, from the Creation unto this Present*, a work expanded in a 1614 printing. In 1619 Purchas again enlarged his work and, while keeping the main title, provided a new terse but explanatory subtitle: *Microcosmus, or The Historie of Man*. Making use of some 1,400 authors, Purchas then published in 1625 his gigantic, four-folio tome—the largest work printed in English up to that time—*Hakluytus Posthumus or Purchas his*

Pilgrimes. A final edition with additional materials appeared in 1626 again under the main title *Purchas his Pilgrimage.*[2]

Although the global voyages of discovery and exploration recounted in Purchas's volumes are accepted today as academic facts, they stimulated heated Renaissance debates over the relative superiority of ancient versus modern learning. Francis Bacon in *The Advancement of Learning* (1625) was one of those who avowed that moderns had explored the world in a manner superior to that of the ancients. By using the information gathered by these modern explorers, Bacon favored the writing of a "mixed species" of history which he termed a "History of Cosmography":

> being compounded of natural history, in respect to the regions themselves; of history civil, in respect of the habitations, regiments, and manners of the people; and the mathematics, in respect of the climates and configurations towards the heavens. . . .[3]

Bacon's claims for the new philosophy and learning gave influential theoretical support to the moderns. But for Milton, the new geographical histories of Hakluyt and Purchas, with their great wealth of substantive materials, were seminal.

Painfully aware of the power of sight after the onset of his blindness in the 1650s, anxious to give indisputable credibility to the supposed "truths" of universal history in his epic, Milton invented *Paradise Lost* by integrating the new, empirical eyewitness reporting techniques of contemporaneous travel writing with revelations of inner, spiritual vision of a kind drawn from biblical and classical tradition. The Bible supplied Milton with a supposedly "true" divine history and a pattern of typological epochs; classical and biblical antecedents provided examples of heroic action disclosed through the inner vision of a divinely inspired narrator; Samuel Purchas and his "pilgrimes," gave a "new" historical and geographical method based upon the direct, carefully recorded, and, if possible, repeated sequential observation of places and events. Milton's imitation of reality in *Paradise Lost* accordingly takes the form of a series of eyewitness poetic testimonials that combine a supposed visionary intellectual-intuitive comprehension of immaterial essences with an accurate, selective rendering of external physical appearances.

In Milton's epic universal history is disclosed, not only through medieval typology, but also through a series of heroic or near-heroic acts, recounted by participants or eyewitnesses, and performed during journeys that progressively extend knowledge of the human, the demonic, the divine, the earth and the universe.

Satan and God the Son, and other holy and evil figures, alternately travel to and from hell or heaven to earth. They then return to their respective immortal mansions to engage in divine masquelike triumphs or demonic masquelike pseudotriumphs, theatrical entries and public appearances in part derived from certain of Milton's theatrical writings including *Arcades, Comus* and the early outlines for sacred representations.[4] Travel, biblical, classical, and culmi-nating theatrical materials are thus uniquely fused.

In the first ten books, largely presenting events before the Fall, the journeys are counterpoised in a patterned hierarchy: the de-monic associated with secular sea voyages to India in the East and with cosmological discovery; the divine with visionary theatrical sacred representations derived from scriptural passages. The last two books, depicting events after the Fall, contain the angel Gabriel's rather flat and imprecisely delineated presentation to Adam of the future typological ages of humankind.

Although criticism has convincingly attested to the considerable aesthetic impact of these last two books, it still must be admitted that even the angel Gabriel grows somewhat weary of his long typological narration. "The rest/ Were long to tell," says the angel to Adam,

> . . . how many Battles fought
> How many Kings destroy'd, and Kingdoms won,
> Or how the Sun shall in mid Heav'n stand still
> A day entire[5]

Events in the early books are aesthetically powerful, not alone because of Milton's forceful depiction of Satan and his evil cohorts, but also because the poet renders the tempestuous travels of the Archfiend and the figures Sin and Death with notable originality. Memorable images and episodes, drawn both from secular world voyages and religious theatrical spectacles, are joined with tra-ditional biblical and classical elements. The direct, dynamic voyages of the Son, though more compressed, are also arresting in their unconventional blending of theatrical and biblical sources. But in the depiction of future history in books 11 and 12, the epic is less powerful because Milton as a poet is not deeply stirred by a selective interrelation of masquelike scenes and traditional medieval typology.

Ever since Erich Auerbach revealed the pervasive typological relations in Dante's *Commedia*, commentators have assumed that

Milton's epic too, if only examined with critical precision, would disclose a similar network of clear or perhaps symbolically obscured typological allusions that provide structures for all 12 books. In the early verse *On the Morning of Christ's Nativity* (1629), Milton had, after all, placed the Son's birth at the center of divine history through typological references to the Creation, the Crucifixion, the Last Judgement and the future bliss of souls. Would not the poet incorporate comparable medieval historical figurism into all of *Paradise Lost*?

The impulse to press such a critical search forward is surely understandable. In placing the Fall of the First Parents at his epic's thematic core, Milton confronted an all but insuperable problem in mimetic depiction and historical disposition: how to relate this one, "true" human action—a single ostensibly heroic and mimetic event of a kind dictated by Aristotelian theory—to traditional medieval figurism embracing all of universal Christian history. This enormous problem in disposition and verisimilitude startled even Andrew Marvell who, in a 1674 dedicatory poem, wondered if the "vast Design" could indeed be contained and compressed within a "slender book" of verse.

In *Paradise Lost*, of course, Milton moved toward a resolution of the problem by rearranging the chronological order of narrative episodes in accordance with classical epic practices. Then the poet went further in introducing widely separated speeches—by God the Father and Son in book 3, by the angel Raphael in books 6–8, and especially by the angel Gabriel in books 11 and 12—that do highlight an overarching figurism reflected also in the comments of the epic narrator, a figurism binding together scattered events under epochal periods: the Begetting of the Son, the War in Heaven, the Creation, the Fall, the Flood, the Exodus, the Redemption, the Eternal Kingdom in Heaven. References to the Exodus, the Second Adam, the Second Eve and other biblical persons and events are also selectively present in the foreground action of Milton's epic. This overarching figurism—which has been carefully and most helpfully examined by commentators including Mary Christopher Pecheux, George Wesley Whiting, C. A. Patrides, Albert C. Labriola, William B. Hunter, Jr., James L. Sims, William B. Madsen and Edward Tayler—is sufficiently pervasive to keep scholars and critics searching for "clouded" and therefore ignored typological references.[6] Yet despite the range of diverse biblical and classical allusions and types and symbolic foreshadowings in the foreground action of the poem, readers of *Paradise Lost* eventually discover that there are stretches in the opening and central books in which there are relatively few specific allusions to universal typological history.

Analysis of the epochal typology in the poem thus often takes a familiar course. In general, extensive background information is first provided. Then after a discussion of the scattered historical figurism in the body of the epic, there follows a detailed reading of the visionary "scenes" and the typology in book 11, and a longer and more detailed reading of the richer typology in book 12. There is general critical agreement that Milton in these last books, as a result of his eclectic interweaving of masquelike scenes with apocalyptic statements about future typological epochs, suggests but does not always clearly differentiate the traditional six ages of humankind as established by St. Augustine and other church fathers: namely, the periods from Adam to Noah, Noah to Abraham, Abraham to David, David to the Babylonian Captivity, the Captivity to the Birth of Christ, and the Birth of Christ to the Last Judgment and the eternal Sabbath.[7]

The obvious reason why universal historical figurism has not been uncovered in more of the expansive foreground action of *Paradise Lost* is because such figurism is there limited. Although historical types are manifest in the outlook of the epic narrator and incorporated into the poetry, it should be remembered that, theoretically, in Milton's ideal Eden before the Fall, there is no prefiguring human history to serve as a type and little in the way of future human history to serve as a possible antitype. The First Parents in Eden, in this pre-Mosaic period, are uniquely free. They are subject only to a simple pre-Mosaic law that gives a rule to the conscience and forbids their eating of the fruit, a law that Milton explains in book 1, chapter 11, of *De Doctrina Christiana*:

> Legis nomine primario hic intelligitur, illa hominis menti insita et innata; deinde illa ore Dei prolata; Gen. ii. 17. *de isto ne comedito*: nam lex per Mosen scripta longe posterior fuit

> By the law is here meant, in the first place, that rule of conscience which is innate, and engraven upon the mind of man; secondly, the special command which proceeded out of the mouth of God (for the law written by Moses was long subsequent), Gen. 2.17. "thou shalt not eat of it."[8]

Then, too, Milton displays mixed reactions to medieval typology like that which underlies the structure of Dante's *Commedia*. Indeed, Milton in one passage of *Paradise Lost* emotionally rejects as folly that form of supposed individual typological fulfillment arising from "Roman" pilgrimage to Jerusalem—that is, the individual imitative acting out and figural fulfillment through pilgrimage, by actual persons or even characters in a literary work, of past biblical events associated with those holy sites visited. In book 3 Milton interjects, with coarse satiric humour, 53 lines that mock Roman clerics and other pilgrims—including some donning *"Franciscan"* garb or that of *"Dominic"* (3.480)*—who will "hereafter" wander past the outermost sphere of the cosmos and will eventually be consigned to a Paradise of Fools. "Here pilgrims roam," sings the epic narrator with sharp sarcasm, "that stray'd so far to seek/ In Golgatha him dead, who lived in Heav'n" (3.476–77). By showing the pilgrims being violently blown by a cross wind "o'er the backside of the World" (3.494), Milton reveals his profound aversion both to pilgrimage practices in general and to veneration of even the most sacred Holy Land site. The entire medieval physical-spiritual pilgrimage tradition is in effect swept away as "Cowls, Hoods and Habits" are

> . . . with thir wearers tost
> And flutter'd into Rags, then Reliques, Beads,
> Indulgences, Dispenses, Pardons, Bulls,
> The sport of Winds
>
> (3.490–93)

Physical pilgrimage stations, once providing iconographic form for the medieval Book of the World and mimetic form for Dante's *Commedia*, now for Milton have obviously lost much of their geographical and spiritual significance. Milton in his epic thus linguistically imitates a new global geographic reality. And in criticizing medieval Roman pilgrimage rituals and actions, Milton perhaps even obliquely criticizes Dante's long figural pilgrimage of individual fulfillment in the *Commedia*.[9]

While in *Paradise Lost* some individual actions by Adam and Eve and other characters appear to prefigure future typological episodes—notably the First Parents' wandering leave-taking of Eden with its intimation of the future Exodus—Milton generally employs historical typology for the revelation of great, public, figural events through "flashbacks" to the "historical" past and through accounts or theatrical visions of the "historical" future.[10] It is Milton's often overlooked but extraordinary Renaissance structural amalgamation of counterpoised voyages, balanced theatrical anti-

---

* References are to book and lines.

triumphs and triumphs, tragic as well as comedic and pastoral elements, and sequential biblical typology—all within a traditional 12-book epic frame—that makes *Paradise Lost* so difficult to compare structurally to Dante's *Commedia*.[11] For Dante's work, with its 100 cantos bound together by a progressive figurism, has been seen to be focused upon the author's own individual typological reenactment of the biblical Exodus, Redemption and Transfiguration.

Yet while Milton restricted his use of medieval universal typological history in the foreground narrative, he also lost confidence in the 1640s in the reliability and "method" of British chroniclers narrating early English history. "England," the poet reported in *The Reason of Church Government Urged Against Prelaty* (1642) "hath had her noble achievements made small by the unskillful handling of monks and mechanics."[12] Milton's *A History of Britain*, while containing some praise for accurate chroniclers, is also larded with the author's open contempt for early English writers who accepted fable and legend for historical fact. "He who can accept Legends for good story," writes the poet, "may quickly swell a volume with trash." He thinks that Geoffrey of Monmouth, Bede, Holinshed, all, to a greater or lesser extent, are factually unreliable; so he reaches a troubling scholarly conclusion: "this we find, that of British affairs, from the first peopling of the island to the coming of Julius Caesar, nothing certain." Accusing Malmsbury and Henry of Huntingdon of unscrupulously adorning "obscure and bloakish Chronicles" to foster their own ambitions, Milton emotionally embraces another source: "them rather than imitate, I shall choose to represent the truth naked, though as lean as a plain Journal."[13]

One small clue pointing to Milton's conception of how history might be authoritatively presented survives as a single sentence scribbled in longhand in the dairy of Samuel Hartlib, the proponent of practical education to whom in 1644 Milton dedicated the prose tract *Of Education*. Hartlib, himself the author of *Some Proposals toward the Advancement of Learning* and many other texts on education, records in his diary what he has been told by his friend Theodore Haak of Milton's then-current literary activities. Hartlib in 1648 observes that "Milton is not only writing a universal history of England but also an epitome of all Purchas's volumes."[14]

Hartlib's reference to a "universal history of England" would be, of course, to Milton's *A History of Britain*; and the second reference to an "epitome" of Purchas would then allude to the poet's *A Brief History of Moscovia*. Could there be in fact a basis for calling Milton's brief history an "epitome" of Purchas's encyclopedic compendium of voyage literature?

In 1625 Purchas was "Rector of All Hallows, Bread Street Church" and, as Francis Harris Fletcher points out, was "probably known personally to Milton."[15] The poet in his *Commonplace Book* mentions Purchas twice, and at the end of *A Brief History of Moscovia* he cites Purchas as a source.[16] Commentators having an awareness of the note do not support the view that Milton wrote an "epitome" of Purchas. "No epitome of Purchas by Milton is known," writes J. Milton French.[17] "There is no record," comments G. H. Turnbull, " . . . of Milton ever having embarked upon the task of writing an epitome of the works of Purchas."[18] And William Riley Parker remarks that "neither he [Milton] nor any of his early biographers spoke of the epitome of Purchas, which must have been abortive."[19]

Yet Milton in his brief history *did* write an epitome of Purchas. And Purchas's writings, along with related maps and historical-geographic works, served as far more than just a source of imagery and information for selected passages in *A Brief History of Moscovia* and *Paradise Lost*, an influence examined by Robert Cawley.[20] In actually epitomizing Purchas to create a new and advanced example of historical writing, Milton further developed an empirical point of view, an empirical method of historical organization and presentation, and a rich new fund of empirical materials. These he used, integrating them with the visionary poetics of his later years, to produce an epic with special internal form contained in tension within a classical 12-book structure.

Part of the difficulty over the question of influence may come from the fact that Purchas gave the final version of his work a somewhat misleading title ending with the word "Pilgrimes." For Purchas's folios, containing only some pilgrimage materials, represent an attempt to produce that mixed or grand universal history of humankind so desired by Francis Bacon and members of the Hartlib circle. The subtitle to the 1625 edition better describes Purchas's aims and what the author calls and discusses as his "method": "A History of the World, in Sea Voyages, & Lande Travells by Englishmen & others . . . by a world of Eye-witness authors Related."

Purchas begins with accounts of biblical history and what he labels the "fabulous voyages" of the Argonauts, Ulysses, Aeneas and other literary figures. The biblical and classical background soon gives way to documents and firsthand statements on the journeys of the "moderns": first, circumnavigations of the globe; second, voyages around the Cape of Good Hope to the East; third, English voyages to the East; and fourth, other selected voyages to the eastern and western parts of the world. The volumes on the "moderns" take emotional fire with narrations of the prodigous sufferings and startling discoveries of new lands and peoples by, among others, Ferdinand Magellan, Sebastian and John Cabot, Henry Hudson, Vasgo de Gama, and English Admiral Hugh Willoby who died seeking a northeast sea passage through the Arctic Ocean to India.

In a revision of medieval pilgrimage traditions, Purchas now cites India as the goal of journey instead of Jerusalem. He generally abandons the division of history into foreshadowed and fulfilled typological epochs, that is, except in his earliest chapters when he relies on the Bible in discussing Old and New Testament events including King Solomon's sponsorship of a voyage to Ophir, taken by Purchas to be India. In the great body of his folios, he stresses and seeks to uncover an empirical cause-and-effect chronology in history.

In an "Address to the Reader," this author openly acknowledges what are his obvious failures: "the Method, I confesse, . . . could not be therein exact: first because I had such a confused Chaos of printed and written Bookes, which could not easily be ordered; . . . partly because this Method by way of Voyages often repeates the same Countries . . . by diverse of our authors . . . observed." Purchas then invites new authors to use his primary materials and to give practical and theoretical ordering to the work. "Here Purchas and his Pilgrimes," he writes, "minister individuall and sensibile materials (as it were with Stones, Brickes and Mortar) to those universall Speculators for their Theorticall structures" (p. xl).

In a letter to Samuel Hartlib dated 27 June 1648, Benjamin Worsley, a member of the Hartlib circle, lamented the fact that Purchas's invitation had not been accepted. According to Worsley, Purchas's work had been "neglected . . . by our great Bookemen, whereas there is scarse a Genius lives, that may not find some delight in them."[21] This was in the same year, 1648, in which Hartlib wrote in his diary that Milton was working on an epitome of Purchas.

In fact, this longest work then printed in the English language has been cited as inspiring Coleridge's dreams of Xanadu in *Kubla Kahn* and Wordsworth's ruminations on eastern religions in the fourth book of *The Excursion*.[22] But first it influenced John Milton.

In composing *A Brief History of Moscovia*, Milton simply went selectively through the first volume of Hakluyt's *The Principal Navigations* of 1589 and then through the related volumes of *Hak-*

luytus Posthumus or Purchas His Pilgrimes of 1625, choosing and using as sources various accounts of English sea voyages originally launched to find a northeast sea passage to the East. This point had to be researched among the recounted voyages to Russia within the approximately 5,000 folio pages of Purchas's work, for Milton leaves one guessing. He lists 20 different sources at the end of *A Brief History of Moscovia*, Hakluyt and Purchas being just two among the other 18. Yet 19 of the sources appear in the works of both Hakluyt and Purchas, the one exception being Milton's last citation of Jansonius whose name was used only in Purchas.

Milton constructed his brief history, as more than 80 accurate marginal notes show, by using the records of attempted northeast passages to India and China, or later actual journeys to Russia, by Hugh Willoby, Richard Chandler, Clement Adams, Richard Jonson, Henry Lane and others. He almost always uses these records in the order in which they appear in the first volume of Hakluyt's *The Principal Navigations*. Then he turned to *Hakluytus Posthumus or Purchas his Pilgrimes*, where these writings appeared in full or abbreviated form, and went on to study the accounts of Randolph, Josias Logan, Thomas Smith and others. The fact that Milton included a list of sources at all—and only in this one among all his published works—is a tribute to Purchas who, in explaining his new method, insisted upon citations, "Marginal references and annotations" (p. xiv).

In Milton's "Author's Preface" written after the first drafts of his brief history, the poet explains in the manner of Purchas that he is seeking a new historical "Pattern or Example, to render others more cautious hereafter." Milton adds that "What was scatter'd in many Volumes, and observ'd at several times by Eye-witnesses, with no cursory pains I laid together, to save the Reader a far longer travile."[23] And in condensing previously published voyage literature, Milton imitated even Purchas's subtitles. Milton's own subtitle reads: "Relations of *Moscovia*, As far as hath been discover'd by English *Voyages*; Gather'd from the Writings of several Eyewitnesses" (p. 331). With his sensitivity to sight doubtless heightened by his approaching blindness, Milton in advancing his list of sources again emphasizes that the "Relations" are by "either Eye-witnesses, or immediate Relaters from such as were." By substituting a few words, one can see how even this subtitle would have stirred Milton's poetic intuition. Consider the following imagined description of the early books of *Paradise Lost*: "Eden; Or, Relations of Eden, As far as hath been discover'd by Satanic voyages; Gathered from the statements and reactions of an Eye witness."

In the 1640s and early 1650s when Milton was writing his histories and tutoring his nephews, the two Phillips brothers, he was also composing outlines of the proposed theatrical work "Adam Unparadiz'd" which contained lines later to appear in *Paradise Lost*. Milton was then well known to the Hartlib circle. Among Hartlib's papers is a notation mentioning "Mr. Milton's Academie," with "Mr. Milton's" crossed out, probably acknowledging that the poet did not formally establish an academic institution. In his 1644 prose tract *Of Education*, Milton displays his debt to Hartlib's practical educational theories by suggesting that students study trigonometry to learn, among other things, "navigation"; that they take to the sea to grasp what "they can in the practical knowledge of sailing"; and that they study the "use of globes and all the maps, first with the old names and then with the new."[24] Years earlier in his Third Academic Exercise delivered in the 1620s at Christ's College, Cambridge, Milton mockingly denounced scholastic philosophy, explaining exactly how his audience of students should use and benefit from maps:

> But how much better were it, gentlemen, and how much more consonant with your dignity, now to let your eyes wander as it were over all the lands depicted on the map, and to behold the places trodden by heroes of old, to range over the regions made famous by wars, by triumphs, and even by the tales of poets of renown.[25]

Milton's remarks echo those of Abraham Ortelius in his address to the "Courteus Reader" introducing the 1606 edition and other editions of his popular geographic-atlas-history *Theatrum Orbis Terrarum*:

> the reading of Histories doeth both seem to be much more pleasant and indeed so it is, when the Mappe being layed befoe your eye, we may behold things done, or places where they were done, as if they were at this time present and in doing.[26]

Ortelius then remarks upon what he says "any student in Divinitie, or History hath oft made triall":

> how much we are holpen, when as in Holy Scripture, we read of the journey of the Israelites, which they made from Egypt, through the Red Sea, and that same huge Wildernesse, into the Land of promise, when as looking upon the Mappe of Palestina, we doe almost as well see it as if we were there.[27]

Ortelius was named by Milton in 1641 in the tract *Animadversions upon the Remonstrant's Defense*, and some maps from Ortelius's atlas were reproduced in *Hakluytus Postumus or Purchas his Pilgrims*.

In the very popular and famed work *Theatrum Orbis Terrarum*, Ortelius placed "new" world and regional maps, together with extended commentary, in the first section of his study. The second section contained "old" maps with ancient names plainly marked. On these, one could trace the journeys of Jason and the Argonauts, Alexander the Great, Ulysses, Aeneas, Abraham, the 12 tribes of Israel, St. Paul, and other classical and biblical figures.

The evidence suggests that Milton would himself have examined, and would have directed his students to examine, such maps as an aid to the study of biblical and classical literature and history. And it was during this time, Edward Phillips records in his *The Life of Milton*, that the poet wrote and read aloud ten lines of verse describing Satan's journey to Eden, as part of what Phillips calls a projected "tragedy." This passage was later incorporated as lines 31–42 into book 4 in *Paradise Lost*, lines in which Satan laments his fallen state as he descends toward the Garden of Eden.

After blindness struck Milton in the early 1650s, he began to display in written works ever more intense absorption in themes of physical and spiritual vision. Now, understandably, Milton grows conscious of an assumed inner vision, the intuitive-rational conformity of his mind with the supposed immaterial essences of being. But his empirical tendencies remain. Writing to Peter Heimbach in a letter dated 8 November 1656, Milton remarks, "As far as I am concerned, pictures are of little use to me, whose blind eyes wander in vain over the real world." Still, the poet's admission was prompted by inquiries Heimbach had made for Milton about Jansson's *Novus Atlas*, a multivolume work containing world and regional maps elaborately illustrated with miniature line drawings. "Inform me on your return," the poet writes, "of how many volumes the work consists, and which of the two editions, that of Blaeu or Janson, is the more complete and accurate."[28] Completeness and accuracy: these were Milton's empirical requirements for knowledge of the physical world even after he lost his sight.

In providing internal forms for the revelation of history in *Paradise Lost*, Milton, having so pointedly dismissed medieval chronicle histories, elaborated upon heroic journey themes in the literature of the ancients. He drew upon Hakluyt and Purchas in giving these themes a "modern" cast. History is in large measure unveiled in Milton's epic through the sum total of great acts performed during a structured series of voyages.

In books 1–10, the perilous, wandering journeys of Satan and his legions are rendered through allusions to the earthly journeys of exploration by English Admiral Hugh Willoby, the English seamen Adventurers, and the navigators of the Cape of Good Hope. Satan voyages to Eden, corrupts humankind, and returns to Hell to participate in a theatrical pseudotriumph, a demonic entry and public appearance. The figures Sin and Death follow Satan and, though initially turned back, finally succeed in constructing a causeway over Chaos to the Earthly Paradise.

By contrast, the direct, swift journeys of the Son and the angels, dispersed throughout the epic but stressed particularly in the "flashback" narratives of books 6–8, are compactly depicted through terse reference to visionary biblical passages, mainly from the Psalms and the Apocalypse, and to visionary sacred representations. The journeys end in ever more important heavenly theatrical triumphs: the theatrical triumph after the battle with the rebel angels in book 6, the theatrical triumph after the Creation in book 8, and the future theatrical triumphs of the Redemption and of the World's End in book 12. The Son's voyage to Eden to judge humankind in book 10, moreover, is set forth with counterbalancing references to the Son's future triumphs of the Redemption and the World's End. Through the Son, the human race after the Fall will be paradoxically rejoined spiritually to heaven.

The somewhat loosely introduced medieval typology of the last books provides the epochal matrix for a generally ascending line of future spiritual journeys by Noah, then Abraham, next Moses, and finally the Son. The focus of action then returns to the present when, at the conclusion of the epic, the fallen First Parents begin their journey through life.

The "voyage structural elements" in *Paradise Lost* show unmistakably that Milton was subject to the "modern," revolutionary epic conceptions that also inspired Luis de Camões in his composition of the sixteenth century Portugese epic *Os Lusiadas*, a poetic account of Vasco de Gama's voyage around the Cape of Good Hope to India.[29] De Camões's epic had been translated into English by Richard Fanshawe in 1655 and was readily available to Milton. Both de Camões and Milton, moreover, were intrigued by the notion that the voyages of the moderns might actually be more heroic than those of the ancients, a position that Milton, unlike de Camões, never came to accept. Both studied the literature associated with attempts by mariners to find a sea route to India and the East. And both sought "historical" national heroes for their epics. But while de Camões clearly believed in the historical reality and the superior heroism of Vasco de Gama, Milton, after mentioning British King Arthur as a possible figure of heroic song in

Epitaphium Damonis (1639–40), eventually questioned the historical existence of Arthur in book 3 of *A History of Britain*.[30] Then in writing *A Brief History of Moscovia*, Milton pondered the question of whether national heroes could be found in English Admiral Hugh Willoby and those English voyagers who were seeking a northeast sea passage to the East, the British equivalent to the Portugese sea passage around the Cape of Good Hope.

Under the influence of the epic views of the "moderns," of Purchas's "method," and of biblical-classical tradition, Milton ingeniously adjusts point-of-view in *Paradise Lost* by means of a montage of intermeshed eyewitness reports on unfolding narrative episodes. The eyewitnesses react immediately and forcefully to the action, giving powerful emotional emphasis to the supposed reality of what is being seen. All is ultimately observed with human compassion through the mediating intuitive-intellectual vision of the epic narrator.

The first action of the Archfiend in book 1 is to throw round his "baleful eyes" and to look with supernormal angelic vision (1.56); the first act of God the Father is to bend down his eye and so first behold "Our two first Parents" (3.64–65). When the Son in his first great victory triumphs over Satan on the third day of the angelic war in heaven, the virtuous angels are said to have "silent stood/ Eye-witnesses to his Almighty Acts" (6.882–83). Eyewitness corroborative testimony is hardly required here, but Milton the empiricist deems it necessary. In the last two books of *Paradise Lost*, Adam's increasing power to see spiritually and to understand unveils the inward growth of this First Parent, and so helps to give aesthetic coherence to the visions and accounts of future history.

In depicting the journeys of Satan, Sin and Death, a governing metaphor enables Milton to invoke the vast perspectives and dangers of Renaissance voyages. The long and perilous journeys of these demonic beings to that ideal garden said to be "in the East/ Of *Eden* planted" in Assyria (4.209–10)—a place alternately referred to as "another World" (2.347), a "happy Isle" (2.410), a "new world" (2.403)—are events in divine history suggestive of the sights and experiences of mortal explorers searching for or voyaging over eastern sea and land routes to and from India.

On the attempted but impassable northeast route to India around Norway and toward Russia via the Arctic Ocean, whales— a creature associated with biblical Leviathan—were often sighted. Storm battered ships were frequently steered to shore and refitted. Images drawn from Hakluyt and Purchas, as Robert Cawley has shown, relate the prone Satan in book 1 to the seabeast Leviathan "slumb'ring on the *Norway* foam" (1.203). And if Milton wrote of Admiral Hugh Willoby and his northeast voyage in *A Brief History of Moscovia*, the poet in *Paradise Lost* notes that "the tallest Pine/ Hewn on *Norwegian* hills" as a ship's mast for some great admiral is "but a wand" when compared in size to Satan's spear (1.292–94). The speech in hell by Beelzebub proposing a journey to Eden echoes a speech, mentioned in *A Brief History of Moscovia* and recorded by Hakluyt, given by Henry Sidney just before the departure of the Willoby expedition.[31] And the devils who go forth "On bold adventure" (2.571) to explore the "frozen Continent" (2.587) and paradoxical landscapes of hell are in part inspired by Milton's knowledge, as demonstrated in *A Brief History of Moscovia*, of mariners sent out by the English Merchant Adventurers Company to find the northeast passage to India.

But a northeast passage by water, the imagined way, did not exist. And when in *Paradise Lost* the figures Sin and Death are buffeted and halted on their dangerous passage through Chaos, Milton compares their blocked pathway to the great ice fields of the Cronian Sea, the Arctic Ocean, that in fact stopped Willoby and other English on journeys northeast. Sin and Death are trapped in opposing currents of elements

> As when two Polar Winds blowing adverse
> Upon the *Cronian* Sea, together drive
> Mountains of Ice, that stop th' imagin'd way
> Beyond *Petsora*, Eastward

> (10.289–92)

The two evil figures must find another route through Chaos to Eden in the East. In analogy, they go east by land building a colossal bridge over Chaos just as, the epic narrator records comparing "great things to small" (10.306), Xerxes "over *Hellespont*/ Bridging his way, *Europe* with *Asia* join'd/ And scourg'd with many a stroke th' indignant waves" (10.309–11).

The great devils mentioned in books 1 and 2 remain in hell awaiting Satan's return. Many of them were described and drawn in Thomas Fuller's *A Pisgah-sight of Palestine* (1650), a work "hinged" on the view that Old Testament history might be revealed through observation from a mountaintop of the journeys of the 12 tribes of Israel. Fuller describes the wanderings in 12 chapters, and he also discusses certain of the demonic pagan idols referred to by Milton in *Paradise Lost*: Moloch, Astoreth, Thammuz, Dagon and Belial.[32]

The poet in book 1, turning his attention to those sites in the

Near East where the devils have their seats, observes that the chief devils "durst fix/ Thir Seats long after next the Seat of God,/ Thir Altars by his Altar" (1.382–84). Milton thus locates the demonic altars in the general places they occupy on maps in Fuller's *A Pisgah-sight of Palestine*. The altar of the devil Moloch, in fact, appears on a map in Fuller's work in the position described by Milton.[33] Moloch is said to have been

> . . . led by fraud to build
> His Temple right against the Temple of God
> On that opprobrious Hill, and made his Grove
> The pleasant Valley of *Hinnom*, *Tophet* thence
> And black *Gehenna* call'd, the Type of Hell.
>
> (1.401–05)

Though Moloch and the other devils remain in hell, Satan acts as the grand evil voyager and explorer who first discovers, through observation of the oceans and continents of the newly created world, a passage east to Eden. It is a route that the epic narrator compares not to tortuous overland routes east or to the attempted northeast sea passage, but rather to the long, arching southeast sea lane discovered by Vasco de Gama. This sea lane stretches down the west coast of Africa, past the southern tip of the African continent at the Cape of Good Hope, and then on eastward to India.

Satan in hell puts on "swift wings" (2.631), and on these "Sail-broad Vans" (2.927) the Archfiend "scours the right hand coast, sometimes the left" (2.633). He "shaves" the "Deep" (2.634) and journeys to and beyond the Gate of Hell into a tempest-wracked Chaos, "a dark/ Illimitable Ocean without bound" (2.891–92). On a new, far longer and more hazardous voyage than those of the Argonauts or of Ulysses—"ancients" whose voyages were illustrated and available to Milton on maps in Ortelius's volumes—the Archfiend is said to be

> . . . harder beset
> And more endanger'd, than when *Argo* pass'd
> Through *Bosporus* betwixt the justling Rocks:
> Or when *Ulysses* on the Larboard shunn'd
> *Charybdis*, and by th' other whirlpool steer'd
>
> (2.1016–20)

Emerging from Chaos "like a weather-beaten Vessel" with "Shrouds and Tackle torn" (2.1043–44), the wandering Satan flies upward to the lowest stair of heaven where, resting, he views the Gate of Heaven far above.

The epic narrator, revealing the influence of cosmographers' drawings and constructions, states that the gate is so resplendent that it is "inimitable on Earth/ By Model, or by shading Pencil drawn" (3.508–09). Yet the passage implies, too, that the creation below Satan can be to some degree captured in earthly renderings and models. Indeed, the "orbs" observed by the Archfiend that enclose this "pendant world"—the earthly globe "hanging in," not on, "a golden Chain" (2.1051–52)—reflect both classical-biblical conceptions and seventeenth century models of the ordered celestial bodies. Such a model of the earth within the "orbs" could be constructed, according to English cosmographer Joseph Moxon in *A Tutor to Astronomy & Geography* (1665), by stringing a "little Golden Ball" on a brass chain or wire, and by placing this "Ball" of the earth at the center of nested hoops of wood representing "orbs."[34]

When Satan on the lowest stair next looks directly down upon the earth, he sees in a single inclusive view the entire *"Promis'd Land"* with its *"happy Tribes"* (3.531–32). In this instance the Fiend's view is analogous to drawings of all of the Holy Land in atlases by Ortelius and Jansson, and particularly in Fuller's *A Pisgah-sight of Palestine* which also contains illustrations of the 12 tribes of Israel on its maps. Satan then stares upon individual sacred sites identified both on Renaissance maps and in biblical passages such as 1 Kings 4. The Archfiend looks

> From *Paneas* the fount of *Jordan's* flood
> To *Beersaba*, where the *Holy Land*
> Borders on *Egypt* and th' *Arabian* shore
>
> (3.535–37)

Finally, with the scope of his vision growing with surprising swiftness to encompass a new Renaissance world perspective, Satan "Looks down with wonder at the sudden view/ Of all this World at once" (3.542–43). Amazed, he gazes at "far off *Atlantic* Seas/ Beyond th' Horizon; then from Pole to Pole/ He views in breadth" (3.559–61). Here is a vision doubtless inspired by seventeenth century spherical globes that could be turned to show seas beyond the normal horizon, and by conical-lined but flat projections of the whole spherical earth. Like a "modern" who is viewing a graphically delineated model of this world under bright sunlight, Satan sees all with startling clarity:

> Undazzl'd, far and wide his eye commands,
> For sight no obstacle found here, nor shade,
> But all Sun-shine
>
> (3.614–16)

Then hurling himself downward in "flight precipitant" (3.563), the Fiend wends his "oblique way" (3.564) past countless heavenly bodies and through a "new" Renaissance cosmos so vast that, as Marjorie Hope Nicolson has shown, it presages the "sublime" spaciousness that was later to be acclaimed in Romantic poetry.[35] Satan flies in celestial realms that seem even to harbor life:

> Amongst innumerable Stars, that shone
> Stars distant, but nigh hand seem'd other Worlds,
> Or other Worlds they seem'd, or happy Isles,
> Like those *Hesperian* Gardens fam'd of old,
> Fortunate Fields, and Groves and flow'ry Vales,
> Thrice happy Isles, but who dwelt happy there
> He stay'd not to enquire
>
> (3.565–71)

In moving through this universe of the new astronomy, Satan, like a global voyager sailing over uncharted seas on earth, experiences navigational problems.

> . . . Thither his course he bends,
> Through the calm Firmament; but up or down
> By centre, or eccentric, hard to tell,
> Or Longitude
>
> (3.573–76)

On the long journey to Eden, the most formidable barrier to confront Satan is the Gate of Hell. The Gate is significantly compared to the African Cape of Good Hope, the stormy southern strait that often blocked mariners on their way to India. The Archfiend, approaching the Gate with illusions of hope, is first said to be like a drug-laden merchant fleet reflected, mirage-like, in clouds as it plies toward a passage around the southernmost tip of Africa.

> As when far off at Sea a Fleet descri'd
> Hangs in the Clouds, by *Equinoctial* Winds
> Close sailing from *Bengala*, or the Isles
> Of *Ternate* and *Tidore*, whence Merchants bring

Thir spicy Drugs: they on the Trading Flood
Through the wide *Ethiopian* to the Cape

(2.636–41)

And having voyaged on through the universe to the earthly gate
and wall of the Garden of Eden, Satan, like those mariners who
sailed safely past the Cape, is entranced by the fragrant odors
similar to those blown by winds from eastern coasts.

. . . As when to them who sail
Beyond the *Cape of Hope,* and now are past
Mozambic, off at Sea North-East winds blow
Sabean Odors from the spicy shore
Of *Araby* the blest, with such delay
Well pleas'd they slack thir course, and many a League
Cheer'd with the grateful smell old Ocean smiles.
So entertain'd those odorous sweets the Fiend
Who came thir bane

(4.159–68)

In *Paradise Lost* the epic narrator rather surprisingly refers even
to regions and persons discovered by voyagers to the Western
Hemisphere. Before the Fall of Adam and Eve, the narrator explains, snow was unknown "From cold *Estotiland,* and South as
far/ Beneath *Magellan*" (10.686–87). And in a most remarkable
analogy, the epic narrator compares the leaves worn by the First
Parents after the Fall to the dress of American Indians:

. . . Such of late
Columbus found th' *American* so girt
With feather'd Cincture, naked else and wild
Among the Trees on Isles and woody Shores.

(9.1114–17)

Here in the 1674 edition of *Paradise Lost* is a new Renaissance
literary vision of a globe transformed. From the northern reaches
of "Estotiland" or Labrador to the southernmost Straits of
Magellan in the New World, from the Cronian Sea or Arctic Ocean
south to the tip of the African Cape of Good Hope in the Old
World, the physical earth stands revealed before the reader in a
fashion that irretrievably breaks the constraints and many of the
correspondences of the old medieval iconographic cosmography.
Through analogies, metaphors, and direct or oblique allusion, the
epic narrator's mimetic verse depiction of this earth—fallen and yet

containing vast and previously unknown continents and seas—
gives further meaning to the sad but spiritually adventurous departure of Adam and Eve from the Garden: "The World was all
before them, where to choose/ Thir place of rest" (12.646–47).
Unlike Dante in the *Commedia* who is constantly led by guides in
human form, the First Parents in Milton's epic will wander
through the world as Reformation figures with an invisible "Providence thir guide" (12.647). Among their progeny will be those few
holy persons who, fired in "Spirit and Truth" by a new Reformation individualism, will become God's

> . . . living Temples, built by Faith to stand,
> Thir own Faith not another's: for on Earth
> Who against Faith and Conscience can be heard
> Infallible?

> (12.527–30)

Milton's representation of a new kind of epic hero, like his
representation of a new earth, arises from unusual sources. In
considering an epic "Subject for Heroic Song," Milton in the
Invocation to book 9 admits that after "long choosing, and beginning late" he decided against an "Argument" centered upon
"fabl'd Knights/ In Battles feign'd" (9.25–30). Not "sedulous by
Nature to indite/ Wars, hitherto the only Argument/ Heroic
deem'd" (9.27–29), the poet obviously searched British history for
some epic "heroic" action performed, if not by warring King
Arthur whose very existence was in question, then by some other
English leader or voyager. Although Milton discovered in ancient
and modern voyage literature that new empirical "method" for
presenting and ordering history—the "method" employed
together with biblical and classical devices to give internal form to
Paradise Lost—he found no suitable epic British action or hero.

Drawing upon his early theatrical writings, Milton then invented *Paradise Lost* from his outlines of the theatrical sacred
representation "Adam Unparadiz'd" that focused, of course, upon
Adam and Eve. He introduced into his epic a series of theatrical
shows and triumphs on biblical themes, and he introduced too the
progressive, counterpoised visionary-empirical voyages that un-
veil universal Christian history through eyewitnesses. All was
then daringly contained within a traditional classical 12 book epic
structure.

But because Milton concluded that the dangerous voyages of the
English "moderns" were only "almost heroick," he used them
primarily as an analogue and metaphor for the journeys of evil

figures in *Paradise Lost*. He thus created in his visionary epic a modern counterpart, focused on evil figures, to the heroic voyage of Vasco de Gama in de Camões's then modern epic *Os Lusiadas*.

"The discovery of *Russia* by the northern Ocean, made first, of any Nation we know, by *English* men," Milton writes in opening the final chapter of *A Brief History of Moscovia*,

> might have seem'd an enterprise almost heroick; if any higher end than the excessive love of Gain and Traffick, had animated the design. Nevertheless that in regard that many things not unprofitable to knowledge . . . are hereby come to light, . . . good events ofttimes arise from evil occasions. (363–64)

Consequently, Milton relates the secular sea voyages east to the journeys of Satan, Sin and Death to Eden in the East. And in so doing, the poet further elaborates what Arthur O. Lovejoy has termed the Paradox of the Fortunate Fall by introducing the Paradox of the Fortunate Evil Journey.[36] Good will come and humankind will be redeemed as the result of Satan's voyage for evil ends.

"For it may be truly affirmed," Francis Bacon stated in the introduction to *The Advancement of Learning* in 1625, "that this great building of the world had never through-lights made in it, till the age of us and our fathers. . . ." The through-lights that Bacon saw, as he endeavored to find effective empirical methods to implement the grand designs of the new philosophy, radiated from sea exploration. Bacon thought that this activity offered experimental proof that theory could predict and grasp something of the true nature of external reality. After more than a century of stunning advances in cartography and navigation, the Lord High Chancellor of England had come to consider the sailing of uncharted oceans an experimental enterprise. For after embarking from the ports of England and Europe, many seamen of Bacon's time risked their lives on the "truth" of fragile navigational calculations and disputed cosmographical theories. Those who were fortunate, sometimes after great physical suffering and agonies of uncertainty, recorded in emotionally charged accounts how their formulations and hopes were at last realized in those moments when the strange shores of a New World, unseen before by people of central Europe, rose like a longed-for dream over the edge of the great ocean. Though Bacon in the *Advancement* and other works turned always to the Book of God's Words as a true text on matters of faith, he sought to open new pages in the Book of Nature by hinging his new philosophy on the experimental method that seemed demonstrated in his own age in voyages of exploration. "And this proficience in navigation and discoveries," he continued in the *Advancement*, "may plant also an expectation of the further proficience and augmentation of all the sciences."[37]

Centuries before, Dante in the *Commedia* reflected the medieval view of the physical world as a true Book of God's Works, a volume teeming with iconographic markings from which humanity could learn of things earthly and divine. Dante accepted that spiritual essences were resident in relics and holy sites, and that persons could grow in spirit through ritualistic meditative-physical pilgrimages past patterned formations of icons that on earth led to Jerusalem, at the center of the geographical world, and to eternal Rome, at the center of Empire. The *Commedia*, like the great cathedrals of the late Middle Ages, thus imitated in its iconographic structures the medieval Books of God's Words and Works. In inventing the literal sense of the *Commedia* in general as a historically true fulfillment of historically true events, Dante focused attention upon his own sequential fulfillment in the world beyond life of the Exodus, Redemption and Transfiguration as pointed to in God's two great books.

Spenser saw the medieval iconographic world, under the pressure of Renaissance exploration and empiricism, shift and alter under his eye. The Book of God's Words, interpreted from Renaissance perspectives, remained a font of spiritual truth that, augmented by classical ideas of virtue, underlay ideology and religious and moral values. But the great cosmic emblems of order depicted in the Book of Nature—particularly the T-and-O icons of the physical world—were disintegrating with each new publication of Ptolemaic and Mercator-inspired representations of the earth. And the popular emblem books of the sixteenth century showed a fractured variety of designs sometimes unabsorbed into the larger medieval iconographic framework. Spenser in his epic, as has been seen, nonetheless mirrored the antique Book of the World with considerable imaginative amusement, but with keen reminders that a new empirical world had been discovered and interposed upon the old. The point within the circle, the medieval icon of the earth and the cosmos, served the poet in *The Faerie Queene* as a basic iconographic structural device. The meandering line of the journey through this world became an emblem for quests and adventures in an imaginative realm. And the iconographic stations, temples, sites, creatures and knights in the antique book served as icons reflected in imaginative emblematic temples and places and characters of the land of faery.

It was left for John Milton in *Paradise Lost* seriously to merge and commingle the new Book of Nature with the old, all the while holding to the spiritual authority of the Book of God's Words.

Changes in iconographic tradition changed heroic poetry. And in England even in Spenser's time, the general decline of the old medieval iconographic vision of nature was perhaps most evident in the decline of ancient "Glassenbury," the British New Jerusalem that for centuries had been linked to the medieval world's center of Jerusalem. Throughout the sixteenth century, the revered tower on the summit of "Glassenbury" Tor, reflected in Gloriana's crystal tower Panthea in Spenser's epic, continued to stand silhouetted against coastal skies above moorlands celebrated in Christian legend and faeryland myth. But in 1536 commissioners of Henry VIII burned Glastonbury Abbey, carried off the sacred relics in bags, and arrested Abbot Richard Whiting. He was later executed on the summit of the Tor. In Elizabeth's reign, legend held that a zealous Puritan, seeking to destroy what he regarded as superstitious relics, cut down a holy thorn tree said to have miraculously sprouted on the site where Joseph of Arimathea first struck his staff into English ground.[38]

The Isle of Glass nevertheless remained sharply in the consciousness of John Dee in his *Perfect Arte of Navigation* (1577). Part new cosmographer and mathematician, part spiritualist and part charlatan, Dee had advised Queen Elizabeth to support the British northeast voyages of exploration to Russia that so absorbed and influenced John Milton. Dee was emotionally drawn to the ancient iconographic world of relics and stations even as, through his cosmographical and navigational studies, he made place for the new. In a sad panegyric reminiscent of the lament of Petrarch for the dead saints in the eternal city of Rome, Dee eulogized the passing of the spiritual glory of ancient Avalon:

> O Glastonbury, Glastonbury: the Treasury of the Carcasses of so many famous, and so many rare Persons, . . . How Lamentable, is thy case, now? . . . the names of many other, most excellent holy Men, and Mighty princes . . . yet, that Apostlelike *Joseph*, That Triumphant *British Arthur*, And now, this Peaceable, and Prouident *Saxon, King Edgar*, do force me, with a certayn sorrowfull Reuerence, here, to Celebrate thy Memory.[39]

200

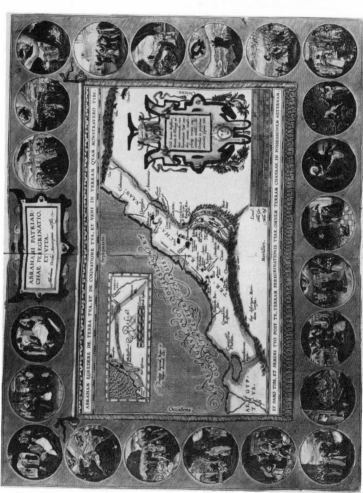

44. A splendid color map of the wanderings of Abraham, including a frame of circular illustrations disclosing the life of the patriarch, that is found in Abraham Ortelius's *Theatrum Orbis Terrarum* (1606). Milton mentions the work of Ortelius in his prose tracts, and the poet introduces Abraham's journey as a typological episode in book 12 of *Paradise Lost. Courtesy of the Huntington Library.*

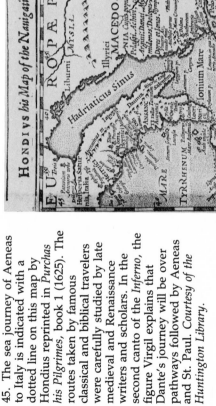

45. The sea journey of Aeneas to Italy is indicated with a dotted line on this map by Hondius reprinted in *Purchas his Pilgrimes*, book 1 (1625). The routes taken by famous classical and biblical travelers were carefully studied by late medieval and Renaissance writers and scholars. In the second canto of the *Inferno*, the figure Virgil explains that Dante's journey will be over pathways followed by Aeneas and St. Paul. *Courtesy of the Huntington Library.*

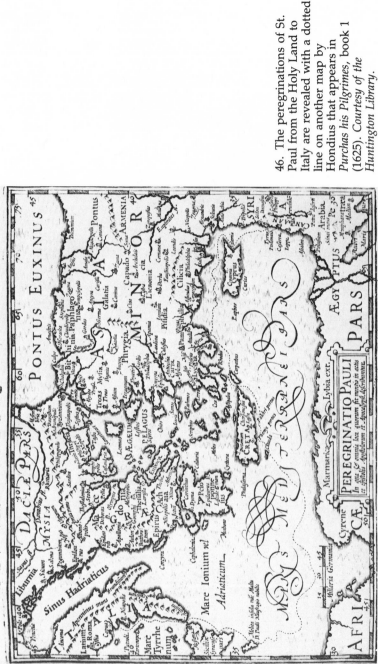

46. The peregrinations of St. Paul from the Holy Land to Italy are revealed with a dotted line on another map by Hondius that appears in *Purchas his Pilgrimes*, book 1 (1625). *Courtesy of the Huntington Library.*

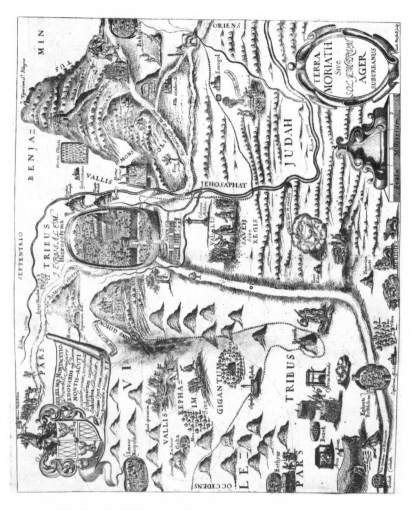

47. The temples of the devils Moloch and Chemosh appear directly to the right of Jerusalem on this map from Thomas Fuller's *A Pisgah-sight of Palestine* (1650). In *Paradise Lost*, Milton similarly depicts Moloch's temple as built "right against the Temple of God," with the "seats" of other devils also "next to the Seat of God,/ Thir Altars by his Altar" (1.383–84, 402). These two devils are referred to in 1 Kings 11.7. *Courtesy of the Huntington Library.*

204

48. Devils of Milton's *Paradise Lost*. In this illustrated pantheon of idols, Thomas Fuller presents many of the demonic figures later to appear in Milton's epic—among them, Baal, Dagon, Moloch, Tammuz and Chemoch. *From A Pisgah-sight of Palestine (1650). Courtesy of the Huntington Library.*

I haue here for the Readers pleasure, set before his eyes Mercators *Mappe or Topography of Paradise.*

PARADISUS

49. The Earthly Paradise, here depicted in general desert regions to the east of the Dead Sea, on a Holy Land map by Mercator and reprinted in Samuel Purchas, *Purchas his Pilgrimes,* book 1 (1625). Milton, writing of Eden in *Paradise Lost,* also avoids locating the garden exactly, but the poet does refer to the Earthly Paradise as "this Assyrian Garden" (4.285) and so implies that it existed in the Near East. *Courtesy of the Huntington Library.*

50. In the Bishops' Version of *The holy Byble*, printed by Richard Iugge in 1574, Adam is shown in the company of friendly animals in Eden. The frame is composed of scenes from Genesis, scenes very similar to those represented by Milton in book 11 of *Paradise Lost*. *Courtesy of the Huntington Library.*

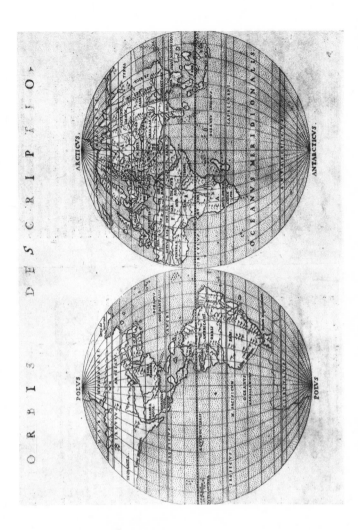

51. Sixteenth century projection of the entire world from Claudius Ptolemaeus, *La Geographia di Clavdio Tolomeo Alessandrino*. Maps of this kind would have influenced Milton who in *Paradise Lost* depicts Satan in flight viewing "all this World," gazing "Beyond th' Horizon; then from Pole to Pole" (3.554, 560). *Courtesy of the Huntington Library.*

52. Map of Norway, the northern seas and countries from Ortelius's *Theatrum Orbis Terrarum* (1606). English merchant adventurers of the sixteenth and seventeenth centuries sailed around Norway vainly seeking a "Northeast Passage" by water through Russia to India, a hoped-for passage that Milton called the "imagin'd way" (*Paradise Lost* 10). *Courtesy of the Huntington Library.*

53. The Capes and Pole referred to by Milton in *Paradise Lost*. This striking projection of the Old World Cape of Good Hope (*upper right*), the New World Straits of Magellan (*upper left*) and the unknown continent at the South Pole appears in Ortelius's *Theatrum Orbis Terrarum* (1606). The framed space for a caption remains mysteriously empty, a suggestion that further designations depend upon the discoveries of future explorers. *Courtesy of the Huntington Library.*

54. Ezekiel's fiery wheel with its four creatures as illustrated in the Geneva Bible (1576), printed by Christopher Barkar. This biblical wheel, signified in the figurism of some wheel windows, is also alluded to in Milton's description of the Chariot of the Son: "Flashing thick flames, Wheel within Wheel, undrawn,/ Itself instinct with Spirit, but convoy'd/ By four Cherubic shapes. . . ." (*Paradise Lost* 6.751–53). *Courtesy of the Huntington Library.*

Dante's Alleged Subversion of Divine Order

Inferno 10

It has long been held that Dante, by giving such powerful individuality to Farinata degli Uberti and the elder Cavalcante in *Inferno* 10.31–130, subverts a sense of their low position in the divine order and so undermines the spiritual hierarchy of the *Commedia*.

The critical argument for Dante's supposed subversion of the hierarchical poetic cosmos was put forward by Erich Auerbach in *Mimesis: The Representation of Reality in Western Literature*, trans. Willard Trask (Princeton, 1953), 174–232, and is quoted by Giuseppe Mazzotta in *Dante: Poet of the Desert* (Princeton, 1979), 231–32.

"By virtue of this immediate and admiring sympathy with man," writes Auerbach:

> the principle, rooted in the divine order, or the indestructibility of the whole historical and individual man turns *against* the order, makes it subservient to its own purposes, and obscures it. The image of man eclipses the image of God. Dante's work made man's Christian-figural being a reality, and destroyed it in the very process of realizing it. (202)

Auerbach bases this conclusion on Dante's extraordinary power and poetic virtuosity in unveiling the human, earthly passions and thoughts of the two heretics. Under the influence of the Reformation views and philosophical dialectic of Hegel, who is cited, Auerbach says of the contemptuous, caustic and arrogant Farinata who rises from a burning tomb: "We cannot but admire Farinata" (200). Weeping Cavalcante, whose head alone at first appears above the tomb, asks questions about his son on earth; and so is surprisingly found by Auerbach to exhibit a "belief in the autonomous greatness of the human mind" (172). Thus Auerbach restates a Hegelian argument in claiming that Dante, by means of character representation, "opened the way for that aspiration toward autonomy which possesses all earthly existence"; and "we" are said to wish to "weep with Cavalcante" (200).

Human sympathy, at least for Cavalcante, is indeed elicited by the representation. But the difficulty with Auerbach's aesthetic-ideological critique is that it reflects a nineteenth century Hegelian outlook but makes no mention of medieval Averroism, a central theme of the episode and one of the abiding explicit and implicit themes in Dante's *Commedia*. Through the *contrapasso* actions and speeches of the excessively arrogant Farinata and the excessively helpless Cavalcante, the poet by means of event and radically individualized characters presents an aesthetically effective satire of heretics dedicated to Averroistic doctrines. Such doctrines are attacked and in some measure unveiled in St. Thomas Aquinas's *De Unitate Intellectus Contra Averroistas* (ca. 1270), trans. Beatrice H. Zedler (Milwaukee, 1968). Aquinas, organizing his treatise under two main topics, first offers a rebuttal to the Averroistic contention that the intellect is separate from the body, a view that Dante bluntly mocks by having Farinata rise in body and mind from an infernal tomb. Next, Aquinas takes issue with the Averroistic doctrine that there is for all persons one universal intellect that apprehends universal ideas in the present, a doctrine that Dante stunningly satirizes by creating heretics who have highly individualized knowledge of the past and future, but who lack and yet desire highly individualized knowledge of the present.

Dante's characterizations are unforgettable. But given the prominence of Averroism as a heresy in the poet's period, educated medieval readers would, it seems to me, have considered the Farinata-Cavalcante scene as an embodiment—not a refutation—of traditional hierarchical scholastic views of the person and the universe.

Anthony K. Cassell in *Dante's Fearful Art of Justice* (Toronto and Buffalo, 1984) urges that the "stance of both Farinata and Cavalcante, once the latter too rises to full height," is the figural antithesis of "a new Gothic vision of a naked Christ," a vision captured beginning in the twelfth century in icons and art works showing Christ standing "'waist-up,' alone and unsupported in his sarcophagus." Noting that Emile Mâle believed the prototype for this new devotional image to be the twelfth century mosaic icon of the Passion in the Church of Santa Croce in Gerusalemme, Rome, Cassell points out that the Santa Croce mosaic "commanded particular veneration as a pilgrim station especially on Passion Sunday and Good Friday." Cassell records that the subject matter and origin of the mosaic are in dispute, but he maintains that "there are certainly enough examples of the 'Imago pietatis' dating close to Dante's time and experience to prove the Poet's most intimate familiarity with it." He writes of the Santa Croce mosaic, however, that "if Mâle's thesis were right, we could be sure that Dante viewed it on his Roman pilgrimage during the Jubilee Year of 1300" (24–25).

Dante's Journey in Body and Spirit

On the Allegory of the *Commedia*

Although total consistency in Dante's long and complex poem is not to be expected, a general critical posture toward the allegory of the *Commedia* is surely necessary. This study takes exception to the once traditional view that the *Commedia* is primarily an allegory of the poets with a fictional literal sense, a view recently restated by G. Paparelli in "Ficto: la definizione dantesca della poesia," *Ideologia e poesia di Dante* (Firenzi, 1975), 53–138. Charles Singleton in *Dante Studies I* (Cambridge, Mass., 1954) and *Dante Studies II* (Cambridge, Mass., 1958) has persuasively urged that Dante in the *Commedia* should be considered as writing theological allegory with a "historical" literal sense. Readings of the spiritual senses of Dante's theological allegory have been offered by Robert Hollander in *Allegory in Dante's Commedia* (Princeton, 1969) and Pompeo Giannantonio in *Dante e l'allegoismo* (Firenzi, 1969).

Recent reinterpretations of the poet's allegory often tend to overstate, in my view, genuine themes and elements in Dante's verse. John Freccero in "The Dance of the Stars: *Paradiso* X," *Dante: The Poetics of Conversion*, ed. Rachel Jacoff (Cambridge, Mass. and London, 1986), 224–25, reprinted from *Dante Studies* 86 (1986): 85–111, calls attention to fictional elements in *Paradiso* in cautiously suggesting that Dante, supposedly using the "technique and terms" of Plato while under the "inspiration" of the Bible, "seems to fashion his representation according to what might be called the allegory of the poets." Freccero notes in particular Beatrice's statement in *Paradiso* 4.37–63, that the physical appearance of souls in the sphere of the moon, far from their true seats in the Empyrean, is arranged by heaven so that Dante can have appropriate sensible matter from which to abstract intellectually and so to understand. Interpreting this physical appearance as Dante's accommodation of Platonic myth, Freccero too quickly abandons distinctions in claiming that "the structure of the *cantica* depends, not upon a principle of *mimesis*, but rather upon metaphor: the creation of a totally new reality out of elements so disparate as to seem contradictory by any logic other than that of poetry" (222).

The "reality" of the canto, however, is not "totally new." While the positioning of souls in lower spheres can in part be considered a possible concession by Dante to Platonic myth, it is nevertheless again apparent that in *Paradiso* as elsewhere in the *Commedia*, the souls themselves—through Dante's application of a historical and mimetic worldly and biblical typology—continue to fulfill beyond life their prefiguring earthly reality.

Freccero does not mention that Beatrice also states that these souls in the sphere of the moon are not like—"non e simile"—those discussed by Plato in the *Timaeus*, souls that Plato, according to this lady, falsely says receive their "forma" from Nature in the stars to which they are supposed to return (*Par.* 4.49–54). Beatrice adds that Plato may possibly be correct only if he means that the influence of the souls is evident in the stars (*Par.* 4.58–60). By contrast, Beatrice defends the souls' outward manifestation in the moon's sphere by an appeal to the authority of the Bible. This lady explains to Dante, as Freccero observes, that the truth of Scripture similarly "condescends to your capacity, and attributes hands and feet to God having other meaning" (*Par.* 4.43–45: "condescende/ e vostra facultate, e piedi e mano/ attribuisce a Dio e altro intende").

Something more than vague biblical "inspiration" is at work here. Freccero chooses to emphasize certain external and adjusted accidental material forms—elements in the sensible veil shrouding transcendent reality—that are in part based upon the poet's seeming accomodation of Platonic myth. Dante mentions the myth but emphasizes the necessity of adjusting accidental material forms to reveal an underlying reality resting upon biblical truth. The poet in theory as well as practice, while introducing mythic elements, thus continues to present souls as figural creations in what is essentially a historical "allegory of the theologians." Dante's "artistic" problem in depicting souls as moving beings with transformed physical bodies in changing or changeless realms beyond life is taken up in my "Three Typological Modes," *The Invention of Dante's Commedia*, 112–15.

Examining what he regards as Dante's special visionary and yet secularized "theological allegory," Gian Roberto Sarolli in his forcefully argued *Prolegomena alla Divina Commedia* (Firenze, 1971)—aware of how the other world of the poem points back *in figura* to Empire, Church and society on earth—strains his interpretation, it seems to me, in transforming Dante the reformer into a kind of divinely ordained prophetic missionary, and the *Commedia* into a form of fiery prophecy that is assumed to be focused primarily upon issues of earthly world order. And Giuseppe Mazzotta in *Dante: Poet of the Desert*, accepting what is here regarded as Auerbach's *mis*interpretation of the Farinata episode (see Appendix A) and citing the failure during Beatific Vision of some of Dante's faculties, leans too much toward an insistence upon the discontinuity and "fragmentation" of the language and meaning of the *Commedia*.

Taking a modern idealist posture that the "only eternal referent" upon which Dante based the truth of the *Commedia* is a transcendent God, Teodolinda Barolini in *Dante's Poets: Textuality and Truth in the Commedia* (Princeton, 1984), 90–91, elaborating upon an argument espoused by Mazzotta and not addressing the range of criticism on Dante's poetic uses of the Bible and the world, advances forms of the authorial autonomy and the poetic discontinuity theories in insisting that Dante, "unchecked" and with "absolute freedom and authority," reassigns new values entirely on his own to the world and to history. "Because none of us can check with God as to what Dante saw, or . . . as to the fidelity of Dante's transcription," writes Barolini of *Purgatorio* 24 and *Paradiso* 10, "the apparently humble role of scribe results in a license to write the world, in fact to play God unchecked." Barolini assumes that God alone, not the Bible and the world, serves as Dante's only index to truth. Barolini provides most subtle and revealing insights into how Dante acts as an original critic and historian of poetry; but in discussing Dante's philosophic-theological attitudes toward universal history, the iconographic Book of the World and poetic invention, Barolini, by adopting an idealist philosophic perspective, arrives at critical conclusions that, I think, require qualification. "The *Comedy*," she writes, "respects no truth but its own, least of all that composite and approximate truth men know as history"; and she asserts that the poetic "strategy of the *Comedy* is that there is no strategy."

While fundamentally accepting Singleton's view of the *Commedia* as theological allegory, I nonetheless cannot agree with Singleton's claim that the earthly action "shadowed" or "reflected" in Dante's otherworldly pilgrimage concerns *only* the abstract, interior spiritual experiences of heart, mind and soul—the *"itinerarium mentis ad Deum"*—of the reader or wayfarer (see Singleton, especially *Dante Studies II*, 4–12). Rather, experiences of *body*, heart, mind and soul can be seen to be encompassed in foreshadowing earthly action that, for critical and historical theological-philosophical reasons, definitely also needs to be regarded as historically "true." A. C. Charity in *Events and their Afterlife* has properly argued against Singleton's purely "abstract" view of reflected earthly action, observing that the foreshadowing and "historical" earthly "journey is a life lived, not just thought of" (253).

Erich Auerbach, therefore, rightly insisted upon the necessary historicity and continuity of both foreshadowing earthly types and fulfilled otherworldly antitypes. Charity, conscious of Incarnation theology, effectively disclosed that the figurism of Dante's own biblically ordered journey beyond life refers back to foreshadowing concrete, historical events in the poet's earthly life. And in *Dante the Maker* (London and Boston, 1980), William Anderson, who has been seen to be equally aware of Incarnation theology, appropriately integrated material and spiritual elements by interpreting the historical types and antitypes of Dante's twofold Great Circle Egypt-Jerusalem-Rome and otherworldly journey in the light of the spiritual senses of theological allegory and the *itinerarium mentis ad Deum* of meditative tradition.

Notes

NOTES TO CHAPTER ONE

1. Georges Duby in *The Age of the Cathedrals, Art and Society, 980–1420*, trans. Eleanor Levieux and Barbara Thompson (Chicago, 1981), analyzes the cathedrals as types for the cosmos and the city of heaven, and discusses parallel elements in the "cosmic" philosophical-theological views of Abbot Suger, builder of St. Denis in Paris, and of St. Bernard, Abbot of Clairvaux and Dante's last guide in the *Commedia*. Duby, placing primary emphasis upon French structures, concludes his study of cathedral building projects of the 1250–1280 period by remarking that the "*Divine Comedy* may be regarded as a cathedral, the last." Calling attention to one of several clerical teaching orders in Dante's home city, Duby suggests that the poet "based the *Commedia* on what he had learned of scholastic theology from the Dominican preachers of Florence who had studied at the university of Paris. Like the great cathedrals of France, the poem leads in successive stages, according to the enlightened hierarchies of Dionysius the Areopagite and through the intercession of Saint Bernard . . . and the Virgin, to the love that moves the stars. As a poetics of the incarnation, the art of the great cathedrals had wonderfully celebrated the body of Christ, in other words . . . the world itself" (187).

In *The Gothic Cathedral: Origins of Gothic Architecture and the Medieval Concept of Order* (Princeton, 1956), Otto von Simson reveals how the cosmic typology of the medieval cathedral, like that of Dante's *Commedia*, is based upon an imitation of the work of God realized in the created universe, and the word of God realized in the Incarnation. Simson notes too that the cathedral in its symbolism is "at once a 'model' of the cosmos and an image of the Celestial City" (35–37). Commenting upon the "archetypes of the Christian sanctuary" that "actually inspired the medieval builder," Simson makes the now well recognized point that, in general, the figural structure of the medieval "church was conceived as an image of the Celestial Jerusalem, but . . . the Celestial Jerusalem in turn was thought to have been prefigured in the Solomonic Temple" (11).

Other recent discussions of the medieval cathedral as a type of the cosmos include those by Charles Terrasse, in his chapters "Le miroir de la nature" and "Le miroir historique" in *La cathedrale: miroir du monde*, rev. ed. (Paris, 1954), 72–89, 112–14; William Anderson and Clive Hicks, *Cathedrals in Britain and Ireland from early times to the reign of Henry VIII* (New York, 1978), 13–19; and Wim Swaan, *The Gothic Cathedral*, intro. Christopher Brooke (New York, 1969), 48–56.

215

In *L'Italia nella Divina Commedia* (Milano, 1923), Paolo Revelli, citing specific T-and-O world maps and other early geographic-iconographic materials, offers authoritative insights into Dante's medieval iconographic view of the world. See in particular the chapters "Le terre che Dante vide" (1–13), "La cultura geografica di Dante" (3–27), "Dante e le carte del suo tempo" (31–40). Excellent examples of medieval T-and-O maps of the thirteenth and fourteenth centuries—maps showing Egypt, Mt. Sinai and Jerusalem—can be found in *Monumenta Cartographica Vaticana*, 2 vols. (Città del Vaticano, 1944).

Very general comments on the world as a book—without allusion to medieval iconographic cosmography, T-and-O icons, or pilgrimage iconography in literature and churches—appear in Umberto Eco, *Art and Beauty in the Middle Ages*, trans. Hugh Bredin (New Haven and London, 1986), 56–60. "Interpreting the world allegorically meant interpreting it like the Bible," Eco rightly observes, "for the theory of Biblical exegesis was thought to be valid also for nature" (59). In his remarks on cathedrals, however, Eco takes note only of their biblical but not their world book figurism (62). Michel Foucault in *The Order of Things: The Archaeology of Human Sciences*, trans. n.n. (London, 1970), 17–36, writes on what he believes to be four kinds of similitudes in pre–sixteenth century prose representations of the world as a book of signs and symbols; but he does not examine comparative poetic, visual and architectural world book iconography nor the early ideology governing artistic and architectural disciplines.

2. *Chroniche Fiorentine*, trans. Rose E. Selfe, ed. Philip H. Wicksteed (London, 1906), book 8, sec. 36, pp. 320–21. See too *Inf.* 18.28–33, for Dante's well-known and presumably eyewitness reference to pilgrims in the Jubilee Year of 1300 crossing the bridge of Castel St. Angelo before St. Peter's Basilica.

3. A reproduction of the illustration appears in Peter Preiger, Millard Meiss and Charles S. Singleton, *Illuminated Manuscripts of the Divine Comedy* (Princeton, 1969), vol. 2; plate 6b of Chantilly Musee Conde MS 579, fol. 33.

4. John Leyerle includes an interpretation, diagrams and photographs of the San Zeno wheel window in "The Rose-Wheel Design and Dante's *Paradiso*," *University of Toronto Quarterly* 40.3 (Spring 1977): 280–307. Leyerle maintains that the iconographic meaning, movement, form, and the optical and light effects associated with both spoked wheel windows and petal or floral wheel windows are variously reflected in passages in the *Roman de la Rose* and the heavenly rose episode of the *Commedia*. The passages suggest, Leyerle argues, that merged elements in the wheels were recognized in the thirteenth century as "rota-rosa" iconography. This point is supported in this study, in the case of Dante, given the nature and pattern of the unfolding, "temple" pilgrimage typology evident in the *Commedia*. B. Knapp offers further arguments for the "rota-rosa" interpretation, first proposed by Leyerle at a conference, in "A Note on Roses and Wheels," *Comitatus* 1 (1970): 43–45. See also Giuseppe C. Di Scipio's contextually unlikely and yet still possible claim in "The Symbolic Rose in Dante's *Paradiso*," City University of New York Doctoral Dissertation, 1977, pp. 150–77, that the eight personages mentioned as appearing in the outer ring of Dante's rose are the *only* ones in the ring; and that they

must be considered as located, not in an arc at the top as traditionally supposed, but evenly spaced around the entire circumference like outer figures in an eight-petal, wheel-rose window. Di Scipio presents a symbolic and numerological analysis favoring this view in "The Structure of the Rose in Dante's *Paradiso*," *Canadian Journal of Italian Studies* 2.1–2 (Fall–Winter 1978–1979): 19–39.

5. For example, see Erwin Panofsky, *Gothic Architecture and Scholasticism* (Labrobe, 1951) and H. O. Tayler, *The Classical Heritage of the Middle Ages*, rev. ed. (New York, 1911), 315ff. See also the comparative, analogical structural analysis of Dante's *Vita Nuova* and figural elements in Gothic cathedrals in Jerome Mazzaro's *The Figure of Dante: An Essay on the Vita Nuova* (Princeton, 1981), 51–70.

6. Giovanni Fallani in *Dante e la cultura figurativa medievale* (Milano, Firenze, Roma, 1971) shows the influence of a great range of medieval art works upon Dante, including the Byzantine, but without associating the works specifically with architectural figurism.

7. For citations to the voluminous body of pilgrim texts, together with readings of Great Circle Egypt-Jerusalem-Rome pilgrimage typology in the *Vita Nuova* and the *Commedia*, see John G. Demaray's "Patterns of Earthly Pilgrimage in Dante's *Commedia*: Palmers, Romers, and the Great Circle Journey," *Romance Philology* (Nov. 1970): 239–58; and *The Invention of Dante's Commedia* (New Haven and London, 1974). The especially famed pilgrimage practices on the Jerusalem "ring" of Redemption stations, involving the greatest number of Latin pilgrims and Crusaders to the Near East through the centuries, are figured in varying ways both in Dante's Eden and in later Roman Catholic stations-of-the-Cross ritual. Practices on the remote stations of the Exodus, involving fewer persons, were generally lost to Catholic ritual but are apparent in figured actions on the slopes of Dante's Mt. Purgatory. The Transfiguring stations of Rome, figured at the end of Dante's *Paradiso*, entered formally into Catholic Jubilee Year ritual, of course, with Boniface VIII's proclamation of the Jubilee pilgrimage of 1300. Dante's wide knowledge of Holy Land pilgrimage sites has been documented by a former Franciscan Custodian of the Holy Land, Fr. P. Ferdinando Diotallevi, in the inclusive *Dante ed i luoghi santi* (Jerusalem, 1921). Fr. Diotallevi draws attention to a range of references in the *Commedia* to medieval Holy Land pilgrimage stations, but he does not develop a structured interpretation of the poem.

In reading the *Commedia* as an allegory of the theologians, William Anderson in *Dante the Maker* (London and Boston, 1980) relates the great circle Egypt-Jerusalem-Rome pilgrimage typology of the poem's literal sense to the spiritual senses of allegory, particularly as reflected in the steps of traditional meditative literature. Anderson, striking a welcome critical balance in discussing Dante's medieval conflation of the physical and the immaterial, reveals how spiritual and visionary meanings are joined in the *Commedia* with a "historical," figural imitation of worldly and biblical events. Elaborating upon the identification of Dante's Eden as a fulfilled antitype of the earthly Jerusalem, and of the poet's heavenly city of the rose as the fulfilled antitype of Rome, Anderson maintains that "just as Jerusalem is a stage on the Great Circle pilgrimage for reaching the final goal of Rome, so Beatrice points to the civilization that will appear with the world emperor and the Christianization of the themes of antiquity" (372–73).

Peter Armour in *The Door of Purgatory: A Study in Multiple Symbolism in Dante's Purgatorio* (Oxford, 1983) has recently argued that the "special religious and redemptive significance" of the Jubilee year of 1300 pilgrimage to Rome accounts for the central symbolism of the *Commedia* (154). In this symbolic reading that leans heavily upon empirical facts about Dante's life, Armour accepts that Dante's movement to the rose in *Paradiso* reflects an earthly Romer's pilgrimage to the eternal city; but by placing what seems to me too much weight upon empirical biographical evidence at the expense of medieval figural relations, he takes issue with the view that the poet's journey beyond in *Purgatorio* is the fulfillment in the literal sense of a foreshadowing terrestrial pilgrimage from Egypt to Jerusalem. "The main difficulty in this theory," he writes, "is, of course, that, whilst there is some evidence that Dante made a pilgrimage from Florence to Rome, there is none at all that he ever made one to the Holy Land" (160). Armour, however, incorporates the symbolic meaning of the full Great Circle journey into his interpretation of Dante's pilgrimage to the heavenly rose: "Under one aspect, his journey is an exodus and pilgrimage of a living man from the Egypt of this world to a Holy Land and the New Jerusalem (*Par.* 25.55–56). Perhaps it is that pilgrimage which, because of Boniface's indifference, Dante was unable to make in his real life (cf. *Par.* 9.126, 136–38). Under another aspect, it is also a transformation of a pilgrimage which he almost certainly did make to Rome, and so he chose to express the personal and the universal redemptive significance of the poem, setting it also in the Jubilee year" (159). For a typological analysis of what constitutes Dante's "real" past life and earthly pilgrimage, see footnote 44 and Appendix B.

8. The text of the *Commedia* used throughout is Dante Alighieri, *La Divina Commedia secondo l'antica vulgata*, ed. Giorgio Petrocchi, 4 vols. (Milano, A. Mandadori for the Società Dantesca Italiana, 1965–69) and reprinted in the edition of C. H. Grandgent, rev. Charles S. Singleton (Cambridge, Mass., 1972).

9. See Charles S. Singleton's notes for *The Divine Comedy: Paradiso, 2. Commentary* (Princeton, 1975), 576–78.

10. For comments on Dante's Beatific Vision in *Paradiso* as the "inceptive cause" of the *Commedia*, see Helen Dunbar, *Symbolism in Medieval Thought* (New York, 1961), 29–30; Anderson, *Dante the Maker*, 335–37; Erich Auerbach, *Dante: Poet of the Secular World*, trans. Ralph Manheim (Chicago, 1961), 94; and Demaray, *The Invention of Dante's Commedia*, 59–63.

11. As John Freccero has shown in "The Sign of Satan," *Modern Language Notes* 80 (1965): 11–26, Satan with his six grotesque wings in the "tomba" of the pit of hell is an antitype for the Redeeming Christ on the cross in Jerusalem.

12. Grabar in his comprehensive *Martyrium: Recherches sur le culte des reliques et l'art Chretien antique*, 3 vols. (Paris, 1943–1946) provides an analysis of how religious edifices such as old St. Peter's, St. Paul's, the Lateran, St. Vitale in Ravenna, San Stefano in Bologna and other European structures were designed to a significant degree as figural reflections of the round Church of the Holy Sepulchre or Byzantine basilica Martyria in the Near East. Martyria in Rome and elsewhere in the west, Grabar shows, were constructed over the relics of saints and holy persons and used as pilgrim shrines. In disclosing the Near Eastern Byzantine influ-

ence on the typological form of European medieval religious edifices, Grabar, in volume one (1946) includes actual or projected ground plans of the fourth century Church of the Holy Sepulchre (fig. 37); the Church of the Nativity, Bethlehem (fig. 27); Old St. Peter's, Rome, with its two southern circular Martyrii (fig. 22); Old Maria Maggiore, Rome (fig. 46); the crypt of St. Apollinare, Ravenna (fig. 118); medieval plans for circular Martyrium structures by Fra Giocondo, Florence (fig. 74); and the old Abbey of St. Augustine with its round Martyrium, Canterbury, about 1050 A.D. (fig. 91). Photographs are contained in volume three (1946) of fifth century Byzantine mosaics, in the apse of St. Pudenziana in Rome, of pilgrimage sites in Jerusalem (pl. 39); and of a number of Byzantine Transfiguration mosaics of similar design in the Church of the Transfiguration, St. Catherine's Monastery, Mt. Sinai; in St. Apollinare, Ravenna (pl. 41); in St. Vitale, Ravenna; and in SS. Cosma and Damiano, Rome (pl. 42). See also Jean Paul Richter, *Die mosaiken von Ravenna* (Wien, 1878), 103–04, for an early comparison of the Transfiguration mosaics at St. Apollinare and the Church of the Transfiguration, Mt. Sinai.

Numerous medieval bottles and amulets, excavated in the small northern Italian town of Bobbio and depicting images of the cupola of Christ's Jerusalem tomb and other Holy Land pilgrimage sites, are examined by André Grabar in *Ampoules de Terre Sainte* (Paris, 1958). See also Grabar's *l'iconoclasme byzantine; dossier archeologique* (Paris, 1957).

In an important study, Richard Krautheimer examines figural architectual reproductions of the Rotunda or Anastasis of the Holy Sepulchre in "Introduction to an 'Iconography of Medieval Architecture,'" first published in the *Journal of the Warburg and Courtault Institutes* 5 (1942), 1–33, and reprinted with a postscript and additional bibliography in Krautheimer's *Studies in Early Christian, Medieval, and Renaissance Art* (New York and London, 1969), 115–50. Krautheimer argues that even the "Baptistery of S. Giovanni at Florence" and other baptisteries, though having forms derived in part from those of ancient mausolea, at times "went further and actually copied the model of the Anastasis in Jerusalem, where Christ had risen from His tomb, setting the prototype of resurrection and symbolically of baptism" (138–39). And Ernest Hatch Wilkins, without referring to the wider literature and iconography of the Latin-Byzantine pilgrimage tradition, maintains that the thirteenth century, Byzantine-style mosaics on the lower band of the S. Giovanni Baptistery copula influenced the depiction of Dante's entry into the Earthly Paradise, the otherworldly realm that has been found to contain actual antitypes for the "Temple" of the Holy Sepulchre in Jerusalem ("Dante and the Mosaics of his 'Bel San Giovanni,'" *Speculum* 2 (1927): 1–10, reprinted in *Dante in America: the First Two Centuries*, ed. A. Bartlett Giamatti (Binghamton, 1983), 144–59. Also see note 39). Giovanni Fallani, concentrating in detail upon edifices and art works in medieval Italy in *Dante e la cultura figurative medievale* (Milano, Firenze, Roma, and other cities, 1971), 99–100, has called attention to iconographic similarities in the processional Byzantine mosaics of St. Apollinare, Ravenna and St. Paul's, Rome; and in the figural representation of Beatrice's processional appearance with her train in the Earthly Paradise.

European and English figural imitations of the Church of the Holy Sepulchre and other Jerusalem edifices are discussed by Alfred W.

Chaplan, *St. John of Jerusalem, Clerkenwell* (London, 1922), 38–42; and by
Elizabeth Wheeler Schermerhorn, *On the Trail of the Eight-Pointed Cross:
A Study of the Heritage of the Knights Hospitallers in Feudal Europe* (New York,
1940), 300–05. English round churches as types of the Holy Sepulchre are
examined by William St. John Hope, "Round Naved Churches of
England," *Report of the Chapter General for the Year 1916* (London, 1916) in a
contemporary British Hospitallers Association publication; Henry W.
Fincham, "The Priory Church of St. John at Clerkenwell," *The Journal of the
British Archeological Association* (December 1911): 183–89; Charles Lucas,
"Eglises Circulaires," *Des Annales de la Societe Central des Architectes* 12, first
series (1881): 39–64.

13. For accounts of the long pilgrimage recorded in an international
body of pilgrim texts, see the fine compendium of twelfth and thirteenth
century texts recently gathered together with notes by Franciscan editor
Sabino de Sandoli in *Itinera Hierosolymitana Crucesignatorum*, 3 vols. (Jerusalem, 1978–1981). A bibliography of medieval French pilgrim texts on the
Exodus route, published by the French Oriental Institute, appears in
Mahfouz Labib's *Pèlerins et Voyageurs au Mont Sinai* (Cairo, 1961). A great
variety of representative Holy Land pilgrimage narratives have been
collected in *Itinéraires à Jérusalem et Descriptions de la Terre Sainte*, ed. Henri
Michelant and Gaston Raynoud (Geneva, 1882); *Itinera Hierosolymitana et
Descriptiones Terrae Sanctae*, ed. Titus Tobler and Augustus Molinier (Osnabruck, 1966); *Itinéraires Russes en Orient*, ed. B. De Khitrowo (Osnabruck,
1966); and *Deutsche Pilgerreisen nach dem Heiligen Lande*, ed. Reinhold
Rohricht (Osnabruck, 1967). Selected narratives of medieval English pilgrims to the Holy Land, along with a bibliography of medieval pilgrim
texts published in English, can be found in Franciscan editor Eugene
Hoade's *Western Pilgrims* (Jerusalem, 1952).

14. In an incisive exposition affording insight into Dante's processional
pilgrimage typology based in part upon the Book of God's Words, the
Scriptures, Georges Duby points out that "history was a song of glory . . .
fitted into the liturgy." Universal history, he notes, was conceived as
unfolding in "one continuous procession." He adds that "the Scriptures,
which were no different from a history, described it [universal history] as a
gradual ascension in three phases. The New Testament—the second
phase—had smoothed out the rough spots that remained in humankind
during the first phase, prior to the Incarnation. . . . The processions to
and within the abbey churches were symbolic realizations of history. They
completed the last phase as they mimed the entry into the Kingdom of
Heaven" (*The Age of Cathedrals*, 79–80). For an account of the influence of
Jerusalem pilgrimage traditions on the medieval liturgy, particularly in
Rome, see Johan Chydenius, "The Typological Problem in Dante," *Societas
Scientiarum Fannica: Commentatione Humanarum Litterarum* 25 (Helsingfors,
1958): 70–86. The figurism of Holy Land places and events, as expressed in
medieval liturgy and then reflected in the *Commedia*, is analyzed by
Fr. Dunstan Tucker, "The *Divine Comedy* and the Liturgy of Holy Week,"
Orate Fratres 14 (1940): 204–11; "Baptism in Dante's *Purgatorio*," *Orate
Fratres* 15 (1940): 112–22; and by Lizette Andrews Fisher, *The Mystic Vision
in the Grail Legend and in the Divine Comedy* (New York, 1917), 87–116. See
also the study of the development of religious ritual from pilgrimage
traditions in chapter 16, "Medieval Christianity: Religion to Ritual," in

Jonathan Sumption, *Pilgrimage: An Image of Medieval Religion* (Totowa, New Jersey, 1975), 289–302.

15. Referring to classical and medieval rhetorical works on the poetic uses of memory, Barbara Nolan in "The *Vita Nuova*: Dante's Book of Revelation," *Dante Studies* 88 (1970), shows how Dante as narrator "first of all aligns the story of his love for Beatrice with the pattern of Old and New Testament accounts of man's gradual growth in love and knowledge of God"; and then by disclosing his "personal history, in Florence over the course of fifteen years, participates by imitation in the cosmic history of salvation" (53). Cast in "figurative, enigmatic revelations," this personal history, she writes, is a demonstration of "human memory discovering meaning in history" and "indicates directions which point unmistakably to the *Commedia*" (51, 53, 76). Marianne Shapiro in "Figurality in the *Vita Nuova*: Dante's New Rhetoric," *Dante Studies* 97 (1979), further discusses Dante's rhetorical techniques and figural participation in biblical history, including the Christological typology of the *peregrino spirito* of sonnet 41 in the *Vita Nuova*, in reading the work primarily as an "allegory of the theologians" (107–27). V. A. Kolve in *Chaucer and the Imagery of Narrative: The First Five Canterbury Tales* (Stanford, 1984), 9–58, cites Dante, among many other medieval authors, in presenting illustrations of how medieval writers employed memory in their selection and disposition of imagery. Dante, Kolve observes, uses "images born of sense experience with the secular world" in creating an allegory of "multivalent significance" that is "anchored in history" (46, 296). See also Philip H. Wicksteed, *From Vita Nuova to Paradiso: Two Essays on the Vital Relations between Dante's Successive Works* (London and New York, 1922), for general remarks on two "visions" of Dante, one at the end of the *Vita Nuova* and the other at the end of *Paradiso*.

16. All quotations from the *Vita Nuova* are from *Le Opere di Dante Alighieri*, ed. E. Moore, rev. Paget Toynbee, 4th ed. (Oxford, 1924).

17. A detailed reading of Dante's full Egypt-Jerusalem-Rome Great Circle pilgrimage and biblical typology, together with references to primary pilgrimage sources and related scholarship and criticism, appears in the notes and text of Demaray, *The Invention of Dante's Commedia*, 9–92, 133–85. This study is an elaboration of earlier publications: "Pilgrim Text Models for Dante's *Purgatorio*," *Studies in Philology* (Jan. 1969): 1–25; "The Pilgrim Texts and Dante's Three Beasts, *Inferno* I," *Italica* (Winter, 1969): 233–41; and "Patterns of Earthly Pilgrimage in Dante's *Commedia*: Palmers, Romers, and the Great Circle Journey." Carol V. Kaske in "Mount Sinai and Dante's Mount Purgatory," *Dante Studies* 79 (1971): 1–18, offers an excellent interpretation, referring to past figural studies including the work of A. C. Charity, of the typological relationship of Mt. Sinai and Mt. Purgatory. See also the early study by Rodolfo Benini: "Il grande Sion, il Sinai e il piccolo Sion," *Rendiconti della Reale Accademia dei Lincei*, 5th ser. 23: 1–25. Benini presents original but somewhat impressionistic readings, using medieval geographical writings but not pilgrim texts, in arguing that Mt. Purgatory is modeled after a partly mythical, partly geographical "Grand Sion," a mountain that was thought to rise to the sphere of the moon and that was composed of the combined peaks of Horeb, Pharan and Sinai. Interpretations of Dante's journey up Mt. Purgatory have been related to the biblical Exodus by Charles Singleton, particularly in "'In

Exitu Israel de Aegypto,'" *Seventy-Eighth Annual Report of the Dante Society* (1960); 1–24; and by Fr. Dunstan J. Tucker, "'In Exitu Israel de Aegypto': The Divine Comedy in the Light of the Easter Liturgy," *The American Benedictine Review* 11 (March–June 1960): 43–61. See too Singleton's "'Sulla fiumana ove 'l mar non ha vanto,'" *The Romanic Review* 39 (December 1948): 269–77; and John Freccero's "The River of Death: *Inferno* II, 108" in *The World of Dante: Six Studies in Language and Thought*, ed. S. Bernard Chandler and J. A. Molinaro (Toronto, 1966), 26–41.

Among studies associating the *Commedia* with the Jubilee Pilgrimage of 1300 are C. Carboni, *Il Giubileo di Bonifazio VIII e la Commedia di Dante* (Roma, 1901); R. Zingarelli, *Dante e Roma* (Roma, 1895); Lonsdale Ragg, *Dante and His Italy* (New York and London, 1907); Thomas Caldecot Chubb, *Dante and His World* (Boston and Toronto, 1966), 23–46; Fr. Herbert Thurston, *The Holy Year of Jubilee* (Westminster, Maryland, 1949), 10–27; William Anderson, *Dante the Maker*, 152, 278–381; and Peter Armour, *The Door of Purgatory*.

Julia Bolton Holloway in *The Pilgrim and the Book: A Study of Dante, Langland and Chaucer* (Berne and New York, 1987) adds considerably to pilgrimage readings by showing how the biblical Emmaus pilgrimage episode, mentioned by Dante in *Purg.* 21.7–11 and acted out in the medieval *Officium Peregrinorum* liturgical drama, merges thematically with Exodus and related pilgrimage motifs in the *Commedia*. Holloway offers further Exodus pilgrimage analysis in "Dante's *Commedia*: Egyptian Spoils, Roman Jubilee, and Florence's Patron," *Studies in Medieval Culture* 12 (1978): 97–104; and also in her presently circulating manuscript on the medieval 42 pilgrimage stations of the Exodus and Dante's *Vita Nuova*.

18. See Demaray, "Invention from the Book of God's Words," *The Invention of Dante's Commedia*, 116–31.

19. *Life of Constantine*, trans. John H. Bernard, intro. and notes T. Hayter Lewis (London, 1896), 89.

20. Vergilio C. Corbo in *Il Santo Sepolcro di Gerusalemme: Aspetti archaelogici dalle origini al periodo crociato*, 2 vols. (Jerusalem, 1981) presents a reconstruction of the fourth century Anastasis or Rotunda of the Holy Sepulchre, based on recent excavations and early texts, in the form of a circular nave within a lower ambience, semicircular in the back and rectangular in front. (See the outlined reconstruction in vol. 2, Tavola 3). After examining the site and the evidence, however, I agree with Richard Krautheimer's reservations, cited in the Postscript to "Santo Stefano Rotondo and the Holy Sepulchre Rotunda," *Studies In Early Christian, Medieval, and Renaissance Art* (New York and London, 1969), about Corbo's proposed plan: namely, that "this reconstruction is so contrary to the descriptions beginning with Egeria's in the late fourth century and continuing with Arculf's that . . . the results of further examination of the structure" should be awaited (105).

See the discussions, supported by illustrations, of the Near Eastern Byzantine influence on the processional-pilgrimage designs of medieval European round churches, basilicas and cathedrals in André Grabar, *Martyrium*, 3 vols.; Richard Krautheimer, *Studies in Early Christian, Medieval, and Renaissance Art*; G. Bandmann, *Mittelalterliche Architektur als Bedeutungstrager* (Berlin, 1951); and Otto von Simson, *The Gothic Cathedral*.

21. *The Gothic Cathedral*, 81.

22. See Hermann Kern's comprehensive *Labyrinthe* (Munchen, 1982), particularly the chapter "Kirchen-Labyrinthe" (206–18). A catalog of known medieval church labyrinths is provided together with photographs and drawings of various designs (219–41). Included too is a catalog of known labyrinths of the Chartres type (211), and a chapter on medieval church and outdoor labyrinths in Great Britain (243–53). See also Paolo Santarcangeli, *Le livre des labrinthes: Histoire d'un mythe et d'un symbole*, trans. from the Italian by Monique Lacau (Paris, 1974), 272–301. Santarcangeli gives accounts of inlaid stone labyrinth floors over which medieval pilgrims and sometimes holy ritualistic dancers moved in figured imitation of Exodus or divine peregrinations to the earthly and heavenly Jerusalem (215–20, 296–98). Because, as Santarcangeli notes, many of these floors in France and elsewhere were destroyed during religious wars and during the French Revolution, the full number once existing cannot be accurately fixed. See also the description and photographs of the twelfth century world T-and-O mosaic map in the floor of the romanesque Church of St. Salvatore, Turin, materials published by Ernst Kitzinger, "The World Map and Fortune's Wheel: A Medieval Mosaic Floor in Turin," *Proceedings of the American Philosophical Society* 117, no. 5 (Oct. 1973): 344–73.

23. See William H. Matthews, *Mazes and Labyrinths: Their History and Development* (New York, 1970), reprinted from the 1922 edition, 65–68, for speculations on the possible medieval uses and significations of church labyrinths. Erwin Panofsky in *Early Netherlandish Painting: Its Origin and Character*, vol. 1 (Cambridge, Mass., 1964), 132–39, though not directly commenting upon labyrinths, points out how in late medieval and Renaissance paintings and illuminations, new Gothic structures were represented as arising from the depicted earthly ruins of earlier pagan or other constructions. It should be noted that even pilgrim Dante, on Mt. Purgatory's terrace of the proud, walks upon sculpture showing the ruins of Troy (*Purg.* 12.61–69).

24. *Rose Windows* (San Francisco, 1979), 98–99. See also Santarcangeli, *Le livre des labyrinthes*, 291–92. The Chartres labyrinth was known to medieval pilgrims as the "station of Jerusalem." A ninth century manuscript from the Abbey of Saint-Germain-des-Pres contains a drawing of an identical labyrinth with a minotaur at the center, leading to speculation that in early times the Chartres labyrinth may also have signified the pathway to the pagan world center at Crete.

Jean Vilette in "L'enigme du labyrinthe," *Notre-Dame de Chartres* 58 (March 1984): 4–12, has recently called attention to the figural relation of the west wheel-rose and the labyrinth. Even the size of the two structures, he notes, is similar, for the labyrinth is only about half a meter smaller in diameter than the rose window. John James in "Chartres: Les constructeurs," *Societé Archéologique d'Eure-et-Loir* 3 (1982), finds the labyrinth a second axis of the church nave, corresponding in ground plan to the main axis at the intersection of nave and transept (206).

Labyrinth designs, as Kern in *Labyrinthe* points out (206–18), lead to medallions or hubs sometimes signifying *in figura* unholy as well as holy centers. The focal point of journey can sometimes be interpreted as representing, in hierarchical order: the center of hell or the underworld; the old pagan center of Troy; the later pagan center of Crete; and on a higher level of figural fulfillment, the "true" spiritual-geographic center of the earthly Jerusalem, a type for the heavenly city.

Dante in the *Commedia* reflects a traditional medieval view of earthly directional figurism evident in the labyrinths, but the poet causes this earthly directional figurism to converge on the city of Rome as a center and goal. Dante states that he will follow in the footsteps of Aeneas, who in the *Aeneid* is described as journeying from Troy to the eternal city (*Inf.* 2.20–33). Dante refers also to the statue of an Old Man signifying humanity standing at the pagan center of Crete, a statue with eyes turned toward Rome but with shoulders pointing toward Egyptian Damietta (*Inf.* 14.103–120). Studies have shown how the shoulders indicate a traditional crusading-pilgrimage pathway, one followed even by St. Francis, to or past the old pagan world center to Damietta and then to the Holy Land. The statue faces the final goal of long pilgrimage: Rome.

See Rodolfo Benini, "Il grande Sion, il Sinai e il piccolo Sion," *Rendiconti della Reale Accademia dei Lincei*, 5th ser. 23 (Roma, 1915): 8–10; Demaray, *The Invention of Dante's Commedia*, 150–54; and Anderson, *Dante the Maker*, 290–93. See also Anderson's diagram of the statue and the travel route to Jerusalem via Crete, Damietta and Mt. Sinai; and to Rome from Jerusalem or Troy (292, fig. 13).

Church labyrinth figurism can be seen in a general way as an analogue to Dante's labyrinth-like circular hell arranged in tiers leading down to Satan, and to the more ordered circular terraces of Mt. Purgatory leading up to an Eden that figures Jerusalem. However, the poet's movements in Eden and soaring ascent through the spheres both fulfill and transcend the figurism of nave labyrinth designs, and, in developing further analogues, the wider earthly and cosmic figurism of churches needs to be examined.

In a work that has just appeared, *The Idea of the Labyrinth from Classical Antiquity through the Middle Ages* (Ithaca and London, 1990), Penelope Reed Doob perceptively relates labyrinth themes and patterns in the *Commedia* to pagan legends, particularly of Cretan Minos and the Minotaur, while pointing out that such pagan labyrinth materials are "subsidiary" to "the definitive importance of Exodus as a shaping influence" (279). Doob sees the labyrinth pattern as influencing the form of Dante's *Inferno*, *Purgatorio*, and what she terms "the amphitheater of the elect in *Paradiso* 30" (285); and she offers helpful readings of the Minotaur and Minos as figures in Hell. But because Doob does not study the Christian pilgrimage typology of the physical world and the cathedrals—a typology in which the circle of a Christian holy city fulfills and transcends the winding labyrinth of Crete, just as cathedral wheel windows fulfill and transcend nave labyrinth floors—she tends to overstress the significance of "subsidiary" pagan labyrinth designs upon Dante's Christian rose of heaven in *Paradiso* 30. The perfect circle of the rose, like the heavenly temple of the angels in *Paradiso* 28, fulfills and transcends pagan labyrinth patterns. The perfected Christian icons are quite different, containing at most only shadows or vestiges of their subsidiary pagan types.

25. Kern, *Labyrinthe*, 211. The manuscript of the *Commedia* is catalogued in the Vatican Library as Ms. Barb. Lat. 4112, Fol. 209r.

26. Cowen, *Rose Windows*, 8–10.

27. See Corbo, *Il Santo Sepolcro di Gerusalemme*. Georges Duby in *The Age of the Cathedrals* rightly claims that the origins of European typological

imitations of the "Temple" of the Holy Sepulchre can in large measure be traced to pilgrims. "When the pilgrims to the Holy Land arrived at their journey's end and entered the Holy Sepulchre," he writes, "the structure they entered was round. . . . Hence the popularity of this type of architecture. In the eleventh century it spread through the Empire as far as Slavic borders" (24). In *Il S. Sepolcro Riprodotto in Occidente* (Jerusalem, 1971), Damiano Neri, examining the plethora of medieval figural imitations of the Holy Sepulchre built by the Knights Templar and others throughout Europe, maintains that by the eleventh century such construction projects had become a European "mania" (95). Neri discusses the figural models of the sepulchre erected in numerous Italian cities including Rome, Florence, Pisa, Bologna, Milan and Borgo S. Sepolcro. Neri observes too that the Holy Sepulchre Ceremony of the Holy Fire, an Easter candle-lighting ceremony that commences in the cupola tomb of Christ at the center of the round Anastasis in Jerusalem, was imitated *in figura* annually at Easter in medieval Florence after pilgrims were said to have brought reports of the ceremony from the Holy Land (78–79).

In writing of the Knights Templar constructions in Florence, Neri points out that the Knights were associated with an eleventh century hospital with a church attached near the Ponte Vecchio, and that two Florentine documents dated 1189 and 1299, respectively, refer to a temple of the "Sancti Supulcri" near the "Pontis Veteris" (68–69). In *Inf.* 10, Dante, speaking to the heretical Florentine Farinata, remarks upon orations given in "nostro tempio," presumably the existing temple in their home city (10.87).

See George Jeffery's "The Holy Sepulchre in Jerusalem Reproduced as a Pilgrim Shrine in Europe," and "Lesser Copies of the Holy Sepulchre in different parts of Europe" in *A Brief Description of the Holy Sepulchre* (Cambridge, England, 1919), 195–219. See also Pamela Sheingorn's *The Easter Sepulchre in England*, Early Drama, Art and Music, Ref. Ser. 5 (Kalamazoo, 1987), which contains an opening chapter on architectural reproductions of the Holy Sepulchre in Europe and later chapters on the relation of Easter ritual to medieval drama.

28. See Jeffery's *A Brief Description*, 8–9, for an analysis of the St. Pudenziana mosaics in the light of the pilgrimage tradition.

29. See E. Venturini, *The Eternal City* (Roma, 1963), 108–16; Herbert Thurston, *The Holy Year of Jubilee: An Account of the History and Ceremonial of the Roman Jubilee* (Westminster, Maryland, 1945), 171–97. The location and appearance of sites and churches in Rome can be found in the medieval work, translated into several languages and available in the French version entitled *Les Merveilles de la Ville de Rome* (Roma, 1650). See also Constantine Carboni, *Il Giubileo di Bonifazio VIII e la Commedia di Dante* (Roma, 1901); and the recent association of specific Jubilee Year 1300 pilgrimage sites in Rome with Dante's rose of *Paradiso* in Peter Armour's *The Door of Purgatory: A Study of Multiple Symbolism in Dante's Purgatorio* (Oxford, 1983), 154–68.

30. The design of Constantine's Old St. Peter's, together with an account of the rose window added in the sixth century in the eastern facade, appears in James Lees-Milne's *Saint Peter's* (London, 1967), 63–122. In Paul Letarouilly's *The Basilica Of St. Peter* (London, 1953), an analysis of the structure and ornamentation of the basilica is accompanied by 16

plates showing reconstructed elements of the ediface. See also the reconstruction of St. Peter's as drawn by Frazer in Richard Krautheimer, *Studies in Early Christian, Medieval, and Renaissance Art*, fig. 12; and the reconstruction by Alfarano in André Grabar, *Martyrium*, vol. 1, fig. 22, with commentary, 293–305.

31. *Croniche Fiorentine*, 320.

32. Heinz Skobucha, *Sinai* (New York, London, and Toronto, 1966), 88–89.

33. Skobucha in *Sinai* discusses the chapels and offers evidence of the excellent relations between the seventh century Sinai bishop, John Climacus, and later bishops of Sinai and the Papacy (78, 84, 94–98). In the seventh century Pope Gregory the Great corresponded with Bishop John Climacus and warmly praised him; and in Dante's period, Popes Gregory X (1271–1276) and John XXII (1316–1334) both issued written statements renewing the traditional Papal protection given to St. Catherine's Monastery and its possessions. Pope John XXII alone produced 11 documents affirming his fatherly love for the Greek monks of the monastery, and this Latin pope repeatedly supported, in written briefs, the rights of the Greek monastery to property on Cyprus and Crete against the claims of the Venetians.

The Monastery of St. Catherine and its legendary "angelic" desert monks rested secure in a deep desert location beyond the bloody conflicts of the Crusades and even somewhat removed from Eastern and Western political and religious rivalries. This monastery, constructed largely in the sixth century, had never been sacked. It was unique in containing within its walls a twelfth century mosque and, in its library, a spurious firman from Mohammed granting protection. At this famed pilgrimage center where clerics and pilgrims of different nationalities and cultures intermingled, language barriers were overcome as Copts, Greeks, Latins, Syrians, Russians and others shared common Exodus pilgrimage experiences in climbing the holy mountain of God. The pilgrimage pathways and carved rock steps leading from the monastery up terraced Mt. Sinai included, in Dante's time, a stone Gate of Confession through which pilgrims passed, sometimes confessing their sins to a guardian monk, and a ring of Old Testament stations ascending to the supposed rock on which Moses received the Law.

It is sometimes assumed that, because in the last few centuries there has been little cultural or artistic interchange between the Greek monastery of Mt. Sinai and the Latin West, there was little or none in earlier periods. Yet the body of Latin pilgrim texts from the fourth century through Dante's period—together with historical evidence of the surprisingly good relationship between Popes, Latin clerics and pilgrims, and the "heretical" but honored Greek desert fathers—suggests that such interchange was steady and influential.

34. Paul Sabatier, *Life of St. Francis of Assisi*, trans. Louise Houghton (New York, 1894), 234–300. Sabatier includes a useful critical study of primary sources, 347–432. P. Girolamo Golubovich, *Biblioteca Bio-Bibliografica della Terra Santa e dell' Oriente Francescano* (Firenze, 1906) 1.1–7, contains historical records on St. Francis's period in Egypt and the Holy Land.

35. An account of the history of the La Verna area, of the holy shrines and stations of the "Pellegrino alla Verna," and of the medieval "scala"

ascended by pilgrims on the mountain La Verna, appears in Piero Bargellini and Vittorio Vettori, *Amoroso viaggio in terra francescana* (Firenzi, 1949). The Camaldolese eremetical movement and establishments are reviewed on pp. 34–45. See also Johannes Jorgensen, *Pilgrim Walks in Franciscan Italy* (London and Edinburgh, 1908), 171–76.

36. *Patrologiae Cursus Completus*, Series Graeca, ed. J. P. Migne (Paris, 1860), vol. 88, p. 582. The Latin translation of the *Scala Paradisi* appears in vol. 88, pp. 581–1210. In the *Scala Paradisi*, John Climacus's 30 meditative steps to God are illustrated with stories of virtue from the lives of the "angelic" desert fathers. Step seven includes an account of the Mt. Sinai cell and holy activities of St. Stephanos, the sixth century monk who gained legendary fame as the Warder of Mt. Sinai's stone Gate of Confession.

Greek and Latin manuscripts of Climacus's *Scala Paradisi*, often with illuminations showing pilgrims in postures of penitence or climbing a ladder, circulated in Europe in Dante's period. See, for example, John J. Tikken's review of the eleventh or twelfth century Vatican illuminated manuscript copy in "Eine illustrierte Klimax-Handschrift der Vatikanischen Bibliothek," *Acta Societatis Scientiarum Fennicae* 19, no. 2 (1893): 3–16; M. Heppell's study of more than 30 manuscript copies in Slavic monasteries in "Some Slavonic Manuscripts of 'Scala Paradisi,'" *Byzantinoslavica* 18, no. 2 (1957): 233–70; and John Rupert Martin's published collection of ladder illustrations from Greek and Latin sources in *The Illustration of the Heavenly Ladder of John Climacus* (Princeton, 1954). Martin confirms that the Latin translation of the work appeared "at least as early as the thirteenth century" (6). Climacus and Bonaventura were apparently associated as meditative writers, moreover, in the late Italian translation *Santo Iouanni Climacho Altrimenti Scala paradisi* (Venezia, 1492), for the small pietas illustrating leaf 2b had previously appeared in an edition of the works of Bonaventura.

37. P. Girolamo Golubovich in *Biblioteca Bio-Bibliografica della Terra Santa e dell' Oriente Francescano*, vol. 2 (Firenze, 1913), cites records showing that the Franciscans established houses in Egypt and the Holy Land at Damietta in 1220; Jerusalem, 1230; Jaffa, 1252; and Acre, 1217; and he provides evidence of the approximate dates for the establishment of other Franciscan houses at Nicosia, ca. 1252; Alleppo, ca. 1251; Sidon, ca. 1253; Tripoli, ca. 1255; and Tyre, ca. 1255–1256. Further information on the considerable chain of Franciscan houses in the Holy Land, a chain staffed almost exclusively by clerics from Italy who assisted pilgrims, has been published in Martiniano Roncaglia, *Storia della Provincia di Terra Santa* (Cairo, 1954), vol. 1, pp. 34–63; and P. Agustin Arce, *Miscelanea de Terra Santa* (Jerusalem, 1974), vol. 3, pp. 77–81. Fr. Sabino de Sandoli in *Il Primo Convento Francescano in Gerusalemme: 1230–1244* (Jerusalem, 1893), 1–33, maintains that the first Franciscan house in Jerusalem opened in 1217 near what is now the third Station of the Cross on the Via Dolorosa. Golubovich in *Serie Cronologica dei Reverendissimi Superiori di Terra Santa* (Jerusalem, 1898), 3–11, lists the Italian Franciscans, a number of them from Tuscany, who in Dante's period served as the reverend superiors of the Holy Land.

Paolo Revelli in *L'Italia e il Mar di Levante* (Milano, 1917), provides an informative and most revealing analysis of the strong commercial and cultural associations between Italian and Near Eastern cities in the thirteenth and fourteenth centuries, associations studied in his review of the eastern Mediterranean outposts and colonies of Rome (32–50), Venice (66–78), Genoa (79–97) and other Italian cities. Revelli discloses some 31 Italian colonies or establishments, some of considerable size, in the eastern Mediterranean in the fourteenth century.

38. See the account of the Oratory of St. Bonaventura in Marino Bernardo Barfucci, *Il Monte della Verna* (Città di Castello, 1982), 77–78; and Mariano Ughi da Firenze, *Dialogo del sacro monte della Verna* (Pistoia, 1930), 87. The Chapel of the Stigmata is discussed by Barfucci, 61–76; by Bargelli and Vettori, *Amoroso viaggio*, 21–22; and by Jorgensen, *Pilgrim Walks*, 171–76.

39. Georges Duby in *The Age of the Cathedrals*, for example, rightly records that, beginning in the eleventh century and extending through the centuries of cathedral building, the "humanity of the Son of God" became the "pivotal point" of a "new" Christian religion, and that icons of the crucified Christ and relics of the Passion were then prominently placed in medieval cathedrals (86–107). See also Johan Chydenius, *The Typological Problem*, 85–98, for remarks on typological commentary of the period stressing the earthly Jerusalem and the humanity of the Son.

40. In an idealistic philosophic interpretation of history propounding views that still influence Dante criticism, G. W. F. Hegel in *The Philosophy of History*, rev. ed., trans. J. Sibree (New York, 1900) launched a famed attack in the 1830s upon what he regarded as "externals" devoid of spiritual essences—medieval relics, pilgrimage sites and activities, and other medieval manifestations of "mundane existence" (391)—and so established an intellectual "climate" for abstract individualized analyses of even the medieval literal "historical" sense of biblical events and places.

Hegel objects to the medieval union of the spiritual with the concrete. He praises "looking for the specific embodiment of Deity," not in a material "earthly sepulchre of stone," but "rather in the deeper abyss of Absolute Ideality" in a realm of abstraction divorced from matter (414, 420). Hegel properly castigates the barbarism of the Crusades and the nominalism of those Crusaders and pilgrims who were obsessed with the grossly physical. But in failing to take into account complex medieval scholastic conceptions of the union of the accidents of matter with immaterial substantial forms, and in directing a fierce assault upon the medieval identification of the divine with specific "historical" places and events, he advances positions at variance with the medieval belief that a literal, concrete, historical base is necessary for the revelation of spiritual senses in biblical and theological interpretation.

Hegel thus takes exception to that medieval religious faith grounded in part upon the historicity of "mere finite things— . . . the belief that such or such a person existed and said this or that; or that the Children of Israel passed dry-shod through the Red Sea—or that the trumpets before the walls of Jericho produced as powerful an impression as our cannons" (415). He accordingly proclaims, in a radical break with the medieval notion of the literal historical sense of theological allegory, that "all relations that sprung from that vitiating element of externality which we examined above, are *ipso facto* abrogated" (416). Hegel then replaces concrete medieval historical typology with abstract historical dialectical ideology.

Hegel's critical comments on Dante in *Aesthetics: Lectures on Fine Art,* trans. T. M. Know, 2 vols. (Oxford, 1975) are, of course, colored by his philosophic posture. In maintaining that a "chief interest" of poetry consists in revealing idealistic, abstract *"universal* doctrines" that "shall be known and believed as universal truth," Hegel argues that in poetry "concrete representation must remain subordinate and indeed external to the content, and allegory is the form which satisfies this need in the easiest and most appropriate way. In this sense Dante has much that is allegorical in his *Divine Comedy.* So there, e.g., theology appears fused with the picture of his beloved Beatrice." Hegel insists that Dante "put into the chief work of his life" very little of the mundane and external, but rather the "inner subjective religion of his heart" (vol. 1, p. 402). Overlooking the social content particularly of *Paradiso,* Hegel contends that in the poem the individual is "an infinite end in himself. . . . In this divine world, concern is purely for the individual" (vol. 2, p. 980). But while imposing a philosophic idealism upon Dante's medieval theological allegory, Hegel perceived that in some respects the other world of the work pointed back to events in the earthly world: "the poem comprises the entirety of objective life: the eternal condition of Hell, Purgatory, and Paradise; and on this indestructible foundation the figures of the real world move in their particular character, or rather they *have* moved and now in their being and action are frozen and are eternal themselves in the arms of eternal justice" (vol. 2, p. 1104).

It should be added that Hegel's criticism, though exposing Dante's true spiritual inwardness, nevertheless exaggerates the poet's individual subjectivism. For Dante, as he presents himself in the *Commedia,* is not autonomous. During the poet's processional education through a wondrous love of Beatrice and under the primary guidance of her eyes, Dante's increasingly holy movements of *body,* mind and soul unquestionably reveal, not a turn from external form, but rather a full and extraordinary merging of external form with spiritual inwardness. Dante's "freedom" is in his conformity to that divine love which he depicts as giving underlying hierarchical order by means of natural law to society and to the entire universe.

41. For discussions of Dante's knowledge of the Jerusalem temple and of the poet's figural allusions to the temple in the Eden passages, see Robert L. John, *Dante* (Vienna, 1946), 174–81; and *Dante and Michelangelo: Das Paradiso Terrestre und die Sixtinische Decke* (Koln, 1959), 18–21, 45–71; Demaray, *The Invention of Dante's Commedia,* 119–23, 169–74; Rene Guenon, *L'Esoterisme de Dante,* 3rd ed. (Paris, 1949), 9–22; Helmut Hatzfeld, "Modern Literary Scholarship as Reflected in Dante Criticism," *American Critical Essays on The Divine Comedy,* ed. Robert J. Clements (New York and London, 1967), 206–07; and William Anderson, *Dante the Maker,* 277–80, 344–45, 367–70.

An earlier allusion in *Purg.* 15 points forward to the appearance of Beatrice, a type of Christ, in an otherworldly location figuring the Old Temple. On the terrace of the wrathful, Dante dreams of the Virgin Mary as she looks for but cannot yet find Christ in the "tempio" (1.87). The Virgin and her actions serve as an exemplum of that gentleness that is the opposite of wrath.

42. Anderson in *Dante the Maker* rightly observes that Beatrice's descent

to Eden at the core of a holy procession is "remarkably like the splendid peregrinations performed in the cathedrals and great churches of the Gothic period, especially during Lent and Easter" (370). Other critics have found that Dante's meeting with Beatrice and her procession suggests an earthly encounter with clerics bearing Christ in the form of the Host; see Lizette Andrews Fisher, *The Mystic Vision*, 102–16; and Bernard Stambler, *Dante's Other World* (New York, 1957), 27–35. Johan Chydenius in *The Typological Problem*, 70–73, gives an example of how the church of Santa Croce in Gerusalemme, Rome, served in the literal sense as an antitype for the earthly Jerusalem as manifest in the earliest preserved epistolary: the seventh century *Comes* of John of Wurzburg. "The texts for the stational mass," Chydenius writes, "which was said *ad Hierusalem* on the fourth Sunday in Lent were specially selected to be appropriate for this locality." He adds that "in the mass in question, the idea of pilgrimage to Jerusalem is prominent to the end" (71–72). Margaret R. Miles in "The Fourth Century: Architecture, Images, and Liturgy," *Images as Insight: Visual Understanding in Western Christianity and Secular Culture* (Boston, 1985), traces the correlation between early Roman liturgy and church processional architecture more widely, noting that "Christian liturgy was markedly peripatetic" (52). See also Jeffrey T. Schnapp's *The Transfiguration of History at the Center of Dante's Paradise* (Princeton, 1986), for readings of Transfiguration and church typology in *Paradiso* 14–18. Schnapp, studying what he terms Dante's "poetics of martyrdom," finds the apsidal mosaics of the Transfiguration in the Byzantine church of St. Apollinare in Classe, Ravenna, to be reflected in their general typal outlines in the Transfiguration iconography of Dante's sphere of Mars.

43. Giuseppe Mazzotta in his chapter "Allegory" in *Dante: Poet of the Desert* (Princeton, 1979), 227–74, discusses Dante's limitations and failures of memory, the poet's images of "scattering" and closure, and the poet's constant admissions that poetic depiction falls short of reality. Mazzotta, on the basis of his own critical analysis, then accepts Eric Auerbach's "hesitant conclusion that Dante disrupts the order he creates" (270). But by not exploring the earthly and heavenly figural "inversions" that sustain even as they reorder typological relations, and by leaning away from the progressions of medieval "historical" typological allegory and toward the assumed "contradictions" of Hegelian abstract dialectic in his independent criticism, Mazzotta advances an extreme case for the fragmentation of Dante's verse in suggesting the possibility of a "double reading of the poem. The *Divine Comedy*," he writes, "overtly tells the story of the pilgrim's progress from the sinful state of the 'selva oscura' to beatific vision of *Paradise* 33. . . . It also tells the story of persistent ambiguity of metaphoric language in which everything is perpetually fragmented and irreducible to any unification" (269). These two possible "opposed readings," he urges, "do not deconstruct and cancel each other out, but are simultaneously present and always involve each other" (270). Dante's text for *Paradiso* 33 and elsewhere "actually, originates from the confusions and fragmentations of a blotted memory, the only trace of which," Mazzota adds in a phrase echoing the subjectivism of Hegel, "is the impression of sweetness in the heart" (265).

Ambiguities in the metaphoric language of medieval vision, of a kind reviewed from a scholastic hierarchical perspective by Jacques Maritain in

The Degrees of Knowledge, trans. under Gerald B. Phelan from the fourth French edition (New York, 1959), are indeed pervasive in the *Commedia.* These ambiguities are particularly noticeable in *Paradiso,* for there Dante is constantly transcending his slowly acquired awareness of earthly centers below, even as, having turned from pilgrimage goals on earth to heaven, his powers are only partially capable of understanding paradisal centers above. But through an encompassing language giving expression to Dante's imitative and often "inverted" figural actions and associated experiences, an essentially harmonious, hierarchical pattern of linguistic meanings emerges throughout the text. As an unfolding structure of words, the poem allows for the connatural aesthetic illumination of the reader if not, in every case, of Dante himself.

44. Using medieval theological, philosophical and literary works, A. C. Charity in *Events and their Afterlife: The Dialectics of Christian Typology in the Bible and Dante* (Cambridge, England, 1966) convincingly shows how the poet grounded his otherworldly pilgrimage in such an autobiographical "back-reference to a history prior to that directly narrated." Dante's pilgrimage beyond based upon this "back-reference," Charity notes, is adjusted—after the manner of medieval legendary lives of St. Francis, St. Paul and other holy persons—so as to be interpreted as an imitation of biblical events ultimately focused upon the life of Christ. Citing Fra Bartolomeo's *De Conformitate Vitae B. Francisci ad Vitam Domini Jesu* as an example, Charity writes that "undeniably, a historical basis exists for the most part behind each unit of narrative," but that "the fundamentally theological point in the *imitatio Christi* is brought out by setting event opposite event from the life of the Saviour and servant. In the earlier 'Lives' of St. Francis, stylization of the incident and evocative phrase together do the same work." Commentators should "look further back still," Charity urges, to "New Testament narratives" for examples of how back-references to "historical" episodes help to mold the depiction of holy lives. "There too," Charity remarks, "in St. Paul's journey to Jerusalem, a self-conforming with the life of Christ is presented by indirect means, in phraseology and echo." Dante's journey beyond life, Charity adds, "retains still an autobiographic substance with which it never loses contact" through back-references to the true "literal sense" of the poet's past historical life. He adds that "the figuring, the stylizing, of Dante's life, on this view, remains vital, a necessary means of expressing something he felt about it. It is done for the sake of making a point of theology, or better, for the sake of a claim made by means of typology. . . . [T]his, Dante may say, is my own self-conforming with Christ" (253–55).

Although Charity contrasts the historicity of the foreshadowed earthly events with the many mythic qualities implicit in the depiction of fulfilled events beyond life, he also refers to Auerbach's comments on the historicity of both earthly and otherworldly figurism, stressing that there is a "certain historical dependency and continuity between the events which typology relates" (199). He thus finds, giving attention to the allegorical statements in Letter X, that the fulfilled events beyond life in the *Commedia* embody "typological back-references as well as forward ones," that in the other world "Dante's journey is a type of his future" (247–49).

William Anderson in *Dante the Maker,* also addressing the question of the importance of Christ's life in history to allegorical interpretation, critically reviews "the method of *figura*, a method which depends on the historicity both of the character or event described and the people or happenings with which it is compared, as the strength and sufferings of Samson were regarded as a type of the strength and sufferings of Christ, or as in Dante's journey the Great Circle pilgrimage is a figure of his own travels from the spiritual Jerusalem to the eternal Rome. But this method can easily be related to the allegorical level of the fourfold method, which relates past and present events in the light of the role of Christ's life in the history of the world" (331–32). For an analysis of the Redemption typology in the Eden section, and of the pervasive fourfold allegorical meanings as they relate to Dante's typology, see also Demaray, particularly the chapter "Three Typological Modes in Dante's *Commedia*: Biblical Imitation, Internal Recurrence, and Worldly Imitation," *The Invention of Dante's "Commedia,"* 93–115.

Excellent examples of imitation-of-Christ typology appear in paintings of the life of St. Francis by Taddeo Gaddi (ca. 1327–1366), paintings that once hung in the sacristy of the "New Jerusalem" of Santa Croce and which are now exhibited in the Accademia, Florence (See Inv. 1890, del n. 8581 n. 8593). Twelve medallions showing the life of Christ, including the Crucifixion, are set against matching medallions showing the life of St. Francis, including the reception of the Stigmata. In the Crucifixion painting in this series, as in three other Crucifixion paintings now hanging respectively in the Chiesa di Ognissanti, Museo Bardini and the Accademia, Gaddi depicted the skull of the First Adam below Christ on the cross and so followed the typological tradition manifested at the Golgatha station of Constantine's "New Jerusalem" of the Holy Sepulchre.

45. In *The Political Vision of Dante* (Princeton, 1984), Joan Ferrante, in a thematic reading of political and mercantile references in the *Commedia*, places special emphasis upon the "sixth canto of each cantica," which, she argues, "focuses on the political entity that serves as the model for that cantica: in Hell, it is Florence, in Purgatory, Italy, and in Paradise, the Roman empire" (47). Certain distinctions—rephrased from an earlier article "Florence and Rome, the Two Cities of Man," in the *Divine Comedy*, *The Early Renaissance Acta* 5 (1978), 1–9—are used in advancing the case for models. Purgatory is said to be "like Italy" (46). "The Italy evoked in Purgatory is partly the physical entity," she writes, "in that Purgatory is a mountain surrounded by sea; but it is primarily cultural" (47). By contrast, the model for hell is found to be "the physical and historical reality" of just "contemporary Florence," not the Florence of the past or the future (47). She adds that "Paradise is based on an idealized Rome"(47).

Ferrante helpfully points out allusions to the infernal political and social evils of "contemporary Florence" as a mercantile city state, and to Rome as the idealized center for world order and justice. Nevertheless, Italian and related political allusions together with mercantile references, however numerous or strongly felt by Dante, do not fully reveal the all-embracing "models" for otherworldly realms in a political-philosophical-theological poem such as the *Commedia*. By neither citing nor critically engaging the rich commentary on Dante's biblical allegory involving alternative and complementary "models" for the poet's realms beyond life, Ferrante provides restricted perspectives on Dante's meaning.

It should be noted that even corrupt, mercantile Florence is advanced as a model for hell only by means of arguable distinctions resting on the word "contemporary." In the remembered "present" of actions in the *Commedia* that might well be considered "contemporary," Florence despite all of its evils remains the city of the blessed Beatrice's life and death; the "sheepfold" beset by wolves but still "fair" to which Dante wishes to return (*Par.* 25.4–9); the city that, as Ernst Robert Curtius discerned, gave up 32 of its citizens to Dante's hell, but also four citizens to the poet's purgatory and two citizens to the poet's paradise. Florence is thus depicted as a place of much evil but also of some exceptional holiness.

Although Dante was powerfully influenced by mercantile matters and by "visionary" and practical politics involving Florence, Italy and the "Holy Roman Empire," he can be seen to cast political and mercantile elements and types, together with the myriad details of his poem, within the all-embracing figurism of universal Hebraic-Christian history as disclosed with ultimate authority in the Bible and in the iconography of the full world and Cosmic Book of God's Works. The final cantos, not primarily the sixth canto, of each cantica best reveal the virtuous guides, the "source books," and the figured sites and characters that provide the dominating earthly "models" for the realms beyond life.

NOTES TO CHAPTER TWO

1. *Purg.* 21.121. All quotations from the *Commedia* are cited from Dante Alighieri, *La Divina Commedia secondo l'antica vulgata*, ed. Giorgio Petrocchi, 4 vols. (Milano, A. Mandadori for the Societa Dantesca Italiana, 1965–69).

2. John Leyerle, "The Rose-Wheel Design and Dante's *Paradiso*," *University of Toronto Quarterly* 40.3 (Spring 1977): 280–307; and James Miller, "Three Mirrors of Dante's *Paradiso*," *University of Toronto Quarterly* 46.3 (Spring 1977): 263–79. A most revealing analysis of mirror images in selected medieval works appears in V. A. Kolve, *Chaucer and the Imagery of Narrative* (Stanford, 1984), 52–60. Historical background on knowledge of optics in the twelfth century can be found in A. C. Crombie, *Robert Grosseteste and the Origins of Experimental Science: 1100–1170* (Oxford, 1953).

It needs to be observed that Dante's analogic and metaphoric references relating to mirror images in general point to a language that— through ever more tenuous yet brilliantly chosen intermediary analogies, metaphors and allusions—captures by "degrees" a limited and glancing discursive or intuitive apprehension of what are regarded as transcendent objects beyond direct, full human knowledge. Scholastic and Thomastic philosophic attitudes, joined with medieval mystical theology, clearly govern Dante's linguistic practices. Jacques Maritain, adopting such philosophic and mystical views toward language in an analysis employing references to mirrors in *The Degrees of Knowledge*, trans. under Gerald B. Phelan from the fourth French edition (New York, 1959) has called attention to how, from the Thomastic outlook, transcendent objects or "transobjective subjects" that "do not fall at first within our grasp . . . are known by the intermediary of the primordially apprehended analogate. They are known in the latter as in a mirror," Maritain continues, "in virtue of the likeness it has with them. This is specular knowledge or knowledge by analogy. . . . Strictly speaking, the transobjective subjects in which they are realized are not subject to our intelligible grasps, do not give themselves up to us as objects. It is not their essence or their first intelligible constitutive which is objectivized for us by means of their presentative forms and of our concepts. They are known, however, intrinsically and properly designed, constituted as objects of intellection, but as it were at a distance and not in themselves. The ray of the intellect that attains them has been refracted or reflected, and they always remain above the knowledge we have of them, superior to the grasps that reach up to them, separated from our mind in the very act which unites it to them" (210–11).

See Étienne Gilson, *Dante the Philosopher*, trans. David Moore (London, 1948) on Dante's individualized integration of traditional elements in classical philosophy, medieval rational theology and medieval mystical theology. Though Umberto Eco in *Art and Beauty in the Middle Ages*, trans. Hugh Bredin (New Haven and London, 1986), in discussing the "aesthetics" of Thomas Aquinas, emphasizes the discursive or logical operations of the intellect in apprehending objects (72–73); Edgar De Bruyne in *Études D'Asthétique Médiévale* (Brugge, 1946), vol. 3, pp. 283–97, rightly calls attention to the rational intuition of objects as part of Thomastic "aesthetics," as does Maritain. See also De Bruyne's *The Aesthetics of the Middle Ages*, trans. Eileen Hennessy (New York, 1969), 121–24. What is clear is that Dante in the *Commedia* reveals through action both intuitive rational apprehension and discursive or logical apprehension.

3. The poem, written about 1225–1235, contains the lines:

Praebentes germinae jubar orbiculare fenestrae,
Ecclesiae due sunt oculi: recteque videtur
Major in his esse praesul, menor esse decanus.

The twin windows exhibiting a circular splendour
are the two eyes of the church;
and the larger of them is rightly seen to
be the bishop and the smaller, the dean.

The poem was printed in the last century under the title *The Metrical Life of St. Hugh, Bishop of Lincoln*, ed. J. F. Demcock (London, 1860), 35–36; and the lines cited above are quoted and translated by Leyerle in "The Rose Wheel," 300.

Comments on the general influence of wheel windows on Dante's heavenly rose appear in A. F. Ozanam, *Dante et la philosophia catholique au treizième siècle*, 2nd ed. (Paris, 1845), 335–36. P. Savi Lopez, pointing out the obvious variations in design between Dante's rose and earthly wheel windows, depends in large measure in this early study upon external characteristics in denying such influence in *Il canto XXX del "Paradiso" letto nella Sala di Dante* in *Orsanmichele* (Firenze, 1904), 15–19. Because rose images cannot be specifically identified in the designs of floral plain-glass as distinct from some floral stained-glass windows; and because medieval texts provide slight and usually circumstantial written evidence of the association of floral wheel windows with that most spiritual medieval flower of love and Mary, the rose; John Barnes in *"Ut Architectura Poesis? The Case of Dante's Candida Rosa"* in *The Italianist: Journal of the Depart-*

ment of Italian Studies, University of Reading 6 (1986) has drawn the embracing and doubtful conclusion that in Dante's period, presumably without exception, "the rose window without stained glass" was not "perceived as a rose." In phrasing that avoids the issue of typological function, he then maintains—without exploring Dante's unfolding figurism—that the poet had "no need of any fenestrial association" to "justify" his depiction of the heavenly rose (28).

Dante's rose is such a transcendent synthesis of figural elements that, if discussed in relative figural isolation, carefully phrased readings of this kind can understandably be advanced. But it is important, I think, to view the heavenly rose in wide figural contexts.

The case for the general influence upon Dante of wheel windows was made in this century by Filippo Ermini, who argued from figural relations, in "La candida rosa del Paradiso dantesco: Il simbolo e la figura," *Giornale dantesco* 25 (1922): 306–09; reprinted in his *Medio evo latino: Studi e richerche,* ed. G. Bertoni (Modena, 1938), 327–32. Further associations between Dante's heavenly rose and earthly wheel windows have been developed, of course, in works already cited by William Anderson, Painton Cowen, John Leyerle, James Miller, Giuseppe di Scipio and B. Knapp.

The expectation that Dante would simply refer to or copy the "accidental" material appearances of one or two wheel windows—rather than dramatically merge and adjust selected material "accidents" of wheels in a unique attempt to show forth something of the transcendent splendor of immaterial heavenly forms—has been an element in the few claims made against wheel-window influence. Such claims overlook the way in which Dante brilliantly exploits source iconography in seeking to manifest presumed essences. In their concentration upon the heavenly rose passage, these claims also overlook the entire unfolding figural structure of the *Commedia* as it relates to Byzantine round church, basilica, cathedral and wider but corresponding Holy Land and cosmic iconography. In short, such criticism limits appreciation, it seems to me, of the vitality, originality and contextual range of Dante's medieval figural art.

4. See Patricia J. Eberle, "The Lover's Looking Glass: Nature's Discourse on Optics and the Optical Design of the Romance of the Rose," *University of Toronto Quarterly* 46.3 (Spring 1977): 241–62. Optical references, as Eberle notes, are used to establish points-of-view in the *Roman de la Rose* and in a medieval work such as the satirical *Speculum stultorum* (ca. 1190), the "Fool's Glass," also known as *The Book of Burnellus the Ass.*

5. In *Itinerarium Burdigalense,* ed. P. Geyer and O. Cuntz in *Itineraria et Alia Geographica: Corpus Christianorum, Series Latina,* vol. 175 (Città del Vaticano, 1965), 15–16, the pilgrim from Burdigala (now Bordeaux) outlines in the fourth century the Jerusalem city route from the Old Temple to the New on a line parallel to modern King David Street. And in *Itinerarium Egeriae,* ed. E. Franceschini and R. Weber in *Itineraria et Alia Geographica,* 175: 77–78 Egeria (St. Silvia) also in the fourth century describes a Palm Sunday procession moving down the Mount of Olives, through the Golden Gate in the eastern wall of Jerusalem, and then on from the Old Temple to the New. Stephen Graham in *With the Russian Pilgrims to Jerusalem* (London, 1916), 241–43, records in this century Palm Sunday liturgical practices in Jerusalem that still follow the patterns outlined by Egeria. Such Palm Sunday practices remain in use in the Holy City today.

Illustrations of eleventh and twelfth century circular iconographic maps of Jerusalem like those still popular in Dante's time—maps showing the city as a cross within a circle, the Old Temple usually as a circle, and the New Temple as a circle surmounted by a cross—are reproduced in Sabino de Sandoli's *Itinera Hierosolymitana Crucesignatorum*, vol. 2 (Jerusalem, 1980): 391, 413, 422.

6. Allusions to the skull of Adam buried beneath Golgotha appear, for example, in two twelfth century pilgrim texts: *The Pilgrimage of the Russian Abbot Daniel in the Holy Land*, trans. Aubrey Stewart, notes C. W. Wilson (London, 1895), 15; and "Anonymous Pilgrim VI" in *Anonymous Pilgrims*, I-VIII, trans. Aubrey Stewart (London, 1894), 22. For recent studies comparing episodes and places in Dante's Eden to those in Jerusalem as it was known in the poet's time, see chapter one, n. 7, n. 14.

A pagan altar dedicated to Adam, an altar predating Roman shrines to Venus and later Christian shrines, was unearthed in the Hill of Calvary within the Holy Sepulchre in the 1970s as the result of excavations sponsored by the Greek Orthodox Patriarch, Jerusalem. See Christos Kalsimbinis, *The Uncovering of the Eastern Side of the Hill of Calvary and its Base* (Jerusalem, 1977), 197–208.

7. See Painton Cowen, *Rose Windows* (San Francisco, 1979), 100.

8. St. Francis's disciple Illuminato, who accompanied the saint to the Holy Land, is said to have worn the "capestro," along with Augustine, in *Par.* 12.132. The early follower of St. Francis, Silvestro, is also identified as wearing a "capestro" in *Par.* 11.87. See the recent discussion of the "corda" and the "capestro" in Helmut Hatzfeld's "Modern Literary Scholarship as Reflected in Dante Criticism," *American Critical Essays on The Divine Comedy*, ed. Robert J. Clements (New York and London, 1967), 206–07; and William Anderson, *Dante the Maker* (New York and Boston, 1980), 362–63.

9. *Abbot Suger on the Abbey Church of St. Denis and its Art Treasures*, trans. and notes Erwin Panofsky, 2nd ed., ed. Gerda Panofsky-Soergel (Princeton, 1979), 114–15.

10. *Abbot Suger*, p. 121.

11. *Abbot Suger*, p. 117.

12. See chapter 120 of that work in *Patrologiae Cursus Completus*, vol. 202, 2nd series, ed. J. P. Migne (Paris, 1885): 125. Belethus in chapter 6, pp. 18–19, discusses the liturgy and the pilgrimage stations in Jerusalem. In *Il Duomo di Lucca* (Lucca, 1982), Pietro Lazzarini notes that in the medieval period dances were presented on Easter afternoon on the labyrinth, now destroyed, of the nave floor in the cathedral at Auxerre. The dean of the cathedral and a circle of dancers joined hands and danced around the labyrinth, Lazzarini observes, as a large ball was thrown from performer to performer (10). Erwin Mehal in "Der Ausweg aus dem Labyrinth," *Festgabe fur Leopold Schmidt* (Wien, 1972) cites a relatively late example of labyrinth dances, performed in 1412 in the cathedral at Auxerre, involving members of the convent. On the basis of the text of the early *Ordinatio de pila facienda*, Mehal explains how chanting performers first moved around the cathedral labyrinth floor and then engaged in an ensemble dance (pp. 402ff.). William Anderson in *The Rise of the Gothic*, photographs, Clive Hicks (London, Melbourne, Auckland, 1985), 156–57,

describes the Easter labyrinth dances at Auxerre and lists other festival-day medieval dances in churches.

See also the historical and critical study of cosmic and sacred dances in James Miller's "Vision of the Cosmic Dance in Western Literature from Plato to Jean de Meun," University of Toronto Doctoral Dissertation, 1979; revised with specialized remarks on the cosmic dance in early Constantinian liturgy in *Measures of Wisdom: The Cosmic Dance in Classical and Christian Antiquity* (Toronto, Buffalo and London, 1986), 511–18.

13. John Freccero, "*Paradiso* X: The Dance of the Stars," *Dante in America: The First Two Centuries*, 345–71; reprinted in *Dante: The Poetics of Conversion*, ed. Rachel Jacoff (Cambridge, Mass. and London, 1986), 221–44. In examining the history of holy classical, Hebraic and Christian "earth dances in consonance with heaven," John C. Meagher in "The Dance in the Masques of Jonson," *Journal of the Warburg and Courtault Institute* 25 (1962): 258–70, analyzes sacred dance passages in the Gnostic *Acts of John* and in texts by Caelius Rhodiginus, Menestrier, Lucian, Plotinus, St. Basil and other writers.

14. See Leyerle on the San Zeno wheel-rose in "The Rose Wheel Design," 280–302. In Painton Cowen's *Rose Windows*, see plate 25 of Sainte-Étienne, Beauvais (ca. 1100), and plate 26 of the modified form of a fortune-type wheel at St. Denis.

15. *Croniche Fiorentine*, trans. Rose E. Selfe, Philip H. Wicksteed, ed. (London, 1906), bk. 8, sec. 36, p. 320. Accounts of the throngs of pilgrims appear in Caldecot Chubb, *Dante and His Italy* (New York and London, 1907), 1–39; Herbert Thurston, *The Holy Year of Jubilee* (Westminster, Maryland, 1949), 19–20; and Peter Armour, *The Door of Purgatory* (Oxford, 1983), 155–56.

16. These pilgrimage practices are discussed in *The Vision of Dante*, trans. with notes by Henry Francis Carey (London, 1929), in commentary on *Par.* 31.95; p. 557.

17. Francesco Petrarch's description of his emotional reactions during his Jubilee Pilgrimage to Rome in 1350 appears in *Epistolae Familiares* (Venezia, 1942), bk. 2, letter 9. See also Petrarch's sonnet 14 in *Le Rime de Francesco Petrarca*, notes by Giosue Carducci and Severino Farrari (Firenze, 1946), 17–18, about an aged man who in his last days makes a journey to Rome to see the famed image of Christ on the Veil of Veronica.

18. Ernest Hatch Wilkins in "Dante and the Mosaics of His Bel San Giovanni," *Dante in America: The First Two Centuries*, 144–59, reprinted from *Speculum* 2 (1927): 1–10, draws a comparison between the image of Mary in Dante's city of the rose in *Paradiso* and the mosaics in the *tribuna* of the Florentine Baptistery showing Mary. In the *tribuna* mosaics, Mary is depicted enthroned on the right outside of and facing away from a circular ceiling design representing eight Old Testament figures, each within bell-shaped compartments. On the opposite side of the circular design, John the Baptist is similarly enthroned outside of and facing away from the central figures (see plate 3, p. 155). If, as is possible, Dante was influenced by the Baptistery mosaics in developing his images of Mary and the celestial rose, it still needs to be emphasized that the unique design of Dante's rose in *Paradiso* illustrates the transforming power of the poet's creative intuition. Unlike the image of Mary in the *tribuna* of the

Florentine Baptistery, the Mary of the *Paradiso* is enthroned within and at the summit of the great rose. From the viewpoint of Dante in the poem, John the Baptist is then directly to her right, and a wall with steps descends from her feet and contains places for both Old and New Testament figures.

19. Cowen, figures 6 and 7.

20. Cowen, figure 31.

21. See Swaan, *The Gothic Cathedral* (New York, 1969), 289–90; plates showing the Siena window with bisecting tracery lines appear as figures 343 and 353.

22. *The Steps of Humility*, Latin text with English trans., intro. and notes by George Boswroth Burch (Cambridge, Mass., 1940), 168–69.

23. Sermon 23 on Canticles 15 in *Opera Omnia*, vol. 1, 4th ed., ed. John Mabillon (Paris, 1839): 2803.

24. *Opera Omnia*, vol. 1: 3193–194.

25. Cowen, 122–23. See also John James, "Medieval Geometry," *Architectural Association Quarterly* 5, no. 2 (1973): 4–10.

26. In an elaboration of medieval mystical writings and neoscholastic philosophic theory, Jacques Maritain in *Man's Approach to God* (Labrobe, 1960) defines those contituants traditionally associated with Beatific Vision of the kind depicted by Dante: a "primary intuitive flash" of apprehension (13–15), "spiritual dynamism" involving a movement of the soul (20–21), and a moment of vision when "all particular representations have vanished away. . . . The God of faith is experienced by his reverberation, His implanting in love" (41). Maritain in *Creative Intuition in Art and Poetry* (New York, 1953) applies a restatement of medieval conceptions of rational discursive and intuitive apprehension to comments on Dante's *Commedia* (370–73, and throughout). Investigations of late medieval and Renaissance views of discursive and intuitive rational apprehension can be found in Demaray, "The Inward Vision" in *Milton's Theatrical Epic: The Invention and Design of Paradise Lost* (Cambridge, Mass. and London, 1980), 1–15; and in the text and notes of Lee A. Jacobus, *Sudden Apprehension* (The Hague and Paris, 1976).

NOTES TO CHAPTER THREE

1. *The Works of Edmund Spenser: A Variorum Edition*, ed. Edwin Greenlaw, Charles Grosvenor Osgood, and Frederick Morgan Padelford, vol. 2 (Baltimore, 1933): 1. All citations of Spenser's writings are from this variorum edition.

2. See the letter in *The Works of Edmund Spenser*, vol. 1 (Baltimore, 1932): 167–70.

3. *Fact or Fiction: The Dilemma of the Renaissance Storyteller* (Cambridge, Mass., 1973), 80.

4. See Dionise Alexandrine, *The Surveye of the World, or Situation of the Earth*, trans. Thomas Twine (London: Henrie Bynneman, 1572). The dot-within-a-circle markings by Harvey on title pages are noted by Virginia F. Stern, *Gabriel Harvey: His Life, Marginalia and Library* (Oxford, 1979), 209.

5. *The Surveye*, First Section, unpaginated.

6. *Mappa Mundi* (London: Robert Wyer), unpaginated and undated. The work was published early in the sixteenth century and is usually dated ca. 1535.

7. Destombes, *Mappemondes: A.D. 1200–1500* (Amsterdam, 1964), 21–23.

8. See Virginia Stern, *Gabriel Harvey*, 231. Stern notes that the copy in Harvey's library was *La geografia di Claudio Ptolomeo Alessandrino* (Venice: Baptista Pedrazano, 1548).

9. Sidney, *The Defence of Poesie*, ed. Albert Feuillerat, vol. 3 (Cambridge, 1962): 29.

10. Heninger, Jr., *Touches of Sweet Harmony: Pythagorean Cosmology and Renaissance Poetics* (San Marino, California, 1974), 296–307. See also Heninger's *The Cosmographical Glass: Renaissance Diagrams of the Universe* (San Marino, California, 1977).

11. See Heninger's *Touches of Sweet Harmony*, and "The Aesthetic Experience of Reading Spenser," *Contemporary Thought on Edmund Spenser*, ed. Richard C. Frushell (Carbondale, Ill.; London and Amsterdam, 1975), 79–89; A. Kent Hieatt, *Short Time's Endless Monument* (New York, 1960); Alastair Fowler, *Spenser and the Numbers of Time* (London, 1964); Jane Aptekar, *Icons of Justice: Iconography & Thematic Imagery in "The Faery Queene"* (New York, 1969); and Josephine Waters Bennett, *The Evolution of "The Faerie Queene"* (Chicago, 1942).

12. Medieval cosmographical-biblical iconography was projected as well into French works such as Guillaume Du Bartas's *Judith* (1573) and *La Sepmaine* (1587). This last poem was translated into English by Joshua Sylvester as *The Divine Weeks of the World's Birth* (1605). In addition, direct or oblique references to the earlier iconography can be found in English poems such as John Donne's "Good Morrow" and "Good Friday, 1613, Riding Westward," and in George Herbert's "The Temple." Spenser's *The Faerie Queene*, however, can be identified as the last major epic written in English to incorporate so pervasively in form and content medieval pilgrimage-cosmological iconography, iconography based on Near Eastern, European and local British traditions.

13. For a discussion of Spenser's actual or possible allusions to early works revealing the medieval world picture, see Lois Whitney, "Spenser's Use of the Literature of Travel in *The Faerie Queene*," *Modern Philology* 19 (1921): 143–62. Whitney discloses that Spenser, along with referring to some sixteenth century travel literature, is indebted to works such as *The Book of Sir John Maundeville*, the *Legend of St. Brandan* and *The Golden Legend*. John B. Friedman in *The Monstrous Races in Medieval Art and Thought* (Cambridge, Mass., 1981), 200–05, rightly maintains that Spenser created certain faeryland character types under the influence of the strange figures drawn on medieval maps and described in medieval writings.

John M. Steadman in *The Lamb and the Elephant: Ideal Imitation and the Context of Renaissance Allegory* (San Marino, California, 1974) stresses past literary tradition in offering insights into Spenser's merger of diverse elements. "Spenser's allegorical vision," Steadman writes, "operates as a solvent, fusing Biblical and classical, medieval and Renaissance, Italian and French and British allusions into a moral pageant that is simultaneously within and beyond time, like the realm of ideas itself. Under the pretext of celebrating the legendary past of his country—the Britain of Prince Arthur in the heroic age of chivalry—he is portraying the virtues and vices of his own society" (40). See also Steadman's incisive comments, in *Nature into Myth: Medieval and Renaissance Moral Symbols* (Pittsburgh, 1979), 23–63, on the application of comparative iconographical and lexigraphical materials to critical readings of late medieval and Renaissance literature.

14. The *Book* is reproduced as *Mandeville's Travels*, ed. M. C. Seymour (Oxford, 1967), 146.

15. Nohrnberg in *The Analogy of The Faerie Queene* (Princeton, 1976) mentions, among other examples of withdrawal, "Calidore's retirement to the world of the shepherds," "Colin's seclusion on Mount Acidale," "the rustication of Timias and Serena" and "Calepine's retreat from Turpine" (657). Citing work by Eric Rosenberg on the theme of embowerment as it relates to Mt. Acidale, Nohrnberg states that "The ring the cannibals form around Serena must correspond to the secondary ring of lusty shepherds around Pastorella, which in turn anticipates the outer ring of the Graces on Mount Acidale" (661).

Ring and compass emblems, found also in early books of *The Faerie Queene*, do receive particular stress in book 6. And in the instance of Mt. Acidale, the outer ring emblem of the Graces appears to embrace in its signification virtuous physical as well as spiritual love, a love that overcomes corrupting forms of lust and desire.

16. Nohrnberg in *The Analogy of The Faerie Queene* has rightly noted that Spenser's *Two Cantos of Mutabilitie* have a "slight precedent: the Garden of Adonis canto in book 3 is followed by the Temple of Venus in book 4. The goddess at the Temple," Nohrnberg adds, "is a veiled androgynous genetrix, as Nature is here, and it follows from this resemblance that the Mutability cantos are reflexive to the present poem, rather than merely sequent to it" (80). C. S. Lewis in *The Allegory of Love* (London, 1953), 353–60, had previously maintained that Spenser's *Two Cantos of Mutabilitie* would have become, if further developed, key cantos at the core of legends of "perfect Maydenhed" in book 3 (3.6.28) involving metaphysical issues of constancy and change.

Resemblances and reflexive allusions on the theme of stasis and change indeed relate the cantos, which conclude with a judgment made by Nature enthroned on Arlo hill, to the Garden of Adonis, the Temple of Venus, and also to the episode on Acidale hill. In the cantos, a sustained single narrative—concerned with the theme of the static and mutable in just the lower realms of creation—supplants what in *The Faerie Queene* is an extremely complex series of interwoven narratives, ultimately involving the three core emblems that are subsumed by the emblem of Cleopolis. These emblems point to unchanging values in ideal realms, and to immaterial substantial forms on all levels of creation that remain constant despite the alteration of accidental forms. Then, too, the cantos differ from Spenser's epic, as Nohrnberg has observed, in that they mythologize objects and central figures. Mythic characters replace the knights and ladies of *The Faerie Queene*.

Though the cantos contain reflexive elements, their individualizing qualities show them to be thematically related to but not integrated into Spenser's epic. Moreover, Nature in canto 7, just before vanishing, confirms that Jove reigns in the universe by implication as an Unmoved

Mover; and in the canto's next to the last stanza, judges that in the lower
realms of creation "all things," though subject to change, nevertheless
hold to their "first estate" and in this sense rule over change.

> . . . all things stedfastnes doe hate
> And changed bee; yet, being rightly wayd,
> They are not changed from their first estate;
> But by their change their being doe dilate,
> And turning to themselves at length againe,
> Doe worke their owne perfection so by fate:
> Then over them Change doth not rule and raigne,
> But they raigne ouer Change, and doe their states maintaine.
>
> (2.7.58)

The disappearance of Nature suggests poetic closure; the questionable
circumstances and manner of Nature's judgment, however, imply the
debate, and therefore the poem could be continued. In any case, the
cantos in their present form philosophically support the existence of the
kinds of constant immaterial values and conceptions signified by the core
emblems of Spenser's epic, emblems that are analogous to configuring
geometrical icons on *mappaemundi*.

Again in the cantos, as in *The Faerie Queene*, Spenser introduces an
essentially "antique" medieval cosmos with the earth located at the center
of the encircling spheres. And again in the cantos, the poet appears to
react to new philosophical-cosmological arguments such as those in Gior-
dano Bruno's *Trattato della Causa, Principio ed Uno*, a work composed
during the author's visit to England in 1583.

17. *The Works of Edmund Spenser*, vol. 1: 167–70. See also the symbolic
and structural analysis of the poem in Angus Fletcher's *The Prophetic
Moment: An Essay on Spenser* (Chicago and London, 1971), a study that
draws upon the archetypal criticism of Northrope Frye in maintaining that
symbols of the "Temple" and the "Labyrinth" are central to *The Faerie
Queene*. Fletcher's definition of the symbols, however, is extremely wide.
"*A templum*," he explains, "is a sacred, separated space. It may assume
various geometric outlines (four-or-five-sided, for example), but ideally it
is round" (14). The "Labyrinth" is found to be "the opposite of the ideal
templar form," that is, a "'perplexed circle'" (24).

18. *Observations* (London: printed for Daniel Frere, 1644), 20.

19. *The Surveye*, First Section, unpaginated.

20. *The Cosmographical Glasse, conteinyng the pleasant Principles of Cosmographie, Geographie, Hydrographie, or Navigation* (London: Ioan Daij,
1559), fol. 170.

21. *Mandeville's Travels*, 57–58. See also Lois Whitney, "Spenser's Use of
the Literature of Travel in *The Faerie Queene*," 146, 156, for comments on
Spenser's employment of Maundeville.

22. See John Hankins, *Source and Meaning in Spenser's Allegory* (Oxford,
1971), 200–05; Isabel C. Rathbone, *The Meaning of Spenser's Faeryland* (New
York, 1937), 194–201; and Charles Bowie Millican, *Spenser and the Table
Round* (Cambridge, Mass., 1932).

23. *The Chronicles of England, from Brute unto this present yeare of Christ.
1580* (London: Ralph Newberie, 1580), fol. 81.

24. *A Summarye of the Chronicles of Englande* (London: Thomas Marsh, 1570), fol. 38.

25. See also Stow, *A Summarie of Englyshe Chroncles* (London: Thomas Marsh, 1565), fol. 30–31.

26. The poem is cited and translated by Geoffrey Ashe in *King Arthur's Avalon* (Glasgow, 1980), 45–46.

27. *De Antiquitate* in *The Works of Sir Thomas Malory*, ed. Eugène Vinaver, vol. 2 (Oxford, 1967), 793, 801.

28. *Here begynneth the lyfe of Joseph of Armathia* (London: Richard Pynson, 1520), unpaginated. In the Trinity College Manuscript of William of Malmsbury's *De Antiquitate*, reproduced from the edition of Thomas Hearne and printed by the Somerset Gazette (Glastonbury, 1932), marginal notes, believed to have been added in the mid-thirteenth century, record Joseph's coming to England (7). For a recent restatement of the view that the early British Church was founded by Joseph of Arimathea, see Lionel Smithett Lewis, *St. Joseph of Arimathea, or The Apostolic Church of Britain* (London, 1955), 26–30. Lewis quotes Polydore Virgil in suggesting that Britain "was of all kingdoms the first that received the Gospel" (15). See the analysis of medieval and Renaissance textual references to Joseph of Arimathea in Geoffrey Ashe, *King Arthur's Avalon*, 30–33, 43–47, 249–54.

29. Richard Warner, *A History of the Abbey of Glaston, and of the Town of Glastonbury* (Bath: Richard Cruttwell, 1826), xxiii–xxiv. See also the *Guide to Glastonbury* (Glastonbury: Avalon Press, 1930), 35.

30. T. Chubb, *A Descriptive List of Printed Maps of Somersetshire, 1575–1914* (Launton: Archeological and History Society, 1914), "Saxton's Map, 1575," Plate II, p. 1; "John Speed's Map, 1610," Plate IV, p. 4. See also "Saxton's Map of Somerset, 1575," B. M. Maps, C. 7 CI, included in Christopher Saxton, *Atlas of England & Wales* of 1575.

31. *The Meaning of Spenser's Faeryland*, 194–201.

32. *Source and Meaning in Spenser's Allegory* (Oxford, 1971), 202–03.

33. See John Dee, *General and Rare Memorials pertayning to the Perfect Arte of Navigation* (London: John Daye, 1577), 56.

34. See Michael Murrin, "The Rhetoric of Faeryland," *The Rhetoric of Renaissance Poetry from Wyatt to Milton*, ed. Thomas O. Sloan and Raymond B. Waddington (Berkeley, Los Angeles and London, 1974), 73–95.

35. For an analysis of this "closure" episode in relation to the general structure of *The Faerie Queene*, see Susanne Woods, "Closure in *The Faerie Queene*," *Journal of English and Germanic Philology* 76 (1977): 195–216; and the comments of James Nohrnberg, *The Analogy of the Faerie Queene*, 657–61.

36. *The Analogy of The Faerie Queene*, 702–03.

37. Lila Green Geller in *The Three Graces in Spenser's Faerie Queene*, a University of California doctoral dissertation, 1969, provides a comprehensive reading of the influence of works by Hesiod, Homer, and the sixteenth century Italian Platonists on Spenser's treatment of the Graces in books 3 and 6. She suggests the relation of the central figure of "Firm Chastity" to conceptions of that providential grace that bestows heavenly care in bountiful fashion (178ff.), and she convincingly demonstrates Spenser's early poetic association of the Graces with the Muses of the Arts. See also James Nohrnberg, *The Analogy of the Faerie Queene*, 698–703, for an analysis of the signification of the Graces and of the theme of providential grace in book 6.

Harry Berger in "A Secret Discipline" in *Form and Convention in the Poetry of Edmund Spenser,* ed. William Nelson 71–72, argues that the three Graces around "Firm Chastity" in book 6 represent an unfolding of the graces of Venus, just as in book 3 Florimell representing Beauty, Belphoebe representing Chastity, and Amoret representing Love, are seen by this critic as a flowering of the traits of Britomart. But it should be noted again that Venus has left Mt. Acidale, and that the Graces appear to signify values that embrace and at the same time transcend those suggested by Berger.

NOTES TO CHAPTER FOUR

1. David Leever, *A Spiritual Song: The Story of the Temple Choir and a History of Divine Service in the Temple Church, London* (London: The Templars Union, 1961), 20–22. The Knights Hospitallers in London, with their round temple church and headquarters buildings, were similarly controlled by a Grand Master in Jerusalem. See accounts of the London Knights Hospitallers and their temple in Henry W. Fincham, "The Priory Church of St. John at Clerkenwell," *The Journal of the British Archeological Association* (December, 1911): 183–89; Alfred W. Clapham, *St. John of Jerusalem Clerkenwell* (London, 1912); and John Wilson, *A Concise Account of St. John's Gate* (London, 1867).

2. Aziz Atiya, *Crusade, Commerce and Culture* (Gloucester, Mass., 1969), 154–55; and *The Crusade in the Later Middle Ages* (London, 1938).

3. "Dr. Leonhart Rauwolff's Itinerary," *A Collection of Curious Travels & Voyages,* ed. John Ray (London: Smith and Walford, 1693), part 3, p. 364. See also the description of the creation of Roman Red Cross Knights of the Sepulchre in *The Theatre of the Whole World: Set forth by that Excellent Geographer Abraham Ortelius* (London: John Norton), 111–12.

4. Moryson, *An Itinerary Containing His Ten Yeeres Travell through the Twelve Dominions of Germany, Bohemerland, Sweitzerland, Netherland, Denmarke, Poland, Italy, Turkey, France, England, Scotland & Ireland,* vol. 2 (Glasgow, 1907): 41.

5. *The Institution, Lawes & Ceremonies of the most Noble Order of the Garter* (London: J. Macock, 1672), 35.

6. *The Golden Legend,* trans. Granger Ryan (New York, 1969), 232.

7. Dionise Alexandrine, *The Surveye,* trans. Thomas Twine (London: Henrie Bynneman, 1572), First Section, unpaginated.

8. *Mappa Mundi* (London: Robert Wyer, ca. 1535), unpaginated.

9. See the Exodus frontispiece illustration, used for both the Old and New Testament title pages, in the *Geneva Bible (Puritans with commentary that disturbed the Anglicans),* (London: Rouland Hall, 1560); and in *The Bible: Holy Scripture* (London: Christopher Barker, 1576), Geneva Version. Maps of the 42 stations of the Exodus appear in the *Geneva Bible* printed by Rouland Hall (1560), verso p. 77; *The holy Byble, conteynying the olde and newe Testament Set foorth by authoritie* (London: Richard Jugge, 1575), 84, Bishops' Version; and *The Bible: Holy Scripture* printed by Christopher Barker (1576), 73, Geneva Version.

10. *Torquato Tasso: A Study of the Poet and his contribution to English Literature* (Cambridge, England, 1965), pp. 236–237.

11. Thomas Brygg, "The Itinerary in the Holy Land of Lord Thomas of Swynburne," *Western Pilgrims*, ed. Fr. Eugene Hoade (Jerusalem, 1952), 78–84. The "Itinerary" was first published in *Archives de L'Orient Latin*, Tome III (1884), a MS, No. 449, of Caius College, Cambridge.

12. Richard Warner, *A History of the Abbey of Glaston: and the Town of Glastonbury* (Bath: Richard Cruttwell, 1926), chapter 2, p. lvii. See also *Guide to Glastonbury* (Glastonbury: Avalon Press, 1934), 26.

13. *Here begynneth the lyfe of Joseph of Armathia* (London: Thomas Pynson, 1520), no pagination.

14. For a description of the holy sites and relics, see Warner, *A History of the Abbey of Glaston*, xx–xxxvii. See also Armine Le Strange Cambell, *The Glories of Glastonbury* (London, 1927).

15. See the "Note on Relics" in C. L. Marston, *Glastonbury: The English Jerusalem* (Bath: Pitman Press, 1925), 98–101. See also the discussion of relics by Roger Sherman Loomis in *The Grail: From Celtic Myth to Christian Symbol* (Cardiff, 1963), 250.

16. See the Trinity College ms. of *De Antiquitate*, ed. Thomas Hearne (Glastonbury: *Somerset Gazette*, 1932), 18.

17. F. Harcastle, *The Chalice Well* (Glastonbury: Chalice Well Trust, 1982), 1–12. Early records of the well are cited in *The Great Chartulary of Glastonbury*, ed. Aelred Watkin, vol. 2 (London, 1952): 323. See also *Guide to Glastonbury*, 7.

18. *The Glastonbury Tor Maze* (Glastonbury: Gothic Image, 1979), 14.

19. *The Works of Edmund Spenser: A Variorum Edition*, ed. Edwin Greenlaw, Charles Grosvenor Osgood, and Frederick Morgan Padelford, vol. 1 (Baltimore, 1932): 5. All citations to Spenser's writings are from this edition.

20. An analysis of Egyptian references appears in C. W. Lemmi, "Monster-Spewing Nile-Mud in Spenser," *Modern Language Notes* 41 (1926): 234–38. Patrick Cullen in *Eternal Triad* (Princeton, 1974) advances a reading, without reference to specific Exodus patterns, of pilgrimage elements in the early books of *The Faerie Queene*.

21. For an account of the sixth century monk St. Stephen's encounters with desert animals, see John Climacus, *The Ladder of Divine Ascent*, trans. Archimandrite Lazarus Moore, intro. M. Heppell (London, 1959), 121–23.

22. See my "The Pilgrim Texts and Dante's Three Beasts, *Inferno* I," *Italica* (Winter, 1969): 223–24.

23. For examples of such pilgrimage meetings on long journeys, see my *The Invention of Dante's Commedia* (New Haven and London, 1974), 160–61.

24. Elizabeth Wheeler Schermerhorn, *On the Trail of the Eight-Pointed Cross: A Study of the Heritage of the Knights Hospitallers in Feudal Europe* (New York, 1940), 74–75. See also A. Mifsud, *The Venerable Tongue of England and Malta* (Malta, 1914), 46–47; and J. H. Round, *The Foundation of the Priories St. Mary and St. John, Clerkenwell* (London, 1899).

Although the Knights Hospitallers had no formal hospital in England, a brother at Clerkenwell Priory with the title *Miles Sagax et discretus* supervised the care of visitors. As pointed out by Schermerhorn in *On the Trail* (73–74), designated categories of persons seeking accommodation at the Priory—members of the order, pilgrims, magistrates, the nobility, and the king and members of his household—were provided, in accordance with governing statutes, with lodging, wine, and other general physical and spiritual assistance.

25. *An Itinerary: Concerning His Ten Yeers Travell*, vol. 2 (Glasgow: James Mac Lehose and Sons, 1907): 44.

26. Judith H. Anderson, *The Growth of a Personal Voice: Piers Plowman and The Faerie Queene* (New Haven and London, 1976), 48–49.

27. John Nichols, *The Progresses and Public Processions of Queen Elizabeth*, vol. 2 (London: Printers to the Society of Antiquaries, 1823): 334–35.

28. *The Progresses and Public Processions of Queen Elizabeth*, vol. 2: 321–29.

29. See Richard Torkington, *Ye Oldest Diarie of Englysshe Travell*, ed. W. J. Loftie (London: Leadenhalle Presse, 1884). In the *Diarie* written in 1517, Torkington notes that "Under the mounte of Clavery ys another Chapell . . . and ther, ryght under the Morteys of the Crosse, was founde the hede of our fore father Adam" (44). Faynes Moryson in *An Itinerary* also observes that "Where they say the Crosse stood, they shewed us stones rent, or the rending of the Mountaine, when Christ died. Under this Mountaine in the corner towards the dore of the Church, they bade us looke in a little window, and there they shewed us a scull, which they say the Mountaine was called Golgatha" (25).

NOTES TO CHAPTER FIVE

1. *The Accedens of Armory* (London: Richard Tottyl, 1568), fol. 206.

2. Quoted from the "Accidence of Armory" in John Nichols, *The Progresses and Public Processions of Queen Elizabeth*, vol. 1 (London: Society of Antiquaries, 1823): 134. In an earlier Tottyl printing of *Accedens* in 1562, the passage as recorded with sixteenth century spelling reads: "the mightye Pallaphilos . . . hyghe constable Marshall of ye knightes Téples, Patrone of the honorable ordre of Pagasus" (fol. 213).

For references to Dudley's role of Marshall in 1652, and to the history of the Knights Templar and Hospitallers in England, see William Dugdale, *Orignes Juridiciales, or Historical Memorials of the English Laws, Courts of Justice, Forms of Tryall* (London: F. and T. Warren, 1666), 144–46, 150–57. The activities of Dudley in support of the Inner Temple, and his participation in the Inner Temple revels in 1652, are mentioned in *A Calendar of the Inner Temple Records*, ed. F. A. Inderwick, vol. 1 (London: Chiswick Press, 1896): 215–18, 311. See also the discussions of English knightly orders and chivalric revels in Frederick S. Boas, *Queen Elizabeth, the Revels Office and Edmund Tilney* (London, 1938), 1–27. As Boas points out, the Revels Office after 1559, under Revels Masters Thomas Benger and then Edmund Tilney, was located in the former Knights Hospitallers' headquarters located at St. John's Gate, Clerkenwell, London (17–18). A library containing revels documents still exists at St. John's Gate, now headquarters for the present, revived English Knights Hospitallers' organization, which operates a British ambulance corps and a hospital in Jerusalem. See the studies of crusading knightly orders, and their influence upon British chivalric and ceremonial activities, appearing in Edwin King's *The Knights of St. John in the British Realm*, rev. and continued by Harry Luke (London: St. John's Gate, 1967), 104–13; H. W. Fincham's *The Order of the Hospital of St. John of Jerusalem and its Grand Priory of England* (London: W. H. L. Collingridge, 1915), 14–42; and Hannibal P. Scicluna's *A Short History of the*

Knights Hospitallers of St. John, of Jerusalem, of Rhodes, and of Malta, with a section on the English branch by H. C. Luke (Malta: Empire Press, 1970), 62–70; and Jonathan Riley-Smith's *The Knights of St. John in Jerusalem and Cyprus* (New York and London, 1967).

3. Fol. 216–217. An excellent analysis of the medieval and Renaissance meanings derived from body and institutional metaphors, particularly as related to royalty, appears in Ernest H. Kantorowicz's *The King's Two Bodies: A Study in Medieval Political Theology* (Princeton, 1957). David Miller in *The Poem's Two Bodies: The Poetics of the 1590 "Faerie Queene"* (Princeton, 1988) effectively applies the political-theology of body metaphors to readings of *The Faerie Queene*.

4. For comments on the mirroring of Leicester in *The Faerie Queene*, see, for example, Alastair Fowler's "Oxford and London Marginalia to *The Faerie Queene*," *Notes and Queries* (1961): 416–19, and John Hankin's *Source and Meaning in Spenser's Allegory* (Oxford, 1971), 175–76.

In Leicester's Arthurian entertainment for the queen at Kenilworth Castle during the summer of 1575, the Earl was repeatedly identified as Arthur's direct descendant. The texts of this 17-day extravaganza— reprinted in John Nichols's *The Progresses and Public Processions of Queen Elizabeth*, vol. 1, pp. 429ff.—disclose that the queen at Kenilworth entered into a theatrical world featuring British Arthur's order of knights and populated by figures comparable to those in *The Faerie Queene*: among them, Merlin, Nymphs, Sibyls, a Savage Man, the giant Hercules and other giants, Sylvanus, a Tryton, and many different allegorical knights. Though widely acclaimed in public accounts and accepted by commentators as a production of great magnificence, this costly theatrical "toy" was marred by a scrambled production and by the amateurism of a number of Leicester's retainers who lacked the performing skills and techniques of formal compliment of professional London musicians and masquers. The comic awkwardness of the Arthurian production is mirrored in Spenser's representation of the confusion, bumbling and excessive theatrical-military posturing of proud faeryland knights like those in the tourney in book 3 (3.4.14–6.23).

5. *The Works of Edmund Spenser: A Variorum Edition*, gen. ed. Edwin Greenlaw with Ray Heffner, James G. McManaway and Ernest A. Strathmann, vol. 2 (Baltimore, 1933): 115; 2.9.22. All citations of Spenser's writings are from this variorum edition.

6. Dingley, *History in Marble*, 1684 ed., (London: facsimile reproduction by the Camden Society, 1866–67), 8. See also the historical remarks on Inner Temple Church statuary and sacred objects in Arundell Esdaile, *Temple Church Monuments, being a Report to the two Honourable Societies of The Temple* (London: George Barber, 1933).

7. Roy Strong, *Splendor at Court: Renaissance Spectacle and the Theater of Power* (Boston, 1973), 54, 144–67.

8. The special Reformation qualities and values of Leicester's tale and of Spenser's Red Cross Knight allegory, both praising Elizabeth, are highlighted by comparison with sixteenth century Catholic allegory in the same knightly quest-and-pilgrimage *genre*. For example, in John Carthenie's *The Voyage of the wandering Knight*, trans. from the French by William Goodyear (London: Thomas East, 1581), the central Wandering Knight in search of "true felicitie" must first hear the Hermit Understanding preach

on the virtues of Mary Magdalene and then must receive Communion before encountering allegorical figures—figures comparable to those in Dante's *Commedia*—of the four cardinal and the three theological virtues. During his allegorical pilgrimage, the Knight is falsely led by Voluptuousness to a Palace of Worldly Felicity in a tangled forest. Upon leaving the Palace, learning of Mary Magdalene's virtues, and receiving Communion, the Knight ascends in a chariot to the Palace of Virtue where the figure "*Faith* from the toppe of her towre, sheweth unto the knight the citie of heaven" (114).

9. Michael O'Connell in *Mirror and Veil: The Historical Dimension of Spenser's Faerie Queene* (Chapel Hill, 1977), 71–89; for example, stresses the respective imperfect and ideal natures of the two chronicles, but he does not give attention to Spenser's satire of history. "Faeryland," he writes, "is not a simple shadowing of Tudor rule but an idealization of it. *Briton moniments* illustrates the moral ambiguities of history, and what is left out of the Faery idealization implies that moral ambiguity and imperfection continue into the present. Faeryland, as the poet's golden world, can present a moral vision in a way that history's brazen world cannot. But such an idealization risks becoming remote, and it is for this reason also, I feel, that the evocation of history is important to Spenser" (81).

For helpful, detailed studies of Spenser's historical chronicles that nonetheless do not include full analyses of wider universal history, see Harry Berger, *The Allegorical Temper: Vision and Reality in Book II of Spenser's Faery Queene* (New Haven, 1957), 97–103; and Carrie A. Harper, *The Sources of the British Chronicle History in Spenser's Faerie Queene* (Philadelphia: J. C. Winsten, 1910), 180–93. Thomas P. Roche, Jr. in *The Kindly Flame: A Study of the Third and Fourth Books of Spenser's "The Faerie Queene"* (Princeton, 1964), 62–66, discusses Britomart's role in British history, concentrating upon how Spenser's imagery in book 3 cleverly plays upon classical themes involving Ulysses and the Trojans.

10. *The First Volume of the Chronicles of Englande, Scotlande, and Irelande* (London, George Bishop, 1577), unpaginated dedicatory page.

11. *The First Booke of the Ecclesiastical History of Eusebius*, trans. Meredith Hanmer (London: Thomas Vautroulier, 1577), II, chapter 3, p. 20.

12. *The First Booke of the Ecclesiastical History*, concluding Chronology, 40–43. See also the merged compendium of chronologies by Eusebius, Socrates Scholasticus and Evagrius gathered together by the editor identifying himself as M. H. in *A Chronographie, with Suppotation of the Yeares from the Beginning of the World unto the birth of Christ* (London: George Miller, 1636).

13. *Eusebius His Life of Constantine* (London: Thomas Coates, 1637), book 3, p. 52.

14. *The Original Chronicle of Andrew of Wyntoun*, ed. and intro. F. J. Amours, vol. 3 (Edinburgh and London: William Blackwood for the Scottish Text Society, 1904): 424; Wemyss Ms., chap. 89, 11.3030–041.

15. *The First Volume of the Chronicles of Englande, Scotlande, and Irelande*, unpaginated dedicatory page, and p. 90.

16. John Eliot Hodgkin, *Fifty Pen-and-Ink Sketches in exact facsimile . . . From a Copy of Polydore Vergil's History of England* (London), unpaginated and undated. As Hodgkin notes, the style of clothing in the drawings dates the ms. at sometime before the mid-sixteenth century.

17. *The Defence of Constantine: With a Treatise of the Popes temporall Monarchie* (London: Bernard Alsop, 1621), unpaginated dedicatory page. See also this same author's *Justinian the Emperor defended against Cardinal Baronius* (London: George Eld, 1616).

As F. J. Levy has convincingly shown in *Tudor Historical Thought* (San Marino, California, 1642), British Reformation writers defending the Tudor monarchy appealed to the worldwide authority of Constantine because, among other reasons, English law was historical in nature and founded upon precedents. Theories of imperial rule allowed British Reformation chroniclers and pamphleteers to rise above troublesome individual cases on issues of authority. To call England "imperial," Levy comments on whether any contemporaneous authority supersedes that of the British Crown, "meant more than to declare the country exempt from the suzerainty of pope and emperor; it meant also that the position of its king vis-a-vis the English church was equivalent to that of Constantine. This to a large extent accounts for the otherwise strangely exorbitant insistence by the Tudor chroniclers on the British origin of Constantine and his mother, Helena" (83). See, too, F. Smith Fussner, *The Historical Revolution: English Historical Writing and Thought, 1580–1640* (London, 1942); and T. D. Kendrick, *British Antiquity* (London, 1950).

18. *Actes and Monuments of these latter and perillous dayes, touching matters of the Church* (London: John Day, 1563), preface. See also the tracing of British "imperial" authority to Constantine and Justinian in Crakenthorp's *The Defence of Constantine*.

19. See John Stow, *A Summarye of the Chronicles of Englande* (London: Thomas Marsh, 1670), fol. 31.

20. *The Institution* (London, J. Macock, 1672), 64–65.

21. *The Register of the Most Noble Order of the Garter*, from its Cover in Black Velvet, usually called *The Black Book*, vol. 1 (London: John Barber, 1724): 27–30.

NOTES TO CHAPTER SIX

1. *The Principal Navigations* (London: Bishop, Newveries, and Barker, 1599).

2. References throughout will be to the readily available, "standard," four-folio 1625 edition, that includes materials employed by Milton, reprinted in 20 volumes as *Hakluytus Posthumus or Purchas His Pilgrimes* (Glasgow and New York, 1905–1907). See also the final edition with its long expository title: *Purchas his Pilgrimage, or Relations of the World and the Religions Observed in all Ages and places Discovered from Creation unto this Present. Contayning a Theological and Geographicall Historie of Asia, Africa, and America, with the lands adjacent. Declaring the ancient Religions before the Floud, the Heathenith, Jewish, and Saracenicall in all Ages since, in those parts professed, with their severall opinions, Idols, Oracles, Temples, Priests, Fasts, Feasts, Sacrifices, and Rites Religious: Their beginnings, Proceedings, Alterations, Sects, Orders and Successions. With briefe Descriptions of the Countries, Nations, States, Discoveries; Private and publike Customes, and the most remarkable Rarities of*

Nature, or Humane industrie, in the same., 4th ed. (London: William Stansby, 1626).

3. See the "Advancement" in *The Works of Francis Bacon*, ed. James Spedding, Robert Leslie Ellis, and Douglas Denon Heath, vol. 6 (Boston, 1861): 198–99.

4. See the analysis of the theatrical background and the theatrical qualities of the antitriumphs and triumphs in John Demaray, *Milton's Theatrical Epic: The Invention and Design of Paradise Lost* (Cambridge, Mass. and London, 1980), 57–72, 95–115.

5. *John Milton: Complete Poems and Major Prose*, ed. Merritt Y. Hughes (New York, 1957), 460; book 12, pp. 261–64. Citations of Milton's prose tract *Of Education* and all citations of Milton's verse will be from the Hughes edition.

6. See Mary Christopher Pecheux, "Abraham, Adam, and the Theme of Exile in *Paradise Lost*," *Publications of the Modern Language Association* 80 (1965): 365–71; "The Pattern of Time and Eternity" in George Wesley Whiting's *Milton and this Pendant World* (Austin, 1958), 196–200; C. A. Patrides, *The Grand Design of God: The Literary Form of the Christian View of History* (London and Toronto, 1972), 84–90; Albert C. Labriola, "The Aesthetics of Self-Diminution: Christian Iconography and *Paradise Lost*," "*Eyes Fast Fixt*": Current Perspectives in Milton Methodology, ed. Albert C. Labriola and Michael Lieb (Pittsburgh, 1975), 267–311. *Bright Essence: Studies in Milton's Theology* with essays by William B. Hunter, Jr., C. A. Patrides, and J. H. Adamson (Salt Lake City, 1971); William B. Madsen, *From Shadowy Types to Truth: Studies in Milton's Symbolism* (New Haven and London, 1968); James H. Sims, *The Bible in Milton's Epics* (Gainesville, 1962); and Edward Tayler, *Milton's Poetry: Its Development in Time* (Pittsburgh, 1979). See also Regina M. Schwartz's largely thematic analysis of what she regards as recurrent creation episodes in Milton's epic in *Remembering and Repeating: Biblical Creation in Paradise Lost* (Cambridge, England, 1988). Citing Augustine and Freud, Schwartz also discusses Satan's "sight" of creation as that of the voyeur, aggressor and spy (54–55).

7. For readings of what have been considered the Augustinian ages of humankind in *Paradise Lost*, see in particular Whiting, "The Pattern of Time and Eternity," *Milton and this Pendant World*, 169–200. See also the analyses of apocalyptic elements in the last books appearing in Joseph Wittreich, *Visionary Poetics: Milton's Tradition & His Legacy* (San Marino, California, 1979); C. A. Patrides, "'Something like Prophetick strain': Apocalyptic configurations in Milton," *The Apocalypse in English Renaissance Thought and Literature*, ed. C. A. Patrides and Joseph Wittreich (Ithaca, 1984), 205–37; and Barbara Kiefer Lewalski, "'Not Less but More Heroic': Prophecy and Transformation of Literary Forms," *Paradise Lost and the Rhetoric of Literary Forms* (Princeton, 1985), 254–79.

For critical arguments on the lessening of Milton's poetic power in the last books, see Louis L. Martz, *The Paradise Within: Studies in Vaughan, Traherne, and Milton* (New Haven and London, 1964), 103–67; John Peter, *A Critique of "Paradise Lost"* (New York, 1960), 138–58; Joseph H. Summers, "The Final Vision" in *Milton: A Collection of Critical Essays*, ed. Louis Martz (Englewood Cliffs, N.J., 1966), 183–206, reprinted from Summers's *The Muse's Method: An Introduction to Paradise Lost* (Cambridge, Mass., and London, 1962); and Demaray, "The Future Triumph of Man" in *Milton's Theatrical Epic*, 102–15.

8. *The Works of John Milton*, gen. ed. Frank Allen Patterson: "De Doctrina" ed. James Holly Hanford and Waldo Hillary Dunn, trans. Charles R. Sumner, vol. 15 (New York, 1933): 179–81. Jason Rosenblatt has called attention to this pre-Mosaic law in *De Doctrina Christiana* and Milton's epic in conducting seminars for Milton scholars at the University of Pennsylvania and the University of Delaware and in *A Revaluation of Milton's Indebtedness to Hebraica in Paradise Lost* (Providence, 1969).

9. Milton's detailed knowledge of Dante has been established by Irene Samuel in her Appendix to *Dante and Milton: The "Commedia" and "Paradise Lost"* (Ithaca, 1966), an appendix listing Milton's over 200 references, or possible references, to Dante's writings.

Milton's rejection of the Holy Land pilgrimage tradition, and of related crusading activities, reflects typical English Reformation views. For example, Thomas Fuller in *The Historie of the Holy Warre* (Cambridge, England: Thomas Buck, 1639) denounces both Holy Land pilgrimages and the Crusades, and the author urges Protestant Englishmen to worship at home and to learn of the Holy Land using books and maps. Dedicatory poems in the *Historie* by a group of such Cambridge "armchair" Holy Land travelers—among them Robert Somersall, James Duport, J. Booth and Clement Bretton—praise Fuller's opposition to pilgrimage. "Stay, Pilgrimes, stay," writes James Duport in his poem, "wander not hence so farr;/ Set up your rest here in this Holy warre." In another poem, Robert Somersall claims that Fuller, because of his outlook, is superior to Tasso who acclaimed pilgrimages and the Crusades in *Jerusalem Liberata*. "Tasso, be silent," writes Somersall, "my friend speks: his Storie/ Hath robb'd thy poeme of its long-liv'd glorie" (unpaginated).

In the Preface to *The Travels of certaine Englishmen* (London: Th. Haveland, 1609), Theophilus Lavender notes with approbation that, though the book contains records of Holy Land journeys by the English, none of the travelers are called *"English Pilgrims."* Lavender declares that "Pilgrims goe with a supersitious devotion to worship Reliques at *Jerusalem*," but he adds that the English group "went thither onely as travelers to see the Holy Land" (unpaginated). One of the accounts in the work, written by Protestant traveler Guiliemus Biddulphus, gives expression to the widespread English Reformation skepticism about the historical authenticity of many Holy Land sites and pilgrimage stories. Biddulphus divides the statements made to him by Holy Land guides and clerics under the listings "apparent Truths," "Manifest Untruths" and "things Doubtfull" (123). English Protestant Fynes Moryson, writing of his visit to Jerusalem in 1596, opens his *An Itinerary: Containing His Ten Yeers Travell*, vol. 2 (Glasgow, 1907) by insisting that "by my journey to this City, I had no thought to expiate any least sinne of mine; much lesse did I hope to merit any grace from God." He opposes what he calls "worship" of the holy "places" in Jerusalem. And although he promises to "relate the situation of the City, and the description of the monuments made to me by the Friars," he admits that he does not "beleeve all the particulars I write upon their report, neither doe I perswade any man to beleeve them" (1).

10. Thematic and typological references to the Exodus in *Paradise Lost* have been traced by John T. Shawcross in *"Paradise Lost and the Theme of Exodus," Milton Studies*, ed. James D. Simmonds, vol. 2 (Pittsburgh, 1970): 3–26. In a theoretical reading that does not draw upon Milton's histories or

sacred representations, Marshall Grossman in *"Authors to Themselves":* *Milton and the Revelation of History* (New York, New Rochelle, Melbourne, 1987) discusses how the "self-authored subject of *Paradise Lost* accumulates experiences through a series of judgments and choices," of how what is considered to be a "new concept of the historical self" arises "through a dialectic that locates the narrated events at the intersection of prospective and retrospective points of view" (vii–viii).

11. Classical elements of form, largely as interpreted by Italian Renaissance writers, have been examined in Milton's poem by John M. Steadman in *Epic and Tragic Structure in "Paradise Lost"* (Chicago and London, 1976). Lewalski in *"Paradise Lost" and the Rhetoric of Literary Forms* has drawn upon an encyclopedic range of recent Milton commentary and criticism, together with Renaissance and other early sources, in concluding that *"Paradise Lost* is, then, an encyclopedia of literary forms which also affords a probing critique of the values those forms traditionally body forth" (23).

12. *Works*, "The Reason of Church Government," ed. Morgan Ayres, vol. 3 (New York, 1931): 237.

13. *Works*, "History of Britain," ed. George Philip Krapp, vol. 10 (New York, 1932): 2, 128, 179–80.

14. Quoted in William Riley Parker, *Milton: A Biography*, vol. 2 (Oxford, 1968): 939.

15. Fletcher, *The Intellectual Development of John Milton*, vol. 2 (Urbana, Ill., 1961): 348.

16. See entries 13 and 57 in *A Common-Place Book of John Milton*, ed. Alfred J. Horwood (Westminster, England, 1876), 3, 6.

17. French, *The Life Records of John Milton*, vol. 2 (New Brunswick, N.J., 1950): 215.

18. George Henry Turnbull, *Hartlib, Dury and Comenius: Gleanings from Hartlib's Papers* (London, 1947), 41.

19. Parker, *Milton: A Biography*, vol. 1 (Oxford, 1968): 295. In the recently published *Complete Prose Works of John Milton*, gen. ed. Don M. Wolfe, vol. 8 (New Haven and London, 1982), George B. Parks, without taking a position on Milton's possible "epitome" of Purchas, does call welcome attention to the poet's general debts to Hakluyt and Purchas. Parks notes that Milton, in composing *A Brief History of Moscovia*, "combed Hakluyt and Purchas for the details he wanted." Parks adds that "the Russian material in Hakluyt occupies some eight hundred pages in the modern octavo edition, and the Purchas material close to four hundred like pages. Our compiler would presumably read through, then go back and mark items to be copied in order or under given heads, then copy and condense in copying." Although Parks does not relate what it seems to me is Milton's new historical-geographic "method" in *A Brief History of Moscovia* to *Paradise Lost*, he offers a general comment on what he terms Milton's "individual approach to geography, that is, extracting from the travel narratives details that would add up to a picture of the country, to make an inductively developed geography" (458).

Parks's published comments, unavailable when views in this chapter were given as a Huntington Library Fellows Lecture in the spring of 1982, offers general confirmation, it seems to me, of the argument here advanced that Milton "epitomized" the northeast voyage accounts in Purchas.

20. Robert Ralston Cawley in *Milton and the Literature of Travel* (Princeton, 1951) shows how voyage literature is used by Milton with rhetorical effect in *Paradise Lost*, but he does not give a structural analysis of Milton's interweaving of counterpoised journeys with medieval typology. See the study of Milton's historical sources in Elbert N. S. Thompson's "Milton's Knowledge of Geography," *Studies in Philology* 16, no. 2 (1919): 148–71. See also J. Milton French's comments on Milton's scientific and critical tendencies in "Milton as a Historian," *Publications of the Modern Language Association* 50 (1935): 469–79. For other studies of source materials and historical traditions influencing Milton's historical writings, see Irene Samuel, "Milton and the Ancients on the Writing of History," *Milton Studies II*, ed. James D. Simmonds (Pittsburgh, 1970), 131–48; Joseph Allen Bryant, Jr., "Milton and the Art of History," *Philological Quarterly* 29 (1950): 15–30; Charles Firth, "Milton as an Historian," *Essays Historical & Literary* (Oxford, 1938), 61–102; and French Fogel and H. R. Trevor-Roper, *Milton and Clarendon: Two Papers on Seventeenth Century Historiography presented at the Clark Library* (Los Angeles, 1965). See also in the *Complete Prose Works of Milton*, 8: 454–538; the preface and notes by George B. Parks to *A Brief History of Moscovia*; and in the *Complete Prose*, vol. 5, part 1 (New Haven and London, 1971), xix–404, with intro. and notes to "A History of Britain" by French Fogel.

21. Quoted by J. Milton French in *The Life Records of Milton*, vol. 1 (New Brunswick, N.J., 1950): 214.

22. See Douglas Bush, *English Literature in the Earlier Seventeenth Century, 1600–1660* (New York, 1952), 179.

23. *Works*, "A Brief History of Moscovia," ed. George Philip Krapp, 10: 328.

24. *John Milton*, ed. Hughes, 634.

25. *Milton: Private Correspondence and Academic Exercises*, trans. Phyllis B. Tillyard (Cambridge, England, 1932), 72. See the study of Milton's use of maps in George Wesley Whiting's *Milton's Literary Milieu* (New York, 1964), 97ff.

26. *Theatrum Orbis Terrarum: The Theatre of the Whole World*, trans. William Tyrius (London: John Norton, 1606), unpaginated introduction.

27. *Theatrum Orbis Terrarum*, unpaginated introduction.

28. The letter is reprinted and translated by J. Milton French in *The Life Records of Milton*, vol. 4 (New Brunswick, N.J., 1956): 12.

29. C. M. Bowra in *From Virgil to Milton* (London, 1943) speculates that, if Milton had written an epic about King Arthur, "it might have been an English counterpart to *Os Lusiadas*." For in discussing the Portugese epic, Bowra insists that Milton "knew Camões, if not in the original, at least in the translation of Richard Fanshawe, who was a public figure at the time and published his *Lusiad* in 1655" (194–95).

30. *Works*, "A History of Britain," 10: 130–31.

31. See Milton's reference in *Works*, "A Brief History of Moscovia," 10: 365.

32. Thomas Fuller in *A Pisgah-sight of Palestine* (London: printed for John Williams, 1650) asks the reader to follow as a traveler: "my humble request to the reader is, that while I goe before him in this my description, he would follow me in his own pace, at his own pleasure, so fast, and so far, as I follow the truth" (48). Fuller calls special attention to individual maps

of the movements of each of the 12 tribes, maps accompanied by commentary, in noting that "none have formerly in any tongue (much lesse in English) presented with distinct Mappes and descriptions together" (1). Discussions of evil idols appear on pp. 120, 133, 290–91, 311, and throughout. See also William Symonds, *Pisgah Evangelica: By the Method of Revelation* (London: Felix Kyngston for Edmund Weaver, 1605), for comments on the 12 tribes from the perspective of the Revelation of St. John.

33. The map showing the altar and temple of Moloch is printed in Fuller's *Pisgah-sight* on pp. 290–91.

34. Moxon, *A Tutor to Astronomy & Geography, or the Use of the Copernican Spheres* (London: Joseph Moxon, 1665), 17. An earlier edition of the book appeared under the title *A Tutor to Astronomy and Geography or An Easie and Speedy way to Understand the Use of both the Globes, Celestial and Terrestrial,* trans. from the first part of Gulielmus Bleau (London: Joseph Moxon, 1654).

35. Nicolson, *The Breaking of the Circle* (Evanston, Ill., 1950), 165–89.

36. Lovejoy, "Milton and the Paradox of the Fortunate Fall," *English Literary History* 4 (1937): 161–79, reprinted in Lovejoy's *Essays in the History of Ideas* (Baltimore, 1948), 277–95. Paradoxical literary themes like those employed by Milton are traced in Rosalie L. Colie's *Paradoxia Epidemica: The Renaissance Tradition of Paradox* (Princeton, 1966).

37. "Advancement" in *The Works of Francis Bacon,* 6: 198–99.

38. See Roger Loomis, *The Grail: From Celtic Myth to Christian Symbol* (Cardiff, 1963), 266; and Richard Warner, *A History of the Abbey of Glaston: and the Town of Glastonbury* (Bath, 1926), c, cii, and appendix.

39. *General and Rare Memorials pertayning to the Perfect Arts of Navigation* (London: John Daye, 1577), 56.

Index

255

About the Author

JOHN G. DEMARAY is professor of English and Renaissance Studies at Rutgers University, and was a recent visiting professor to the Università degli Studi di Firenzi. Dr. Demaray's publications include *Milton's Theatrical Epic: The Invention and Design of "Paradise Lost"* (Harvard University Press, 1980), *The Invention of Dante's "Commedia"* (Yale University Press, 1974) and *Milton and the Masque Tradition* (Harvard and Oxford University Presses, 1968).